JOSEFINA LEYVA

OPERATION PEDRO PAN

THE EXODUS OF CUBA'S CHILDREN

TRANSLATED FROM SPANISH

BY

DEBORAH A. DOUGHERTY

UNIVERSITY PRESS
OF THE SOUTH

2023

Copyright 2023 by Josefina Leyva.

All rights reserved. No part of this publication may be reproduced, stored in a retrieval system, or transmitted, in any form or by any means, electronic, mechanical, photocopying, recording or otherwise, without the prior written permission of the Publisher.

Published in the United States by University Press of the South, New Orleans, LA 70119 USA

Printed by Mon Beau Livre, France/The Netherlands.

E-mail: unprsouth@aol.com
Visit our award-winning web pages: www.unprsouth.com
www.punouveaumonde.com
Acid-Free Paper.

Josefina Leyva.
Operation Pedro Pan. The Exodus of Cuba's Children.
Translated from Spanish by Deborah A. Dougherty (Alma College, USA).
First Edition with University Press of the South, New Orleans (USA): Operation Pedro Pan. The Exodus of Cuba's Children. 2011. ISBN: 978-1-93730-05-6.
268 pages. 2 photos.
Front Cover Design by Stan Duchêne. Cover Photo Printed with Permission.

1. Cuba. 2. History. 3. Operation Pedro Pan. 4. Clandestine Exodus of Children. 5. Aftermath of the Cuban Revolution. 6. Catholic Welfare Bureau. 7. Miami (USA). 8. Father Bryan O. Walsh. 9. Josefina Leyva. 10. Deborah A. Dougherty.

ISBN: 978-1-952799-48-8
2023

CUBAN CHILDREN WAITING IN LINE TO EMIGRATE

FATHER BRYAN O. WALSH AND CUBAN CHILDREN

To the mothers of the Pedro Pans, who risked everything to ensure their children's freedom. And to those who cared for them in the United States, whose guidance and support nurtured their dreams and successes as Cuban-Americans.

Josefina Leyva and Deborah Dougherty

CONTENTS

Prologue	1
Chapter 1	5
Chapter 2	11
Chapter 3	17
Chapter 4	23
Chapter 5	33
Chapter 6	43
Chapter 7	47
Chapter 8	53
Chapter 9	57
Chapter 10	69
Chapter 11	71
Chapter 12	75
Chapter 13	81
Chapter 14	85
Chapter 15	91
Chapter 16	97
Interlude: The Children's Priest	105
Chapter 17	109
Chapter 18	115
Chapter 19	121
Chapter 20	129
Chapter 21	133

Chapter 22	141
Chapter 23	149
Chapter 24	155
Chapter 25	157
Interlude: A Cuban Girl in an American Home	161
Interlude: René, The Boy with Two Mothers	169
Chapter 26	175
Chapter 27	179
Chapter 28	187
Chapter 29	195
Chapter 30	199
Chapter 31	203
Chapter 32	207
Prelude to a Pedro Pan Priest	211
Chapter 33	217
Interlude: Jesús, The Renegade	221
Chapter 34	227
Chapter 35	229
Chapter 36	231
Interlude: The Fernández Sisters	233
Chapter 37	243
Chapter 38	245

ACKNOWLEDGMENTS

I would like to thank my dear friend and colleague, Dr. Margarita Krakusin, Professor Emeritus of Spanish at Alma College for first introducing me to Josefina Leyva and her works and for her support and encouragement as I began translating this author's novels for an English speaking audience. I will be forever grateful to Josefina Leyva for her collaboration during the translation process; patiently explaining cultural subtleties that can be known only to one who lived in Cuba during the time periods in which her novels are set. I wish to thank the faculty and Provost, Dr. Michael Selmon at Alma College for supporting this second translation by awarding me sabbatical leave on order that I might focus my full attention to this project and bring it to publication in time for the Fiftieth anniversary of *Operation Pedro Pan*. A special thank you is extended to Ms. Barbara Tripp, our Departmental Administrative Assistant, who carefully proofread the final manuscript with much-needed fresh eyes. Finally, I would like to thank my husband, John, for his love and support throughout the course of my career and our sons, Shane and Kyle, who mean more to me than they will ever know.

PROLOGUE

In December 1960, a small group of the remaining members of the North American Chamber of Commerce in Havana, Cuba returned to the United States. Those North American businessmen had numerous friends on the island; friends who chose to remain in their homeland, steadfast in their hope of reestablishing democracy by overthrowing a government that was trending toward a dictatorship with Marxist tendencies. Even so, they wanted to save their children by sending them somewhere safe. Some had already sent them to live with family or friends in Miami. However, many found themselves with no one who could care for their children.

By the end of November of that same year, some of the North American businessmen lead by Mr. Jim Baker, Director of the Ruston Academy in Havana, came to me at the Catholic Welfare Bureau in Miami. Unfortunately, few people had such contacts. I understood the need to implement a program to care for the unaccompanied children who were arriving among the tens of thousands of Cuban refugees inundating Miami. The Eisenhower administration had promised to provide funding for just such a program. This was how I could offer my assistance to the Chamber of Commerce group. If they sent the children to Miami, the Catholic Welfare Bureau would care for them until they could return to Cuba or until their parents could join them in exile. We were even able to place protestant or Jewish children with agencies allied with their own faiths. Jim Baker returned to Cuba determined to work toward this goal.

The evening of December 24, I received a phone call from an agent at the U.S. Department of State, Mr. Frank Auerbach. His message was simple: the U. S. government was ready to permit two hundred unaccompanied Cuban children entrance into Miami. However, a non-governmental agency would have to take responsibility for them. He needed an immediate response, so I had no time to consult with my Bishop. I said yes. And at that very moment a process began to unfold that would influence the rest of my life.

On January 3, 1961, the United States severed diplomatic relations with Cuba, making it impossible for Cubans to obtain a visa to enter U.S. territory. A few days later, Frank Auerback called me from Washington to tell me that the Department of State would accept a letter signed by me in lieu of a visa. Such was the beginning of the famous Visa Waiver that allowed the Catholic Welfare Bureau to sponsor the passage of Cuban minors to the United States.

The first Cuban children arrived the twenty-sixth of December 1960. The last, the twenty-second of October 1962, the beginning of the Cuban Missile Crisis or the "October Crisis." Those children, their children, and even their grandchildren remain a part of my life even today. In truth, there are fourteen thousand stories to tell. Relying on the testimonies of just some of those fourteen thousand refugee children, and of some of the adults who helped them, Josefina Leyva tells their stories. They are filled with nostalgia for their homes, the difficulties they faced, the kindness they received from strangers, the misunderstandings caused by linguistic and cultural differences, their adaptation to a new way of life and how they adapted once again when they returned to the bosom of their families when at last their parents arrived.

The "Pedro Pan" children forged their lives in this remarkable land we call the United States. They are Cuban-Americans, but they have never lost their love of their homeland, the "Pearl of the Caribbean." Some have made the pilgrimage back, searching for the street where they lived and the home they vaguely remember. They were shocked by encounters with the places of their childhood, noting how much smaller everything seemed than how they remembered it.

In exile, they have seen their children grow and become adults. Some of the "Pedro Pan" children are now grandparents. Others have passed away here in the United States. Many have buried their parents in this foreign country that now feels like home, although they will always be strangers within its borders. Many have achieved great things in this adopted land. The majority has settled in and become a part of the great American experience as members of the middle class. They see their own children and ask themselves if they would be able to send them into exile if circumstances repeated themselves. Now middle-aged, they ask themselves how their parents could have made such a torturous decision. Since they always felt protected as children, many have never fully understood the choices their parents were forced to make, or the risk and sacrifice it all represents. Josefina Leyva's stories recreate life in Cuba as it was during the early 1970s, and offer some answers.

How did this come to be called *Operation Pedro Pan*? It was important from the very beginning that we in Miami avoided anything that could jeopardize the exodus, or the people in Cuba who worked to make it possible. We were never under the illusion that the Cuban government was unaware of what we were doing, nor that any publicity could easily have been used as propaganda to provoke some reaction. Therefore, we remained silent. Inevitably the Miami press discovered what was going on. When they came to me looking for a story, I told them the truth; but I asked them not to report it. The press cooperated and gave our work the code name *Operation Pedro Pan*, perhaps because the first unaccompanied Cuban child who arrived in Miami under our protection was named Pedro Menéndez.

Family or friends took in approximately half of the children who arrived. We placed the rest in foster homes or in orphanages spread across thirty-five different states. The majority of the children stayed for four years. When the "Freedom Flights" began in December 1965, their parents were given first priority by both governments to come to the United States. Some children remained in our care until adulthood; there were some whose parents never came. Others felt the separation was too much and they returned to the Island of their own accord.

Operation Pedro Pan opened the door to the United States for more than fourteen thousand unaccompanied children. Under the 1965 accord, only those Cubans who had close family members in the United States could come to this country. Perhaps this accounts for the one hundred thousand Cubans who clung to this hope and embarked on the "Freedom Flights" that departed Cuba for Varadero. Still now, in 1993, middle-aged Cubans in possession of a Visa Waiver ask me if it will still allow them to enter the United States. For them, it is too late; the Visa Waivers ended with the Missile Crisis in October 1962.

Monsignor Bryan Walsh

CHAPTER 1

"Sara, my brother René just killed himself at the police station where he was being held." The ardent voice of Manolo Ray, Minister of Public Works for Fidel Castro's government, rang through the telephone and struck Sara del Toro's fierce consciousness like a bolt of lightning.

"They must have killed him!" she gasped. "I just saw him. They were going to release him to me tomorrow!"

"How did he seem to you?" asked Ray, doing his best to control his emotions.

"He was fine; relieved that he was being sent here for house arrest" responded Sara. She said good-bye to Ray, dropped the phone and ran through the sprawling living and dining rooms to find her husband on the terrace at the far end of the first floor. Five of their children clamored around him; beautiful, mischievous youngsters. He is kneeling and they are climbing all over him, full of the joyful exuberance of their happy home.

"Amador! They've killed René Ray at the police station where Amejeiras is!

"Weren't you just there?" Amador Odio stand up smoothly, still balancing one of the children on his shoulders, and looks at his wife with alarm.

"Yes! And they must have killed him! He was completely fine—excited because tomorrow they were going to bring him here to our house since we were going to be in charge of his house arrest." Sara recalls the youthful image of René Ray, whom she had seen just minutes ago. Her maternal eye envisions him—a slim, happy youth of medium height with his dark hair pulled back in a ponytail, dressed as the guerilla he had been in the mountains of Sierra Maestra. He had served there in the Rebel Army lead by Fidel Castro against the government of General Batista.

"Who killed him, Amador? Ifigenio Amejeiras's deputy told me his chief wasn't there, and that tomorrow he was going to release René to me himself," says Sara, a graceful woman with salon-styled hair, wearing a beautiful, ruffled beige dress and a strand of pearls.

"Fidel Castro has to be involved if the Chief of Police, Amejeiras, did it," responds Odio. He sends the children to play out on the terrace, straightening to his full height. His ruddy complexion shines against his gray hair. His broad forehead and handsome, masculine features take on a serious, yet loving, expression giving him an air of staid elegance.

Amador and Sara—true friends as well as husband and wife—exchange looks, shocked by the tragic event. For both of them, the heroic prestige of Fidel's image is unraveling like a beautiful fabric un-knit by its maker's hand.

A while later, on route to the *Caballero* funeral home located in the center of Havana, Sara del Toro and Amador Odio talk, their concern over René Ray's suspicious death mounting. It is the uneasy month of March 1959, and just two months ago Fidel Castro assumed political control of the nation.

"Could Fidel be turning into a dictator? Could this be his first assassination?" wonders Amador, although he is little prone to doubt and inclined toward decisiveness. This time, however, he seems unwilling to give up the hope that Castro has brought to the nation. "Maybe René argued with Amejeiras, and he killed him in a rage. Maybe Fidel didn't know," he tells himself, wanting to believe it.

Amador and Sara enter the funeral home with the uncertainty of these questions hanging over them. They offer their condolences and embrace their friend, the Minister of Public Works, with whom they had conspired against Batista.

The atmosphere at the funeral belies the incongruity of the situation that led to it. The question as to whether René killed himself or was assassinated hovers over those who are paying their respects like a furious swarm of wasps over children on a playground. It is obvious that Minister Ray's grief stems not only from having lost his brother, but also from the suspicion that he was the victim of a crime. A few feet away, a stranger with thick glasses and a mustache murmurs about the event:

"They say they arrested René because he wouldn't give Fidel a hundred-thousand dollars that he brought down from Sierra Maestra where he was responsible for administering the Rebel Army's civilian funds."

"But that's not the whole story," whispers a young, attractive woman. "They say that René told Fidel that he had turned that money over to the Treasury Department, where it was supposed to go.

"René was high up in the Expropriations Department and he resigned," comments an elderly man, exhaling smoke from his cigar. "Could he have argued with Fidel?"

"He was Commander Amejeiras's prisoner. And he's one of the worst, even if he is the Chief of Police," murmurs a woman. But she had sympathized with Batista so no one paid attention to her next assertion: "You know he's a low-class marihuana fiend."

"René had written about his time at Sierra Maestra," explained a young man with intense eyes. "It seems that Fidel didn't like the book because René was anti-communist."

"What does that have to do with his death?" asks the elderly man who had spoken earlier. "I've never heard anything as absurd as that! There are no communists in this government, and Fidel isn't even remotely communist!

"It's a shame," chimes in a man dressed in a dark suit, obviously intended to resemble Fidel Castro. "Men become heroes for getting used to killing. Then later, when they're in power, there's no stopping them."

"And Manolo, what's he going to do now? Continue on as the Minister and keep his mouth closed, or denounce Fidel?" adds a heavy woman who viewed life in imperious mathematical terms.

The Odios had not known René very well. They had contacted him just to help Manolo who asked them to request his brother's transfer to their home. Now they were beginning to think the Minister had attempted the transfer as a last resort to save his younger brother's life. Sara and Amador were convinced of Ray's trustworthiness. He had proved his integrity working side-by-side with them in the plot against Batista. They cannot conceive of René being capable of robbery. And in their heart of hearts they are sure that René delivered the money Fidel asked him to—and to where it belonged, the Treasury Department.

"Manolo, Fidel is here," someone tells Ray. The Minister furrows his brow, evidently bothered by having to endure a visit from his all-powerful Prime Minister, now in charge of the country by virtue of public fascination and his charming image as a romantic guerrilla.

"You go and talk to him, Sara. Try to get him out of here quickly. I don't want to see him," Ray tells Sara del Toro who is ever ready to act decisively without a moment's hesitation. She sets off, determined to help her friend, never stopping to consider whether her resolve might harm her in Fidel's eyes if he is involved with this death. Sara arrives to greet the Prime Minister. Her sure step and her candid smile immediately communicate to any onlookers a complete absence of duplicity. Those present at the funeral turn to watch her greet, with the confidence inspired by this openness, the man adored as an idol by the people of Cuba. Fidel stands before her, striking in his olive green uniform, his dark eyes ablaze with the light of prophecy. The magic of his charisma surrounds him, like a religious icon encased in glass. At his waist hang a pistol and bullets, intended ostensibly to defend against any political coup. His black, unkempt beard frames a Grecian profile, giving him the desired messianic look of Jesus Christ and the *mambises* who had waged wars of independence in Cuba a century ago against Spain's colonial power. Fidel's armed guards surround him, looking in all directions as they move about the funeral home. There is a cluster of people without uniforms around him as well who, although people don't know it yet, are an essential part of his guard.

Fidel's hand is strong and smooth as he clasps Sara's slender fingers. As she meets his sharp gaze, she notes an unexpected change, watching the prophetic light of his intense expression dissolve into the coldness of that of a bird of prey. Images of Fidel flash through Sara's mind: the first time she met him in person, just down from the Sierra Maestra at the agricultural festival outside of Havana. At the time, he recalled that his brother Raúl had been engaged to one of Amador's nieces who lived in Santiago de Cuba on the southeastern-most point of the Island where they were from. He also remembered that Amador was the owner of the largest transportation company in the country, started with a single truck and in partnership with a friend. Fidel had called Amador to offer him the position of Minister of Transportation early in his government, but Odio had turned down the offer in order to avoid any conflict of interest with his highly successful company. "I have a lot of money, Fidel, and people will say that I stole it from the government," he responded frankly. "No. Thank you, but I won't be your Minister. But you can count on me to back you in any way I can." Sara remembers the raffle she organized at the long abandoned *Mazorra* mental hospital when Fidel named her its chief benefactress. Her efforts were supported by the ladies of Havana's high society, still under Fidel's messianic spell as the country's redeemer. They raised more than forty thousand Cuban pesos, which were still equal to the dollar, to repair and transform that depressing and gloomy place.

"How are your children, Sara?" Castro asks her in his role as the thoughtful friend, complete with flawless manners and an exaggerated expression of respect for the dead, in which he is currently immersed.

"My children are well. They remember you fondly," replies Sara, struggling to expel her new image of Fidel as a possible assassin and return to her image of him as a hero.

"Your son, Jorge Carlos, is going to be the ring-bearer at my sister Emma's wedding. She asked me to see if you would host her pre-wedding party at your estate. I told her of course you would agree because you are such good revolutionaries. Yes, marvelous revolutionaries!" repeats with characteristic emphasis the man on whose every word and gesture all of Cuba hangs.

"We would be honored to host it," replies Sara, forcing herself to recall her first image of Fidel as a great nationalist leader and reformer: the man the country needed to fix its widespread political and administrative corruption. "He's a rebel, like me," Sara tells herself, remembering her own cracked ribs, suffered during a protest against the Machado dictatorship nearly thirty years ago when she was still just a girl. She also remembers one morning in her childhood when a school friend dared her on the playground, "I bet you won't walk along the edge of the roof!" Sara climbed onto the terraced roof and when the mayor of Santiago de Cuba saw her slender outline walking at the edge of the abyss, sent an urgent message to her mother: "Principal, one of the girls at your school is walking on the roof. She is going to fall to her death." "It must be Sara," guessed her mother, running out to save her. "Fidel is just like me, fearless," thinks this determined woman, her empathy with her admired leader fully restored.

Fidel again takes her hand, and with the same audacity that propels him past any obstacle put in his path, he goes in search of Manolo Ray who receives him with an expression of complete disgust. Fidel searches his Minister's face with his penetrating gaze, and exits the funeral home, surrounded by the protection of his bodyguards.

"No! Fidel can't be an assassin!" thinks Sara del Toro, the pendulum of her doubt swinging to the other extreme with the passion of her natural vehemence. "René must have killed himself, even it seems unlikely!" and she walks back to her husband, Amador, to share with him her conclusion.

CHAPTER 2

René Ray's death weighed as heavily on Sara del Toro's mind as a shackle on a raw ankle. Nevertheless, she found herself compelled to hide her inner turmoil and feign a celebratory mood for the pre-wedding party in honor of Emma, one of Fidel Castro's younger sisters. The party had been planned before René's death, and was about to begin at *Hurra!*, the beautiful country estate owned by the Odio family just outside of Havana. "Maybe René really did kill himself," thought Sara, refusing to believe that Fidel Castro, the leader Cuba had so suffered to bring forth, could be an assassin. The scandal the Great Leader had unleashed in the press, accusing René of embezzling funds from the Rebel Army, had convinced nearly everyone since Fidel's word carried with it a sort of moral authority.

Amador Odio, an energetic man accustomed to mobilizing and leading others in his many projects, walked among the fourteen servants employed at his country home giving orders so that everything would be perfectly elegant. Later, Amador would mingle with the guests, the majority of whom had come from Mexico to attend the wedding of one of their compatriots to the Prime Minister of Cuba's sister. Flutes of the finest Baccarat crystal balanced on silver trays as the celebratory champagne was served. "And even if Fidel did kill him, it's not Emma's fault. She is good and sweet, charming and refined. Yes, Emma deserves this celebration," thought Sara to herself as she watched her husband mill about.

Fidel Castro had not yet arrived at the party; nor had his brother Raul, recently married to Wilma Espín, a guerrilla from Sierra Maestra who had graduated with a degree in chemical engineering. Also missing was Lina, the matriarch of this unusual family. Of the Castro family, present only was Juanita, whom Sara admired for her frankness and spontaneity.

A banquet of traditional Cuban dishes is served, laid out on both sides of a granite barbeque forming a distinct horseshoe. A few steps away, wrought iron and glass tables lead to the pool, decorated with colored lights. Sweet, melancholy Cuban music drifts from stone benches and leafy trees, controlled from an extraordinary, imported stereo system Amador had installed in the living room. The house is a two-story colonial with balconies and terraces. A few guests enter the bowling alley, admiring the pink granite floor. And the bride-to-be smiles at her good fortune. She stands excitedly at the brink of a new era, like her country for which all the traditional molds of legitimacy will be broken in order to mend old political evils. Cuba's high society has turned out at the Odio's country home, *Hurra!*, their attention to Fidel Castro's sister an expression of their unconditional support of the Revolutionary Government over which the Commander presides.

Sara and Amador's ten children enjoy the dazzling evening. César and Silvia, already grown and married, join in the dancing while the younger children amble about with their nannies, riding in their toy cars. As she smiles, jokes, and attends to her guests, Sara recalls the years of fighting against General Batista, spurred on by the desire to replace him with a true democracy, and the months when Aureliano Sánchez Arango, Minister of Education under Carlos Prío, the last constitutional president, hid in her house in Havana and conspired. Sánchez Arango had secretly come out of exile and entered the capital. One night, the police surrounded him, shot up Silvia's bedroom, and Aureliano had to jump from a balcony into the patio of one of Batista's army officials. As a gentleman and the Odios's neighbor, he showed him the door so that he could escape. "I am a rebel and a revolutionary," thought Sara "Amador, too. We're alike. That's why we're so good together." The days when they met in the bustling city of Santiago de Cuba stir in the recesses of her memory. Back then, in spite of his strong personality, Amador was afraid to approach her for fear that she would reject him. "He befriended my sister so he could figure out how to win me over. And I thought he was in love with her." Sara smiles at the memory. Since Amador does not like to dance, and given her natural chattiness, she seeks out a conversation with a guest to pass the time. Sara tells the woman that the school her mother had founded years ago in Santiago de Cuba was closed because she conspired against the dictator Machado in the early thirties.

"When Machado fell Tony de Varona, a member of the Student Board, came from Havana to look for my mother. He put her in charge of secondary education throughout the country. Amador came with him. He was nineteen when we married, and I was seventeen. He started with nothing and worked hard, driving trucks and building his business until it stretched across the whole country. He made his millions with hard work." Sara tells the story because silence and reflection do not come naturally to her. Silvia, her second daughter, comes looking for her and leads her to Emma. Sister of Fidel—whose charisma as a romantic warrior has crowned him leader of Cuba—Emma is tall, fair, beautiful and poised. She smiles at her Mexican fiancé, and is surrounded by more than a hundred guests from Mexico and Cuba's high society, the majority of whom are progressives at this moment in time. The elite support Castro's nationalism in a way comparable only to the wars of independence from Spain in 1868 when rich islanders fought for political power and defeated the Spanish troops that invaded Cuba. Faced with repression, those Cubans sacrificed everything in battles fought with machetes in the fields.

Suddenly, something like a premonition stirs in Sara's heart. She leaves her graceful and buoyant daughter, Silvia, and goes in search of her husband.

"Amador, what's going to happen to Cuba?" she asks.

"Whatever problems we suspect, we'll have to solve ourselves," he responds, spurred on by her admiration and the seriousness of her expression. "Sara, Fidel is moving toward a dictatorship, and we're going to have to begin to fight it!" Having believed in a promising future for their country, their outlook shifts and the two are gripped once again this night by uncertainty, swaying like a pendulum over an abyss.

Emma's exclusive wedding takes place two days later in Havana's eighteenth century Cathedral. This church, with its baroque exterior and a serene neoclassic interior, opens onto an old plaza filled with birds and shadows, flanked on all sides by colonial palaces with paved porticos supported by columns and arches. Havana's elite attend, demonstrating their support for Fidel Castro's restorative and profoundly reformist government. As of yet, they are unalarmed that the Maximum Leader is not talking about convening elections as he had promised the revolutionary groups that supported him during the insurrection against General Batista. The intellectual and economic leaders of the country applaud his abolishment of prostitution and gambling that had flourished, as the previous regime's police looked the other way. They also support lowering rents, although doing so works to the detriment of many of them, worker protections that conflict with their own interests, and Agrarian Reform that plantation owners' sons support from the universities where they study. The country's rich thank Castro that now Cuba might have a voice in the world since this leader's genius had brought the country to the forefront of international protests against military dictatorships in Latin America. These privileged few hope, in addition, that Cuba will be the spiritual guide for Central and South America, now that it has unexpectedly shed its anonymity.

Amador Odio and Sara del Toro are among Cuba's progressive millionaires who enter the Cathedral arm in arm, where members of the Castro family await. The Odios see Raúl, elegantly dressed; and Lina Ruiz, mother of the two peasant brothers whose popularity has converted into living myths. Lina softens the plainness of her appearance with an expensive mantilla. The bourgeoisie congratulates Fidel and Raúl Castro, these upstarts who lead the progress of the nation day by day, and accepts them without reservation.

Emma arrives in a black Cadillac but Fidel, who is to give her away, has not yet appeared. The bride waits for him in the car, anguished by every tick of the clock. She waits and waits until finally she decides to walk down the aisle with someone else; someone hurriedly selected from among the guests. She enters, concealing her annoyance at her brother's betrayal, and walks to the alter where her groom awaits. Preceding her down the aisle are the ring-bearers: Jorge Carlos, one of Sara and Amador Odios's young sons and another boy, the son of Manolo Ray, the minister whose brother, even in death, is at the center of a scandal over supposed embezzlement. Organ music erupts in the Cathedral, redoubling the solemn atmosphere. As a beautiful soprano voice begins the traditional *Ave María*, Fidel enters the island's principal church, his muddy boots echoing and staining the carpet of the center aisle. He arrives without a jacket or tie. The collar of his olive green military shirt is open and the belt that holds his pistol and ammunition weighs heavily on his strong hips signifying virility. His bodyguards surround him, dirty and in shirtsleeves like him. Sara and Amador see him arrive and hear the Cathedral doors close, in order to prevent any attempt on his life.

Ray, the minister who is at the center of a conspiratory situation in which the Odios are now implicated, whispers to Sarah, "I'm in grave danger here." Sara and Amador feel that Fidel, with his deliberately late arrival, his gun, his heavy footsteps and muddy boots, is insulting God, good-taste, the sanctity of marriage, tradition, and the people who support him. The people, who do not see this behavior, follow him—among other reasons because they think he is religious when they see the medallion of the Virgin of Charity that hangs around his neck, as strong as that of a Greek athlete.

"You're an animal, Fidel! Look at you, showing up like this!" whispers Sara, as if joking, feeling him pass by her. The Leader, masking his cynicism with humor, emits a guffaw that shatters the trills of the *Ave María*. It's like a vow that he will destroy this world that he hates because he feels left out, being the bastard child of a peasant family. Because, although he was educated by the Jesuits, he hates the God that made men unequal, even though he's drawn to the sides of the most disadvantaged. That is why he will bury God, in order to crown himself as the all-powerful god of the masses.

CHAPTER 3

"Sara! Save me a seat at your table. I'm on my way over!" Fidel Castro, an unexpected arrival at *El Carmelo* that darkly foreboding night in 1960, greets Sara and Amador Odio, seated with Pelayito Cuervo, sub-secretary of the Department of the Interior. Sara, Amador and Pelayito look at one another, unnerved by the arrival of the Maximum Leader as they wait for Zurbarán, a Venezuelan diplomat, to pick up Pelayito and take him to the embassy for asylum. Pelayito has left his resignation in a drawer at his vice-ministerial office, and the three hold their breath wondering if Fidel has already found it and that's why he's hovering around, or if his appearance is simply a coincidence.

In this country, it's clear not only that Fidel has initiated a dictatorship, but that it is decidedly communist. He has established diplomatic and economic ties with the dreaded Soviet Union and all of its satellite countries. He has confiscated the assets of all foreigners in Cuba, including the telephone company. He has nationalized industries that were flourishing. He has made Agrarian Reform distinctly socialist. In addition, he has placed troops at the entrances of all Latin American embassies to arrest anyone who seeks asylum.

Amador Odio, quiet and serious when he's not fond of the company, looks around without saying a word. He, Sara and Pelayito Cuervo look at each other again, thinking about Fidel's inopportune arrival at this famous Havana restaurant that has always attracted rich, high-level politicians, intellectuals, dancers from the National Ballet, journalists and members of the social elite. "Fidel's a communist! Who could doubt it now?" Amador ruminates; and he feels that Fidel, this sly fox who is just beginning to show his Machiavellian tendencies, knows that he is conspiring to bring him down.

Meanwhile, the great leader's military escorts don't miss a beat. They have erupted into the spacious salon and fanned out; sniffing the air for any imminent attempt against their commander, ready to defend him with their lives. Devoid of even a hint of decorum, they begin to search the place as has become the custom wherever Fidel appears. So, they look under tables and chairs, they inspect the walls, examine lamps and monitor those present, obviously trying to intimidate them. Outfitted in olive green pants and shirts with heavy belts bearing their pistols and ammunition, they carry in their agile hands the latest model sub-machine guns. They walk with arrogant strides, brazenly gloating over their power. They don't realize, unfamiliar as they are with history's violent turns, that their attitude and their actions represent a tragic return to a centuries old phenomenon that had been eradicated by western political progress—despotism, and its terrible consequences: intellectual slavery, human insecurity and Barbary.

"Fidel is here!" The news spreads from person to person throughout *El Carmelo*, filling the patrons who overflow the chattering tables with anticipation. Some hope that his ardent charisma will inspire them. Others are simply curious to see, for the briefest of moments, the man they have deemed a monster.

Extricating himself from the crowd of people who have surrounded him, hoping to hear his national and international prophecies or to touch him and feel his magnetism, like that of some religious icon, Fidel comes to the Odio's table and sits down with solemn and theatrical flair. His bodyguards stand around him, surveying every detail, looking for some presumed assassin among the well-mannered diners in the room.

"If Fidel knew that I have resigned and am planning to request asylum at the Venezuelan embassy, he would have had me arrested and made an example of me. It's very likely he would have had me shot," thinks Pelayito Cuervo, whose father was assassinated by general Batista's men the night of the assault on the Presidential Palace, March 13, 1956. That night, they arrested Amador and all of the employees of his company, *Shipping and Transport*, implicated by his friendship with Menelao Mora who had died leading that suicidal mission. César, Amador and Sara's oldest son, was also incarcerated that day. He was a member of the Civil Resistance Movement. That night, Commander Ortega, one of the Odio's neighbors, jumped the wall between their homes to warn Sara: "Run! Tonight they're going to kill Pelayo Cuervo and your husband, Amador." Terrified, Sara went to see Anselmo Alliegro, a minister who had been one of her mother's students.

He promised he would speak to Batista and save Amador's life. Pelayo Cuervo was hiding at a friend's house where they found him and killed him.

Taking a seat, Fidel asks Pelayo Cuervo's son, "How's your work at the Ministry going?" examining the fine features of Pelayito's face with his penetrating stare.

"Very well," responds the other, swallowing with some difficulty a spoonful of ice cream.

"Sara, I'm going to recite the names of your ten children, in order," announces Fidel, repeating the feat that had amused the Odio family the year before.

"Let's see."

"César, Silvia, Sarita, Any Laury, Mary Loly, Amador, Javier, Freddy, Jorge Carlos y Marianne."

"You've got the memory of an elephant!" responds Sara, masking the tension of the moment with humor. "You didn't make a single mistake!"

As Sara and Fidel continue to chat, Amador thinks to himself, "I have to get out to the street to tell Zurbarán to keep circling the block until Fidel leaves."

Castro glances with interest at Sara's Rolex watch, to which she responds: "Fidel, you're not going to take it away from me, you already have two!" pointing at his well muscled arm, hardened by exercise and shooting.

They laugh and Castro devours his ice cream. "Amazing," thinks Sara, "since he never eats anywhere these days. Amador wonders, "Is he eating with us in order to fool us? To make us think that he doesn't know we're conspiring against him?" Amador excuses himself and walks toward the restroom. On his way, he turns toward the sidewalk, walking between Castro's military and civilian guards. He stands there, awaiting Zurbarán's car. "Could he have left already? Maybe he thought we didn't show up," he wonders. And thinks, with neither fear nor regret, having carried out similar missions for many others: "If Fidel had found out that we were going to help Pelayito gain asylum tonight, he would have arrested all three of us, Pelayito, Sara and me." Finally, the car appears at the corner. Zurbarán himself is driving, implicating himself to the core in who knows how many conspiracies against Castro, upholding Venezuelan President, Rómulo Betancourt's crusade to defend democracy in the Americas. Seeing Amador, Zurbarán stops and the machine-gun carrying guards watch him, ready to fire at the slightest provocation. Amador walks past the line of new Chryslers used by Fidel and his men and into the street to speak with his Venezuelan friend, as humble and kind hearted as most of his countrymen.

"Fidel's inside," he says. "Keep circling the block until he leaves and I can get my man out."

"O.K." replies Zurbarán, accelerating as Amador returns to the restaurant. Seated at the table, his finely manicured hands clench the napkin and the ice cream spoon, listening to Fidel ramble on, always preferring to listen to himself rather than to others.

"Sara, the Ambassador of Poland went to see your house in Miramar this morning. He would like to rent it. But you shouldn't rent it to him; you have so many children."

"I don't plan to rent it," says Sara.

"He has won without us even noticing," thinks Amador. "He knows everything. He's already established a very efficient network of spies."

"This is communism. Without a doubt," thinks Pelayo Cuervo's son. "That's why I'm leaving. I'll join those on the outside who are preparing to invade Cuba and I'll return with my brothers to fight for liberty."

"And lastly, I'm telling you not to rent your house, Sara. I just left a meeting about the Urban Reform Law. Tenants are going to be given ownership," continues Fidel.

"That's ridiculous!" thinks Amador.

"Just what we needed," Pelayito Cuervo says to himself. "That will be the last straw to set off the chaos that's been hovering over the country. We have got to overthrow Fidel!"

Castro finishes his ice cream and stands up. As quickly as a receding wave, he is out the door, disappearing amid his confidants. Like a bolt of lightening striking a tree, the night fills in the void of his silhouette.

Amador and Pelayito wait a few minutes and then leave. Sara stays seated, praying. When she sees her husband on his way back, she picks up her purse and they walk to their new Cadillac. Driving, with her at his side, Amador alerts her:

"Sara, you have to be prepared. They could pick me up any time. I'm involved in an attempt against Fidel, in helping conspirators gain asylum and in distributing propaganda against the regime. If they catch me, you'll have to take care of the trucking business, as you did when César and I were exiled by the Batista dictatorship. You'll run *Shipping and Transport* until Fidel takes it. He's going to steal everything from everybody.

"I'll take care of it," affirms Sara decidedly, letting neither fear nor the impending situation overwhelm her.

"We've got to get our five older children out of Cuba. You and I will stay and fight this communism. We have to. Morality is not open to interpretation!

"So we'll stay! And we'll fight! You can count on me."

The darkness of the fields consumes these last words as they drive to their country estate, *Hurra!*, where they spend most of their time now so as to hide their activities. And the night strikes their hearts like a dagger, frightening away the happiness that until that moment had been the core of their strength in the ongoing struggle for survival.

CHAPTER 4

"This is where we'll meet Father Walsh," Mauricio Ferré tells Sara as he opens the door to help her out of the car in front of a house just outside of downtown Miami. Sara del Toro has made a brief trip from Cuba to Miami to send her three teenage children, Sarita, Any Laury and Mary Loly from here, where they have begun their exile, to the Dallas area in Texas, where they have received scholarships to study at a high school run by the Ursuline Sisters.

Sara clutches her beautiful Parisian scarf to her throat, bracing against Florida's chill in early 1961. Walking beside Ferré toward the old mansion, she looks at him with admiration. Ferré is a young, Puerto Rican millionaire who is already involved in politics and who will, years later, became Mayor of Miami. She has great faith in people, based on her easy empathy, and looking at his light skin, pleasing features and silky, light hair, Sara is grateful for his collaboration with the exodus of Cuban children, in support of which he has provided the house that they're now approaching. Inside, an Irish priest is living with a group of Cuban children who began arriving in exile from their tragic Caribbean island on December 26 of last year. A moment later, Ferré opens the door to a simple office and a priest appears, about 30 years old, tall, blond, and well built, with bushy eyebrows and piercing blue eyes. He smiles as he speaks to Sara and shakes her hand tenderly. Ferré acts as interpreter since Sara speaks little English, and the priest knows no Spanish.

"Sara, this is Father Bryan Walsh. He's housing the Cuban children who are arriving here alone, escaping from communism. You'll see that he'll pick up Spanish very soon." Turning back to the priest, he says in English that Sara understands: "Father, this is the person I was telling you about. She's agreed to distribute the Visa Waivers in Cuba."

"Welcome," replies the priest aided by Ferré's translation, and adds: "If Ferré has brought you, you have my every confidence."

Father Walsh invites his visitors to be seated and speaks slowly for his interpreter. "Madam, many Cubans wish to remain in Cuba, fighting against the communist dictatorship. But they want to send their children to the United States to protect them. You will be giving Visa Waivers to Cuban children. They will come alone. I wish you luck in your work. We must keep it secret, both here and in Cuba so that Fidel Castro doesn't stop this exodus, since it would be bad press for his regime. I will try to make sure it's not reported here. In Cuba, authorities in the regime will not take kindly to your involvement in this plan. Marxist governments restrict, and even prohibit, emigration.

"That's exactly what's happening in my country," replies Sara, as energetic and expressive in her response and understanding as ever.

"I'm going to give you multiple copies of the Visa Waiver document that replaces a U. S. visa. It's not exactly a visa; it's permission from the government for Cuban children to enter the country. You'll distribute them to the children in your country who need them.

Obviously, Sara does not fear the reprisals that such activity could bring her way. Nonetheless, in Cuba the sole thought of emigrating to foreign soil is considered a serious political treason and is punished with social repudiation by the masses that support Fidel.

Sara says good-bye to Father Walsh and leaves with Ferré. Days later, when she arrives in Cuba, she remembers her encounter with this priest, and another meeting with her friend Manolo Ray, ex-minister of Public Works, exiled now in Miami. Sara was deeply saddened when, despite the friendship they had always maintained, she found herself having to give him a message from "Eugenio," the man who had taken his place at the national level leading the People's Revolutionary Movement, the clandestine anti-Castro movement that Ray had founded. The militants in the group were upset with Ray because he had promised to stay in Cuba, risking his life as they were; but he had escaped to Miami.

"Manolo, 'Eugenio' says that he's not going to follow your directions," Sara told him.

"And who's 'Eugenio' to contradict me?" asked Ray, offended, in one of those terrible moments faced by men accustomed to revolutionary activities.

"He's the one who is there—fighting. People follow him now," was Sara's pained response.

She descends the airplane stairs at the Havana airport, and enters the waiting room to meet Amador who has come, with their five children who remain in Cuba, to pick her up. Amador retrieves his wife's suitcase, which contains the Visa Waivers given to her by Father Walsh at their meeting in Miami.

"Madam, you are under arrest! Come with me," says a man in military uniform.

"Under arrest? Me? Why?" she responds, feigning naïve surprise.

"Come with me, Madam!"

They take her into a room where they begin to interrogate her about her trip to Miami. With every ounce of intensity that her natural animation allows, Sara defends her rights, responding that she went to Miami to see three of her children off to Dallas where they had scholarships to study with the Ursuline nuns.

Amador, seeing that they've detained his wife, calls in favors from people he knows in the airport, even now when no one dares to help a friend estranged from the newly imposed political system. Accustomed to conspiracy, neither Sara nor Amador are intimidated by the arrest; and when they free her, they go home in their Cadillac to the Miramar district of Havana. The children sit on their mother's lap as Amador drives; and exiting the highway that led them away from the airport, they enter the capital. Amador worriedly contemplates the spectacle in the streets, like some tragic carnival in which the zenith of political fanaticism pairs with reactionism, obliterating the familiarity of a life he is prepared to die for.

"This isn't just a political, or even social, problem; it's a humanitarian problem," thinks Odio, looking out his window. Darkness has come early this winter afternoon, and the city begins turning on its lights, minus the formerly joyful tones of everyday contentment. The mood that has permeated Havana since the beginning of 1961 belies the anxious hope of a military invasion backed by the U. S. government to depose Fidel Castro. The United States has broken diplomatic relations with Cuba after canceling their annual sugar quota, the sale of which would have guaranteed the economy of the Caribbean island. The Soviet Union will buy the share, putting Cuba at the mercy of that imperialist country. The first airplanes of the feared invasion could begin bombarding this beautiful capital any minute now. Sandbags form trenches in front of office buildings and machine-gun carrying militia watch enemies of Fidel's cause, surreptitiously radicalized toward communism, although it has not yet been officially declared. Squads of militia travel the streets, their heavy boots aggressively striking the asphalt, with the oppressive, new rhythm of life. Masses huddle in front of the American embassy, now under protection of the Swiss. Gathering menacingly around it, crowds shout vile insults. Not far away, they have toppled the eagle that sat atop the monument to the victims of the *Maine*, the warship whose demolition in a Cuban port occasioned the United States' declaration of war against Spain in 1895, and their alliance with the island's Liberation Army. Near a group of benches under a tree, sits a piano swollen by Cuba's torrential rains. A handful of militants belonging to the Castrist organization "Rebel Youth," stole it from a house abandoned by a family that immigrated to Miami. The piano sat there forgotten, unprotected from the elements, after accompanying a political rally in which participants sang the revolutionary hymns that define Fidel's ardent ideology.

"Sara, we have to bring down Fidel!" exclaims Amador vehemently. "We can't let him poison our children's lives!"

"We'll fight together," vows his wife.

Arriving at their home in the elite Miramar district, they find Sara's hairdresser knocking on their door. The two women embrace and go in to share a cup of coffee.

"Sara, I've come to ask for your help," reveals the hairdresser, as she rearranges with her fingers a lock of her client's beautifully styled hair.

"Tell me how I can help."

"I'm terrified because they say that the government is going to take away our rights as parents. They say they're going to send thousands of children to the Soviet Union if Fidel loses the war that's coming. My husband and I would leave Cuba with our children; but you know that my mother is dying of cancer. She wouldn't survive a trip. Tell me if there's anything you can do for my children; maybe get them a visa from one of your diplomat friends. Do you know anyone in Miami who could take them in?"

"Look, I've got a solution," responds Sara, overjoyed to help her friend. "Your children will be the first to receive a Visa Waiver."

"What's a Visa Waiver?"

"Permission to enter the United States without a visa. Wait here. I'm going to get one from my suitcase. I haven't even opened it yet. In Miami, Father Walsh will take care of the children. Let me tell you what you have to do."

News of the Visa Waivers that could get children out of Cuba spread across the terrified country like water over a drought stricken field. Desperate people learned how to obtain one in the murmuring of churches, secretly through clandestine organizations, visiting their closest friends. From there, they came to Sara's house, or to the country estate, *Hurra!*, overcoming travel difficulties that were already becoming apparent. One of the first people to visit Sara asking for a Visa Waiver is a humble woman whose desperation for her children's future has brought her from the remote city of Holguín on the eastern end of the Island. She arrives dressed in black, with nothing more than a dogged mother's love.

"They shot my husband," explained the woman, used to being a social pariah. "He was in Batista's army. They accused him of torturing and killing. I don't believe he could have done that.... I need to get my children out of Cuba. I have a ten-year-old girl and a four-year-old boy. I don't want them to grow up here, hearing that their father was an assassin. And I can't leave because my only brother is a prisoner. They accused him of distributing anti-Castro literature. I found out about you from a relative of mine who knows a friend of yours."

Sara had fought against general Batista since his *coup d'etat* on the 10th of March 1952. César, her oldest son had participated in the Civil Resistance Movement and had been exiled twice with his father for involvement in conspiracies. She herself, faking a pregnancy, had carried sensitive papers in a padded garment, delivering messages between Aureliano Sánchez Arango, who was hiding in her house in Havana and Carlos Prío, the deposed president who was exiled in Miami. But now, seated next to this peasant woman, Sara is happy to provide her children the opportunity to grow up free from humiliation.

"Here are two Visa Waivers. When they arrive at the airport in Miami they must ask for 'George.' He will meet them and take them to a place where they will be cared for."

"God bless you! But I have another problem, Ma'am."

"What is it?"

"The money to buy their tickets. I don't have a family member abroad who can send them to us and you know that they won't let us buy them here."

"I'll get them for you," says Sara, accustomed to helping people, and she takes the woman by the arm and leads her to the dining room where she is given lunch.

"Ms. Sara, a priest from San Antonio's is calling for you," one of her maids tells her.

"The priests are getting ready in case they have to leave. They're going to arrest them any day now. The havoc that the crowds cause around the churches just tears me apart!" thinks Sara, walking to pick up the phone and assure the priest that Zurbarán, from the Venezuelan embassy, has agreed to give them the visas they need. Next, she receives a black woman who has come to visit her. Sara is impressed by her dignity, her serenity and the objectivity that guides her. She discreetly contains her surprise when she sees the expensive furniture and decorations that fill the house, now even more plentiful since friends who have fled the country have brought them here for safekeeping.

"Ma'am, I heard about you at my church and have come to ask for a Visa Waiver for my six year old son. It kills me that black people are letting themselves be manipulated by Fidel Castro. He's promised to give them the rights we've never had. And they don't see that he's using them to keep himself in power. Thousands and thousands of them have joined the militia, ready to die for him.

Sara gives her the visa, and the money she needs to gain her son's freedom.

The year has kept pace with Cuba's asphyxiating atmosphere, amid military mobilizations, national states of emergency, conspiracies, sabotages, escapes from the country, terror and ever-increasing shootings. As all this takes place, Sara has distributed the Visa Waivers freely, even to strangers. She has forced from her mind the fear that undercover G-2 agents might come to see her. Her goal is to serve, and she has served, ignoring any risk to herself.

On the afternoon of April 14, 1961, Amador's wife is meeting with a group of mothers whose children have received Visa Waivers when Amador arrives unannounced and hurries upstairs.

"Sarah, the invasion's coming very soon," he tells her. "We have to hide some people who have been found out and find them asylum at the embassies. We need medicine and cash, and we have to find somewhere to hide more priests. They're going to arrest them for sure!"

Overwhelmed by the drama this inescapable historic need has placed on her, Sara clutches her rosary as night falls. She has always been very devout and she begins to pray that something will happen to sweep Fidel from power without causing more death or more pain for Cuba. She is still praying when Manuel, one of her most professional employees comes to announce that dinner is ready. Entering the dining room, Sara sees her staff gathered around a television set.

"Ms. Sara! They're burning *El Encanto!*"

"Oh, my God! It's like the world's coming to an end tonight!" they whisper in alarmed tones.

On the screen, they see the most ravaging fire Havana has ever known. The flames leap, like angry giraffes, covering the immense *El Encanto* building, the country's most lavish department store, where the wealthy purchase imported goods from Paris and New York. Never before this deadly night has the fight between the liberty and oppression of Cuba taken to the streets. Lines of militia and civilians form to help the firemen extinguish the blaze. Long human chains of fanatical Fidelists pass the great store's exquisite merchandise from hand to hand, to save it. The sky is choked with smoke, the weight of which falls over the city like a rockslide; and amid the successive announcements that come across the television about the event, one appears on the screen, wounding Sara as she hears it:

"An employee of *El Encanto* has died."

"She was burned to death. There is nothing left of her."

"She was trying to save the merchandise in the children's department where she worked.

"My God! Who is it?" asks Sara, astounded, trying to make her way to the table where the linen tablecloth flutters in the breeze.

"Her name was Fe del Valle."

"Oh, God no!" She was my friend! She dressed my children! She was always so kind to me!"

Sara is overcome by a wave of sadness and weeps for her country that had once been so peaceful and blessed, but is now tearing itself apart.

"Sara, calm down!" instructs Amador, coming downstairs and holding her. "This is a civil war. Worse things will happen."

Sara's sobbing startles the servants and the children, who abandon their toys and bury their faces in her skirt, frightened to see her so distraught.

"Sara! Sara! Pull yourself together!" orders Amador, still holding her.

"Well, what do you expect? She was my friend! She was my friend!"

Now Sara is crying for Amador and their children, wondering if she will lose them, entrenched as they are in this terrifying economic, social and human crisis that has torn through Cuba like a devastating hurricane of historic proportion.

Sara keeps issuing Visa Waivers until September 1961. Father Walsh sends them to her from Miami with Cornellas, an employee of *Pan American* airlines. Many children, and even adults, benefit from Sara's efforts. Many others would collaborate with her in this humanitarian operation. Among them, Pancho Finlay, also an employee of *Pan Am*, and his wife Esther de la Portilla. Bishop Alfredo Muller, in Cienfuegos, a city in the South of the Island. Some people contact relatives already in Miami and ask them for visas, which are smuggled to them in letters. An English woman, Penny Powel, who drove an ambulance during the bombing of London in World War II, would also be implicated in distributing these visas. And Polita Grau, a niece of the ex-president Ramón Grau, would generously distribute Visa Waivers throughout many regions of Cuba. *Rescate,* the underground women's network she led, would get the waivers to many children. Hilda Feo and Alicia Thomas were among its members. Polita would spend fourteen tragic years in prison for her valiant anti-Castro activities; and because of her dignity during those terrible years in the women's prison, she would become a beloved figure among her fellow prisoners. Her brother, Mongo Grau, would also be caught distributing Visa Waivers. Held for anti-communist activities, he would be jailed for more than twenty years. Hundreds, perhaps thousands of people were involved in the distribution of those visas. Risking their lives in an operation deemed illegal by the Castro regime, each of those heroes would provide the hope for freedom to fourteen thousand children who would count among a profoundly revealing exodus indicative of the horrifying situation that continues to envelop Cuba.

CHAPTER 5

The silhouette of Havana's Rancho Boyeros airport emerges like a sluggish worm during the first perilous days of that unforgettable October that swept over Cuba with impending doom. A string of humiliating revolutionary slogans chanted by fanatical groups claw at the still horizon like a talon at a child's tender skin.
—"Fidel, Fidel! Yankees go to hell!"
—"Fidel, Fidel, he's our man! The Yanks can't get him, nobody can!"
—"Cuba yes, Yankees no! —Cuba yes, Yankees no! —Cuba yes, Yankees no!"
—"Fuck Kennedy! Remember the Bay of Pigs!"
—"To the wall! —To the wall! —To the wall! —To the wall! —To the wall!"[1]

"Tonight Fidel is speaking at the Presidential Palace! You must go! It's your revolutionary duty!" The day's instructions echo throughout the island, further oppressing a people who dare not hope of reclaiming a normal existence.

Larger than life images of the Maximum Leader's bearded face inundate the entire country. Thousands of women are infatuated with him because of his good looks, just as they used to adore famous movie stars. His charisma has cast the nation's lifestyle, like an iron fist molding a bit of clay. Hatred and bitterness have enveloped life's former peacefulness.

Race and class issues have lead to extraordinary official reprisals, exacerbated by panic over another invasion. The collective psyche has become paranoid under the treat of such an invasion and is erupting in mounting aggression toward, and persecution of, those suspected of not supporting the regime. The fanaticism of the Fidelists ensures that the next invasion will be defeated like that of the Bay of Pigs, hardly five months ago. An unrelenting vigilance has permeated cities and the countryside, sinking its claws into every inch of the country. And the delusions of grandeur, equally paranoid, foretell the triumph of a worldwide

---
[1] Reference to the firing squad.

Communist Revolution spanning two or three years of war, the leaders of which will be trained in Cuba, enjoying privileges paid for by the hunger of the masses in this country disastrously split between the communists and the anti-communists. Fidel is constantly on the state-run television and radio, covered by the nationalized press as the world leader who, by the end of the decade, will rule the people of Asia, Africa, Europe and the Americas, not to mention the United States.

"This dictatorship is a disgrace," comments Wifredo Chirino, Public Prosecutor of Pinar del Río, dismayed by the loudspeaker at the airport entrance that emits one of Fidel Castro's ominous speeches in which he promises more totalitarianism and increased punishment for traitors to the communist homeland, as well as a perfected Cuba that will enjoy a standard of living never before seen among the world's nations.

Mr. Chirino puts an arm around the hard shoulders of his only son, Wifredito, a tall, wiry boy. They look alike from the side, but Wifredito has his mother's dark eyes and fantastic black hair that falls, disheveled, over his brow stamping his face with an air of uncertainty as he sets off to the United States by himself. The two, father and son, stop at the door of the "fishbowl"—a room constructed with glass walls that will come to be a tragic symbol of the times. At their side, his mother, holding a baby girl in her arms and his nine-year-old sister by the hand, chokes back tears like searing shards of glass.

Mr. Chirino leans over to whisper to the boy, straightening his impeccable gray tie, "Son, now you're on your own. Take care of yourself. Be good. Write to us. We're counting on you. You'll see, in a few months, Fidel will fall and you'll come back to Cuba. We're sending you to Miami so they won't arrest you for being Catholic or for hanging out with boys who pass out anti-communist leaflets. You know, they were going to arrest your sister Marilé's husband."

"Yes, Papá," responds Wifredito, squaring his adolescent shoulders under his suit. Emotion waivers in his impetuous dark eyes as his customary smile fades from his face.

"Find Marilé when you get to Miami. Write to us and let us know if she's O.K. —if there are any problems with the pregnancy. She's been through so much!" his mother says wearily.

Wifredito kisses each one of them and, as he enters the "fishbowl," bumps into a young girl who looks at him in surprise. "She has pretty eyes," he thinks immediately, and he watches her go into the glass room holding the hand of a small, pale girl who's having trouble breathing. She sits down next to her, all the while clutching her hand. Behind him, the silhouettes of airplanes stand out against the runway, heralding the impending trip that will tear them away. Wifredito presses his face to the wall of the fishbowl facing the tarmac so his family, who is still standing in the waiting room, cannot see the emotions that are overwhelming him. The image of his girlfriend appears in front of one of the planes and steps toward him. She is pretty, blond and blue-eyed, just a bit older than he is. "We'll dance at my cousin's fifteenth birthday party next month, Teresita. I won't forget you." And a heart-felt melody begins to play uneasily in his memory.

The glass door between the fishbowl and the waiting room closes, like fate's sword falling on a forsaken family. An arrogant official, dressed in khaki pants and shirt locks the door and walks by an olive skinned, ten year-old boy, tall and strong, who puts his hand against the glass as his parents place theirs opposite it on the other side. Their hands meet, separated by the cold surface of the glass that soon becomes foggy from the warmth and emotion that cling to it.

The official sits down at a table at the front of the fishbowl and hurriedly calls the names of the anxious passengers who are about to leave Cuba. Some have taken seats in the few chairs that line the glass walls. Most are standing, shuffling anxiously around the glass rectangle like fish imprisoned in a tank. Passage through these glass walls represents a rupture in normal life and a brush with the razor's edge of their new one. When they look across the waiting room, they see their families helplessly gathered for the good-bye that might separate them forever.

"Don't cry, Maricarmen," the dark-eyed girl Wifredito Chirino had bumped into on his way into the fishbowl tells her little sister. She adjusts the barrette holding the little girl's hair and reassures, "Don't be afraid, Mari. I'm with you. We're going to stay together." Her cold, delicate fingers clutch the "worm" containing only three sets of clothes, and suddenly her sense of abandonment forces her to assume the enormous responsibilities of motherhood.

"Elisa Vilano." It sounds menacing, coming from the official shuffling paperwork. The two girls stand, and swaying like a pair of delicate reeds, walk toward him and stop in front of his table.

"Which of you is Elisa?" asks the uniformed man. Like all of Fidel's followers, he is in shirtsleeves without a tie.

"I am," says the older sister.

"You, go sit down. I didn't call you."

"Go ahead, Mari and wait for me over there," Ely tells her softly. Her soothing voice revealing her sweet nature.

"Elisa Vilano, fourteen-years-old, address in Guanabacoa." Verifies the officer begrudgingly as he flips through her passport and stares at her. "She looks older. Already filling out. A pretty little thing. Too bad she's a worm," he thinks. "I see you're alone, off to support Yankee imperialism."

"I'm not alone. I'm going with my little sister," replies Elisa trembling with fear.

"Your parents don't want us to turn you into a good communist, eh?

The girl remains silent; afraid that any response she gives might cost her their passage out of Cuba. In her adolescent imagination, she contrasts this harsh official against her first crush, the charming and attractive commander, Camilo Cienfuegos. Memories of his youthful charisma still fill her heart. "He wasn't like them," she tells herself sadly. "That's why they made him disappear."

Meanwhile, Wifredito Chirino looks at his watch. It is exactly ten o'clock and he shrugs off the melody that has been playing in his head and goes to the glass where his family is gathered. The boy notes that each one of them is devastated by this abrupt separation. His baby sister, just one year old, holds out her arms and, wanting Wifredito to pick her up, stumbles into the glass wall of the fishbowl. She bumps her head and starts crying.

His father holds her in his arms and tears spill down the boy's face. He hurries to wipe them away when they call his name.

"Wifredo Chirino!

"Here," he responds, holding out his passport to the official, who inspects in as he looks at the boy suspiciously.

"Fourteen. Born in Consolación del Sur, in Pinar del Río Province... Come here, boy. Is that your father over there holding the little girl?"

"Yes," answers Wifredito, suddenly bothered by the man's rudeness.

"The Public Prosecutor in Pinar del Río. I know him. So, the Prosecutor's sending his son out of Cuba!"

"He's not sending me; I'm going on my own," corrects the boy, hoping to protect his father from any dangerous political allegations.

"You're a minor. If he hadn't signed for you, you wouldn't be going. You're off to Yankee Imperialism. And him, is he going, too?"

"No, he's staying," again trying to defend his father against the risk of suspicion. "Oh, Teresita, I miss you," Wifredito thinks, picking up his passport and leaning against the glass. Suppressing his tears, he pulls himself together and gives his family a sign expressing his hope that he'll be back next month for his cousin's fifteenth birthday party. Today, Wifredito Chirino suffers his first heartbreak: separation from a girlfriend he truly loves. Presently, amid the tears that both he and his family try to hide, memories that they share wordlessly spring to mind: the big house in Consolación del Sur with its enormous Creole railings on the front porch where he used to climb endlessly as a mischievous child. "That boy is hyperactive," his mother used to say as she went off to work as a Pharmacy manager. They share the fleeting scent of the pony given to Wifredito by a friend of his father when he was five years old. In an early example of his adventurous spirit, the boy set out to ride it while no one was watching—until the pony bucked and threw him, leaving him crying and holding a broken arm. The melody that came to him as he said good-bye returns, but this time Wifredito Chirino hears it with a driving beat, like a rumba, different in every way from the classical music his sister used to play, except for the desperate emotion expressed. His older sister, Marilé played the piano; but Wifredito was never allowed to get near it. "Men don't play the piano, only pansies do. You're my only son, and you'll be an attorney like me, with an acceptable career; not some musician." The scent of violets washes over Wifredito and he sees Elisa Vilano, sitting next to her little sister whose face she is dabbing with cologne.

"What's the matter with her?" he asks, in case he can be of help.

"She's asthmatic. She can't breathe."

Wifredito notices that it's stiflingly hot inside the fishbowl—surely because like in almost all stores and public buildings in Cuba, the air conditioning has broken down and there are no parts available to fix it; nor will there be for a long time. According to Ché Guevara, who sits in an air-conditioned office at the Ministry of Industry, "air conditioners are not items of first necessity." Neither, apparently, are record-player needles; fabric for clothing; the ability to vacation abroad; most grocery items; furniture—which can't be found in any store; children's toys—which have completely disappeared; nor housing—impossible to find now; or sheets; or cosmetics; or clocks and watches; pens or pencils; notebooks or textbooks—even at the university where forty students might have one copy to share; or cars, unless you're one of the new political elite; or records; or bicycles; or rope; or shoes; nylons—sold on the black market at exorbitant prices; nor bath soap—restricted to a miserable monthly ration; not butter or cheese, or bottled sodas; not detergents—which inexplicably disappear for months at a time; not flowers, or musical instruments; or books— that are imported in very limited supply in order to save cash; or spices; or oil; or vinegar; not sugar—reserved almost exclusively for export; or gasoline for vehicles; or wood and cement to repair houses; or refrigerators, televisions, radios or any other electrical appliance; or even movies from the Free World. They have all been banned in keeping with the new social regulations. Recreation, technical progress, how people spend their free time— are now all controlled by the State to populate lightening rallies, militia drills, security watches, physical exams for "Civil Defense

Preparedness," required group study sessions for students, assessment and self-assessment meetings for workers. Enjoyment of the present is eclipsed by the illusion of a spectacular future, a common goal that mandates complete sacrifice by the current generation—and possibly those to come over the course of an unspecified period that could last five years, a few centuries or several millennia.

"The plane's late," someone mutters.

"Why don't they make an announcement?" asks an impatient fellow in a quivering voice.

"Because they want to keep us in the dark. That's their plan for the whole country," whispers an elegant, older woman.

"Be careful that the rebels don't hear you," warns a girl, accustomed to the silence imposed on their new lives.

Wifredito thinks to himself, "That Elisa is pretty; but not like my Teresita. I'll be back. In a month, they'll have overthrown Fidel and I'll dance with her at my cousin's party."

Suddenly, the loudspeaker erupts with a menacing and impassioned speech that Fidel Castro had given the night during a torrential downpour to mark the grand opening of a community farm. The speech lasted for four hours, with the assembled crowd forced to stand, unprotected from the weather, to applaud him, which resulted in numerous fainting spells, illnesses and accusations of weakness during the interminable series of rallies they endured the following day at their workplaces.

"Geez! They're going to play that speech again!" Wifredito hears the tall, olive skinned boy who is pressing his hands against the glass opposite those of his family who remains in the waiting room.

"What's your name?" asks Wifredito, hoping to find a friend.

"Juan Couriel," answers the boy, with an air of machismo. "I'm ten. I'm going with my sister, Silvia. She's older. Twelve."

"You Catholic?"

"Yeah, but my dad's a Sephardic Jew."

"Put'er there, man."

Their sweaty handshake seals a new friendship. Two Chinese boys are standing a few steps away, watching everything with the indomitable serenity of the Orient.

"All children who are traveling alone, come with me!" shouts a rebel who has just walked into the fishbowl resting the barrel of his machine gun on his shoulder. "Bring your 'worms' and your suitcases!"

Seven children follow him into a room where another rebel is waiting.

"Girls over here! Boys, come with me!" he orders, walking into an adjoining room where he lays the machine gun on a table and looks at the boys arrogantly. With his big, rough hands, he begins patting down the boys' clothes, looking for jewelry or money that is illegal to take out of the country. He carefully inspects the hems where travelers sometimes hide American dollars obtained on the black market, risking the possibility of losing their exit visa and being imprisoned indefinitely.

As he is roughly searching the youngest Ling brother, he finds a gold chain with a medallion of Cachita, Our Lady of Charity, around his neck. He brutally yanks it off.

"This is gold!" he shouts, boorishly. "It's a crime to take it out of the country! It's valuable! Aren't you afraid of losing permission to leave?" The boy, terrified, looks at the rebel's temple marked by a long, thick scar like a snake's skin, accentuating his threatening appearance.

"Open the 'worms'!" he orders, as if it were a military command. "Take everything out! Count the clothes! Three pairs of briefs; three t-shirts; three shirts; three pairs of pants; three pairs of socks; shoes, the one's you're wearing, that's all! You, China boy; what's your name?"

"Martín Ling," answers the boy, whose emotionless expression reveals nothing.

"Three sweaters, no. Take one. The others are needed here. And you," addressing Juan Couriel now. "You've got four pairs of socks! You thought you'd get away with that? Now you don't get to take anything! These 'worms'! They're so insolent!" he scoffs, rudely gathering the travelers together and taking way the boy's suitcase.

Fists clenched, everyone eyes the rebel with unspeakable hatred.

"Let's see! You, the traitor Prosecutor's son! Empty your bag. I'm going to see what you're taking out of Cuba."

"My father is not a traitor!" affirms Wifredito, burying his fists in his pockets so as not to strike the rebel who has now located, with the tip of his machine gun, a small drum and drumsticks hidden in one of his shirts.

"Give me that drum! It belongs to the revolutionary children who stay here!" proclaims the Fidelist rebel.

"Come with me!" the man with the sinister scar picks up the machine gun and goes to the room where the girls are waiting. Three girls stand there, clutching their suitcases.

"Open them!"

"I already checked them," declares a female rebel. "They don't have anything illegal."

"Open them again, and take everything out!" he repeats. "You know you can't take any money! Not a single penny!"

"Not that, Ely. Don't take that out!" he hears Ely Vilano's little sister gasp softly.

"What do you have there?" Let's see!" inquires the man, and with the tip of his machine gun, he pokes around the little suitcase and uncovers a packet of sanitary napkins, spilling them out onto the floor. Ely, humiliated, stoops to pick them up. Her little sister and Silvia Couriel run to help her.

"You can't take those! Anyone with anything hidden in their clothes, take it out!"

Crouched on the floor between her little sister and Silvia, Ely suffers the humiliation of the Fidelist regime. As the boys avert their eyes to spare her more embarrassment, she studies the rebel staring at her: his rough black boots with thick laces, his khaki pants and his rough cotton shirt. She sees his enormous scar and in his actions senses a long-held bitterness. Suddenly, the rebel reaches into the cloth suitcase they call a "worm."

"Why do you have this picture of Camilo? Give it to me!"

The room fills with the unforgettable charisma of Camilo Cienfuegos, one of Fidel's most famous commanders when they fought in the mountains against the Batista government. The photo accompanying a newspaper clipping captures his heavy beard and joyful smile.

"You can't take this with you!" he tells her. "He was a great revolutionary!"

"At least I didn't bring the photos I had taken with him at that festival," thinks Ely, perspiring as she tries to pull closed the zipper of her worm that has snagged on a pair of underpants. "They wouldn't have let me leave, thinking that I knew some revolutionary secrets because I knew Camilo."

"Those of you leaving Cuba by yourselves to work for the Yankee Imperialism," the rebel gravely begins his speech, "you are missing out on the triumph of Socialism in Cuba. You will speak an enemy's language. You will betray your duty as Cubans." The children realize that the man is repeating Fidel's words and imitating his oratory style. "You will be humiliated because you're not fair skinned, like the Yankees. You'll lose the privilege to be revolutionaries here because you're looking for money there. And when you're there and realize that we have made a country where there will be no rich and no poor, you will regret having left! Stay, and we will support you so you don't have to go back to your worm homes!"

"We're leaving."

"We're going."

"Let's go," whisper the children.

"You will not share in the glory of building Socialism! You'll never be able to return to Cuba, never! Here we say, 'Homeland or Death'!"

"We will be victorious!" echoes the female rebel who is watching him.

CHAPTER 6

That the same morning of October 5, 1961 on which so many children escape to Miami on one of Sara's Visa Waivers, in the intimacy of their bedroom, Amador Odio tells his wife about the decision of the People's Revolutionary Movement. "Tonight will be a turning point for Cuba's freedom! There's a plan to execute Fidel."

"Oh, Amador! My God! How are they going to do it?" she asks, struck by the gravity of the news, but passionately fearless.

"Fidel will give a speech tonight from the North Terrace of the Presidential Palace. The Movement has rented an apartment across the street. There's another anti-Communist group involved. They've already installed a bazooka, pointed at the terrace where he'll give the speech. They've selected a man to fire at him with the bazooka.

"It will be dreadful, Amador! He won't escape alive! The repercussions will be terrible! The communists will kill thousands of people tonight!"

"We have to do it, my love! The Bay of Pigs invasion failed! The rebels in the mountains have been defeated! Killing Fidel is only hope we have of bringing freedom back to Cuba!

"And what do we have to do, you and I?"

"Arrange a dinner for five ambassadors. Four will be here, waiting for anyone from the Movement who survives the backlash from the execution. From here, they'll take them to their embassies. The fifth is the German Ambassador. Since he's here so often, everything will look normal to the servants."

"Ms. Sara! Freddy pushed Marianne's nanny into the pool, shoes and all!" The maid's shouts cause Sara to turn and leave the room so quickly she still has Amador's cufflinks in her hand. Amador follows her, incensed by the misbehavior of one of his children. He punishes him, sending him to his room for the rest of the day; and Sara clips the cufflinks on the sleeves of her husband's impeccably white shirt. Kissing him and watching him ride his bicycle through the estate, she walks off with a carefree air so as to disguise her worry from their fourteen servants. Tonight's mission is dangerous and difficult; and could cost the lives of her husband and many others.

Sara leaves the house, walks toward the bowling alley and kisses four of the children who remain with them in Cuba. Amador, the oldest, is tall and fair. He is ten years old and extremely intelligent, and is reading a book of adventure stories. Jorge Carlos, who was the ring-bearer at Emma Castro's wedding, and his brother Javier are running around the bowling alley. They are handsome and look alike with their black, wavy hair. Javier is eight, and Jorge Carlos, five. Sara is holding Marianne, who is three years old and as pretty as if she had been born to be a child star. Her short, dark hair trembles above her eyes. Still carrying Marianne, Sara goes to Freddy's room to see that he is fulfilling his punishment for the earlier incident with the nanny. She finds him dismantling a toy horse to see how it works, before he puts it back together. Freddy is the quietest of all of Sara's children. He is six years old with an insatiable curiosity about the world. Sara reminds him that he must stay in his room all day. She lets Marianne down to play with the other children who are milling about the yard, and walks toward the pigsty. Trying to distract herself from the worry she feels about tonight's plan, she looks at the pigs, gives the staff their instructions and begins to gather the eggs her hens lay. Once she has completed her rounds, she returns to the kitchen to speak with Eduardo, the chef, about dinner. Eduardo serves her a cup of coffee and leans in toward her. He is as black as onyx and as big as a bear. He is from Martinique, speaks very little Spanish, very proudly calls himself a "Frenchman" and wears an immaculate white uniform, complete with hat and apron, just like the chefs in the movies.

"Oui, Madame, with pleasure," responds Eduardo with a French accent that seems to rob him of his "r"s. Suddenly, a nanny bursts in and announces that Marianne, Sara's three-year-old daughter, is missing.

Sara is alarmed, and questions her. She says they have looked everywhere. Sara begins searching as well, increasingly frightened by the disappearance. She calls for her horse, which they bring to her fully saddled, having been tied under a tree awaiting her summons. Sara mounts *Capricho*, her beautiful palomino, and sets off across the estate in search of her missing daughter. Amador is notified, and accustomed to leadership and directing operations, he comes home to coordinate the search effort. An hour passes slowly, and the child remains missing. Suddenly, from the main road, the Rural Guard arrives, asking if anything is wrong. "Oh my God! Today of all days! Just what I need is to have the military coming here!" thinks Sara. "And anyway, how did they know about Marianne? Are they watching us?"

Two sets of guards get out of the Jeep, sheathed in their tan khaki uniforms. Their wide brimmed hats flapping in the early autumn breeze, they join in the search for Marianne. Sara, frantic, begins to fear that the girl has been kidnapped. She brings *Capricho* to a halt at the stable, although she is sure Marianne could not have walked this far. When she goes inside, she finds the girl tied in a corner with a handkerchief gagging her mouth, just like kidnap victims in the movies.

"Holy Mother of God! This is Freddy's doing!" she exclaims, running to untie Marianne and carrying her out. The sobbing little girl confesses that her brother did it, and Sara tells Amador, who sends him to his room a second time after a sound scolding.

Watching the Rural Guards depart, Sara calms down a bit; and using the prank to rid her mind of the night's impending terror, she orders the dinner be held on the open terrace at the very back of the house.

"Amador, it worries me that the guards showed up. No one told them about Marianne. It's like they've been watching us, waiting for an excuse to come in.

"Don't worry," he tells her. "You have to stay calm. Any of the servants could turn us in if they see you're nervous. Tonight Cuba will be free!"

And Sara begins to pray, with a feeling of foreboding, that God will have mercy on them during the terrifying night that awaits.

CHAPTER 7

"Ely, I'm scared," whimpers María del Carmen, Elisa Vilano's little sister, as they sit in the fishbowl at the Havana airport. It is ten minutes before five o'clock in the afternoon, and due to the disorganization that's ruled the country since Fidel took over, the *Pan American* flight to Miami still hasn't departed.

"Don't be afraid. I'll take care of you since Mamá's not here," responds Ely. "Are you tired?"

"Yes. And it's hot—and I can't breathe."

"Here, smell this," Ely tells her sister, dabbing her forehead with a handkerchief dampened with cologne.

"This Ché Guevara speech is making me feel sick."

"Look, Mamá and Papá are worried enough out there. Don't let them see that you don't feel well."

They have been heralded over the loudspeaker thus far by one of Fidel Castro's four-hour speeches; one by Raúl that lasted an hour; an hour of revolutionary hymns and finally Ché Guevara's speech given from one of the factories he's taken over. Finally, the droning Magnavox relays that it is every revolutionary's duty to gather for the speech at the Presidential Palace tonight.

The golden, afternoon sun shimmers against the airplanes outside, and an elderly woman seated next to Ely Vilano offers, "Let me help you with your little sister. These people should call a doctor for her…. I'm getting out of here, leaving behind two sons who've become Communists. The other two are coming with me. But I won't be able to see my grandchildren here," she wipes her nose with a Dutch linen hankie. "And you, do you have one of the Visa Waivers for children leaving by themselves?"

"Yes, ma'am…"

"Who got it for you, dear?"

"My uncle, who lives in Miami," replies Ely with the secrecy that pervades all conversations now, for fear of being denounced. These days, even your best friend could turn out to be a "rat."

"No one knows anything. No one tells names, or anything else. Anyway, it wouldn't do me any good to find out since my sons would never let my grandchildren leave. This Communism is like a fever that takes a hold of people," she adds in a low voice, the way everyone has become accustomed to speaking.

Wifredito Chirino looks at his watch—five o'clock. "We've been in this fishbowl since ten this morning," he thinks. He watches a soldier clad in an olive green uniform walk toward the door that leads from the fishbowl to the tarmac and open it.

"Everyone out, now!" he commands arrogantly.

The children who are traveling alone or with their siblings run to the glass wall that separates them from the waiting room, squeezing between the adults to say good-bye to their families who are pressed against the other side of the cold glass. This moment is so intense that it is seared into their memories as the worst of their lives. They cry, and their parents and siblings hide tears on the other side. Some press their hands to the hard, clear pane. They wave. They throw kisses. The devastating helplessness of the departure tears at those on either side of the glass, until the crowd of passengers sweeps the children away in the frenzy to escape. The unaccompanied children feel completely abandoned to the unknown world that awaits them. Ely Vilano's little sister leans against her, barely conscious. The Chinese brothers shuffle in front of them, crying. Juan Couriel, the ten-year-old boy with a Jewish father, comes to help them with their suitcases with tears streaming down his face. His sister, just two years older, follows him, trying to choke back her own sobs so he won't feel so frightened. Wifredito Cirino wipes his eyes with his handkerchief after kissing the glass that his mother kissed on the other side. The children go out alone onto the runway and into the most chaotic scene they will ever witness. "Teresita, I'll be here for my cousin's party," Wifredito reassures himself. "Fidel will have been overthrown, and there will be parties everywhere. I'll play the drums with the guys in the band."

"Hurry, so we can sit by a window," Ely tells her little sister, drying her eyes but still crying inside. A moment passes before she can speak again, "Mamá's going to be on the runway holding a red umbrella so we can see her from the plane."

Juan Couriel helps them board the airplane once their documents have been checked yet again at the bottom of the stairs.

Inside the plane, rocked gently by a sudden afternoon breeze, Ely and María del Carmen sit together, and Couriel stands on tiptoe to put their suitcases away before sitting down behind them, next to his slightly older sister, Silvia. The two Chinese boys are seated on the other side, and Wifredito is alone in the back, resting his head against the seat in front of him and watching his tears fall to the floor. The plane begins to race down the runway, like a rabbit pursued by a cat. At the moment of their departure, the unaccompanied children border on panic.

"Look for Mamá on the runway, María del Carmen. Look for the red umbrella," murmurs Ely, the color drained from her face by a brutal feeling of being torn away as palm trees rush past her wide eyes.

"Mamá, where's Mamá?" gasps her sister. The plane takes off and soars to the clouds before the passengers are able to make out their family members who are waving good-bye from the airport terrace. Havana bids them farewell with its whirling throng of rooftops and tall buildings and like a bride lost in a daydream, is left behind in the distance, maybe forever.

"Ely, I'm scared! I'm scared! What if we never see them again?"

"Here, dry your eyes," Silvia tells Juan Couriel. "Don't be afraid. I'll be with you even though Mamá stayed here."

"Martín, what do we do now? What's going to happen to us? What's it going to be like there?" sobs the younger of the Chinese brothers, suppressing his nausea.

"Teresita! Teresita!" whispers Wifredito to the last window of the plane as clouds brush by and they break through into the glow of the afternoon sun.

"We didn't see Mamá. We didn't see her," says Ely.

"We're free! We're free!" shouts a man from one of the front seats. And suddenly, as if in unanimous response to some unspoken cue, a chorus of patriotic and battle-weary voices intones the National Anthem.

> "To arms, Bayameses
> your proud country looks to you.
> Don't fear a death in glory

Die for a life that's true."

Sobs separate the first and second stanzas.

> "Live no more in chains,
> subject to insults and harms.
> Heed the clarion's call.
> To arms, brave men, to arms."

The hymn is followed by the "Our Father," as María del Carmen Vilano and Juan, the younger of the Ling brothers are overcome by unbearable nausea. Wifredito Chirino feels suddenly consoled by a tune taking shape in his head. It is a song for Teresita, the girlfriend he has left in Cuba.

The stewardess brings the unaccompanied children Coca-Cola as someone on the plane shouts the motto of those facing the firing squad, "Long live Cristo Rey! Down with Communism!"

Ely Vilano watches the clouds multiply beneath the airplane like a wide-open highway that could lead anywhere in the world. A torrent of secret tears runs down her throat, and a poem by José Martí stirs in her memory.

> "I have seen the wounded eagle
> soar to the bluest air
> and watched the poisonous viper
> die in the depths of his lair."

Silvia Couriel also remembers Marí's poetry, as she passes the time speechlessly.

> "Buried in my brave heart
> a pain secret from all eyes,
> Son of a country in shackles
> who lives for it, is silenced and dies."

The older siblings, never saying a word, take on the role of parents for their younger brothers and sisters.

The plane glides between two expanses of blue, equal but for one inescapable contradiction: the sky through which they're passing will carry them to freedom, whereas the ocean geographically enslaves Cuba, robbing its people of any hope of escape by land. Juan Ling, who is in an airplane for the first time in his life, is surprised that the clouds cast shadows on the sea.

For the passengers bound for Miami, the wrenching loss of being torn away from everything they knew, including the island that was their touchstone in the world, mixes with the uncertainty of what will happen to them now, and how they will earn a living. Doctors cease being doctors during the course of this flight. Dentists begin thinking about how to buy a car so they can work as taxi-drivers. Lawyers, overwhelmed by the thought of studying the complexity of American laws, written in a language they can barely pronounce, face the prospect of sweeping floors. And the children, who have lost their homes in this exodus, have become adults, never having passed through adolescence. So Ely Vilano holds the little paper bag while her sister vomits. She comes to understand that only two things remain: her little sister whom she'll care for by herself from now on, and the dear memory of Commander Camilo Cienfuegos, whom she had adored since that day at the aquaculture festival in Guanabacoa when they rode horseback side by side. Love came later, when that handsome Cuban idol asked her father for permission to visit her. Silvia Couriel, on the other hand, worries about how they will get along with her mother's friend who is going to pick them up. Martín Ling touches Juan's hand and asks him where the bathroom is. Wifredito watches them pass, tapping with his fingers since the soldier confiscated his drumsticks. He wants to lock the whole experience away in his memory, and the melody tumbles out like colored birds in a cage, crowding the bars to breathe in life.

CHAPTER 8

The afternoon sun is setting over Amador Odio's country estate as the first of his diplomatic guests arrives. It is Alfonso Zurbarán, the key man in president Rómulo Betancourt's conspiracy in support of Cuba's freedom. Zurbarán is tall and athletic, a good-looking man with fair skin and undeniably European ancestry. He is wearing his ever-present dark glasses, and still shows signs of grief over the recent loss of his wife.

"They'll never be able to talk about this period of Cuba's history without mentioning you, Zurbarán," Sara holds out her hand as she greets him, thinking of his wife who died just a few months ago of an aggressive leukemia. "I don't think I'll ever see my three little pigs again," she had told Sara before her death, referring to their three small children who had remained in Caracas rather than risk the dangers of Cuba's current situation. The Venezuelan emissary is dressed formally in a dark, gray linen suit and he crosses the open terrace awash in the scent of native trees to where Amador, also formally attired, awaits. Sara excuses herself for a moment to make sure the children are put to bed. When she returns, she hears the two men talking, maintaining an air of complete nonchalance in front of the estate's fourteen servants. Soon, however, the conversation shifts to the seriousness of the nation's situation.

"The Escambray rebellion will be crushed," Sarah hears the Venezuelan gentleman say; and given his elite diplomatic position, he is very well informed about these things. "The sieges against them are five layers deep. The militia sets the jungle on fire. They've taken rivers, streams, wells. They've captured and shot hundreds of farmers for aiding the rebels. They've taken the women and children from families suspected of helping the insurrection to Havana. They're holding the women in houses in Miramar left empty by people who fled to Miami, and the government's sent the children off to school to indoctrinate them into communism.

"But, the anti-communist rebels continue the fight!" replies Amador hopefully.

"Yes, they keep fighting. But don't fool yourself. With these odds, the insurrection can't hold out for long."

"The economic collapse will help bring down this government, assuming it makes it through today. Only Fidel can convince the people to follow him when they're hungry. The businesses they've confiscated from private owners are being run by inexperienced people who don't know what they're doing…"

The voices fade to murmurs, and Sara goes back to the children's rooms to pray with them. The house is the same as always, except that its previous sense of peace and happiness that have taken refuge in the idyllic realm of memory. Countless miles divide her family. Those who have left cannot return because Fidel has prohibited as much for the thousands of Cubans who chose to leave. César, Silvia, Sarita, Any Laury and Mary Loly, her beloved five eldest children are in exile, and she cannot see them. Meanwhile, she fears for the five younger ones who are at the estate tonight, caught up in the chaos that grips this country where the only hope of restoring democratic order rests on executing Fidel.

Zurbarán and Amador are still talking as the other invited diplomats arrive, one after the other. Although unable to grant asylum, the German ambassador also attends, to maintain the illusion of a typical gathering. After a glass of excellent, imported wine, they walk to the expansive iron and glass dining table, draped with impeccable white linen. No one knows who among their company could be an informant, now that from one end of the country to the other parents have denounced their children, children their parents, and even wives their own husbands.

The five gentlemen and Sara take their seats at the table where they are served in the Russian fashion as is customary among Cuba's elite. Two waiters dressed formally with jackets and gloves approach the guests. They are Rufino and Manolo, extremely polite and polished, and expert at conveying the zest for life that fills the Odio household. The mood at dinner is cheerful; the guests talking about whatever light-hearted subject that comes to mind.

"Oh, my God! What is going to happen tonight? How many will die in the backlash after they kill Fidel? Have mercy,

Father! This is going to be terrible!" thinks Sara, masking her concern with a smile and overlooking the details of her guest's outward appearance while extremely attentive to the personality and intentions of each one.

The representative of Panama is short and slim; and laughs at a joke told by the Brazilian ambassador who is tall and a bit heavy. He speaks Spanish perfectly and is the most jovial of the group. The Argentine, tall and good looking, is doubtlessly the most talkative. They're all young, surely none of them past their thirties. Aware of the gravity of the situation about to unfold, none of them has brought his wife to this dinner, uncertain of its outcome.

Amador surreptitiously glances at his watch and calculates the time left until the planned execution of Fidel is carried out. "After this, we might end up in a civil war," he thinks. "Although, we might be able to avoid it. Either way, at least we'll be free. Freedom is worth any sacrifice and any risk."

The favorite desserts are a strawberry tart and flan. They are such consummate culinary feats that the ambassadors call for Eduardo, the Martinican chef, to congratulate him on his exquisite offering. He is humbly pleased and offers a sweeping bow before he exits, smiling.

"That poor man, he has no idea that we're at the brink of a catastrophe," Sara thinks, watching him. "This is all going to be so horrible! We're surely going to have to hide people who are wounded! Some of the men involved have orders to go directly to our friends' embassies; others will surely come here so they can be taken into asylum. But enduring Communism for the rest of our lives would be worse!"

When dessert is finished, Amador instructs his wife, in front of his guests and servants, "Go up and watch the television. Fidel is giving another speech and I want to know what he says. Let me know what else he plans to steal."

Sara, understanding the order, excuses herself and walks up the stone staircase that leads to the second floor. She knows that her mission is to inform Amador and the five diplomats when the execution has been carried out. Upstairs, she sits in front of the television set. The crowd shouts their support of the Maximum

Leader and Dorticós, his front man, who now occupies the presidency and has just returned from a tour of socialist countries. Dorticós, an attorney who rose from anonymity in the south of the Island, in a spectacular gesture of modesty, has not yet taken up residence in the Presidential Palace. He has, however, moved into a mansion in the wealthiest district of Havana, confiscated from a rich émigré. Fidel does not live in the Palace either; no one knows where he lives. It is rumored that sometimes he takes over an entire floor of the luxurious *Havana Hilton*, now called *Free Havana*.

"How is this going to play out?" Sara wonders. "They say that the crowd won't be injured because the bazooka will only fire at the north terrace of the Palace where the government officials are. So many ministers and commanders are going to die."

Castro's bearded face appears on the screen, angry and menacing; and Sara begins to pray for all the people who will surely die in the darkness of this tragic night when the government's survivors exact fierce reprisals for the execution of their Maximum Leader.

CHAPTER 9

The plane carrying the Cuban exiles approaches Miami at twilight, that hour in the summer that brings with it a deathly sadness. The children see familiar, puffy clouds, like those that populate the skies over the Caribbean islands, and realize they are completely alone. "We're just as vulnerable as those clouds. We don't know what's going to happen to us, either," thinks Ely Vilano. Her little sister has not stopped crying the whole flight, and she squeezes her hand. Before they surrender to the turmoil of their arrival, which is cloaked in uncertainty, each of the unaccompanied children thinks of the home they have left in Cuba and the loved ones they were so abruptly torn away from: Ely thinks of the piano she would be playing now, her memory framed by the crisp notes of Debussy's lyrical *Claire de lune*. She remembers that she had played it that afternoon when Camilo Cienfuegos, so handsome and gallant, helped her mount a palomino mare and rode along beside her on a lively, white stallion. His smooth, black beard glistened on his handsome face, his friendly, dark eyes complimenting an enchanting smile. That is when Ely fell in love with him, as she showed him around the festival, unable to imagine the tragic death that awaited him in a maze of personal and political betrayal. Wifredito Chirino remembers kissing Teresita for the first time on an afternoon like this one, caressed by her blond hair and timid, blue eyes. "I'll be with you next month," he conveys to her telepathically.

"Ely, who's going to pick us up at the airport?" María del Carmen Vilano asks her sister, as resilient as a delicate, tropical reed, impervious to danger.

"Someone named George."

"Who is he?"

"I don't know."

"Well, how are we going to find him? Nobody there speaks Spanish."

"They'll know what to do at the airport; don't worry. Let me take care of it."

"Martín, Who's going to meet us in Miami?"
"Mamá said it'd be some of Papá's friends."
"Do you know them?"
"No, but we'll find them. Don't worry."

So goes the conversation between the two Chinese boys who begin thinking about the restaurant where they served Chinese and Cuban food. Their family had made it a success with years of hard work stacked atop one another like precarious domino towers built by children.

"They took it over, anyway," says Martín.
"Took over what?"
"Our restaurant. Even though we set up a socialist cooperative with the employees at the last minute, they took it. It belongs to the State now." Martín remembers himself carrying a tray filled with plates of fried rice and tender spring rolls to some customers' table.

Wifredito Chirino is still improvising a rumba, tapping it out with his fingers on the armrest. The music swirling in his head escapes, tangled with images of his home: the entrance gate; the huge bedrooms; the dining room where he use to roller skate years ago; the garden full of violets and other colorful flowers; the orchards of chirimoya, lemon and orange trees that he climbed as a child, and his sister Marilé's piano that his father wouldn't let him touch. Suddenly, he sees himself dressed like a sailor on this trip. The improvised melodies in his head envelop the image, but don't seem to jell. Wifredito chokes back one last sob before he leaves the plane. Armed with the optimism and strong will that will accompany him throughout his life, he prepares to face this challenge imposed by circumstance.

The plane abandons the sea and searches out the Miami airport. The children see the runway approach, getting bigger and bigger as if they are looking at it through a magnifying glass. It spins before their eyes before settling under the plane. The stewardess gathers all of the unaccompanied children together at the top of the stairway. They look outside, where the night lies in wait.

"Come with me," the stewardess tells them, walking quickly through the busy airport. The children clutch the handles of their 'worms' and suitcases, and follow the woman leading them.

"Where do we have to wait for George?" asks María del Carmen Vilano hanging on to her suitcase and her sister's arm for dear life.

"We'll look at all of the men. You'll see; we'll find him." The children become aware of a new face among them, someone they had not noticed before. She is swinging a little patchwork 'worm' made mostly of purple squares. She takes a little mirror and comb out of the pocket of her shirtdress and shyly combs her blond hair. Her slim body sways gracefully as she walks, and she looks to see if anyone is watching her. "She's pretty, and must be twelve or thirteen," thinks Martín Ling. "She's cute, but not compared to Teresita," Wifredito Chirino tells himself, comparing his girlfriend's blue eyes with this girl's dark eyes. The new girl's fingernails are painted with clear polish, and her pretty features are strained with fear. Everyone is looking around, searching for anything familiar. They look at each other, driven to spark a friendship that might alleviate their desperate sense of abandonment and their agonizing fear of the unknown.

"Martín, what if they don't come to get us?" the younger Ling boy asks his brother.

"They won't just leave us here. Don't worry."

"It's just that we don't have any money."

"Are you all coming from Cuba?" The friendly, male voice with its Caribbean accent causes all of the children to turn to him in unison, as if an alarm clock had just awakened them.

"Yes, we are," responds Ely Vilano. Overcoming her youthful shyness, she takes a step toward him, her dress hinting at the silhouette of her agile, adolescent body.

"I'm George!" the man introduces himself, smiling. "Hearing his magical name, the children are drawn to him like students on a playground swarming around a teacher giving out candy. In a matter of moments, each one takes their stock of him: Ely sees a good man, medium height, olive-skinned and slim. To

María del Carmen he seems very tall and strong, and his Cuban *guayabera*, with its many tiny pleats, reminds her of her father and makes her feel better. Wifredito Chirino suspects he is a good dancer with natural rhythm and a flexible body. Juan Ling envisions him a soccer player, while Martín sees a serious and responsible man. Juan Couriel, who is starving, notices the plastic bag he is carrying in his left hand, and the Coca-Cola emblem he can see through it. Silvia scrutinizes George, noting his lively and carefree expression, his ears that stick out from his head, his wavy hair combed straight back—as was the style in those days—and that he's clean-shaven. At the same time, she wonders if he would take her and her brother with him if the family who is supposed to meet them does not show up. Lastly, the newest girl to join the group tries her best to get him to notice her, brazenly offering him a flirtatious smile and hoping he will respond.

"Your parents are all very proud of you," asserts George, still smiling and looking at each of the young travelers. "You've all been very brave to come by yourselves. Don't worry! You're going to be fine with us. You'll be back with your parents very soon. Father Walsh has asked that everyone who's helping you be Cuban. Almost all of us are new here. But you'll feel better soon." He concludes his warm welcome and begins handing out sandwiches, Coca-Colas, and gum as the children watch him, comforted.

"Come with me," he says and they start walking.

"Mister," Silvia Couriel addresses him, "a friend of my mother's is supposed to pick up my brother and me. Could you tell us where the people wait for arriving passengers?"

"I'll take you there. But are you sure someone's coming to pick you up?"

"We hope so," she responds.

Juan Ling elbows his brother Martín, prodding him to speak.

"Someone's supposed to pick us up, too." Martín says, aligning himself with George. "But if they don't come…" the boy grips his right fist with his left hand.

"If they don't come, I'll take you with me. Don't worry."

George looks through the children's passports and writes their names in a book he has been carrying under his arm. In the main immigration area, American agents ask the children questions in English—which they don't understand—and mark a page of their passports with six letters: PAROLE. With gestures and simple words, the agents send the children down a long ramp, disoriented and scared, again walking behind George who is their only hope for protection in the unfamiliar world that surrounds them with dizzying images. They draw closer to him again when they reach Customs, a word they have never heard before. And finally they arrive at the baggage pick-up area, where they have nothing to retrieve.

When they arrive in the area where people await arriving passengers, an ill-humored woman approaches and looks at the Couriel children, with a tremendous display of impatience. She is tall and fat, and they're surprised that she's Cuban since she has quickly adapted to wearing shorts, something you only see on the beach in Cuba.

"I've been waiting for you all day," she says accusingly. "I had to miss work today to pick you up. Why was the plane late?" Silvia and Juan remain silent, taken aback by this rude reception, and George delicately suggests, "If you can't take them, Ma'am, I will. Father Walsh has room in his camps for all of the children."

"Who's Father Walsh?" Juan Ling quietly asks his brother.

"I don't know, but it seems like he must be in charge of some camps they have for kids coming in."

"No, sir," the woman responds to George, "they're not going anywhere except home with me. Their parents sent them to me." "Don't you have a suitcase?" she asks Juan after giving him the once over.

"No, Ma'am. They took it away from me at the airport in Havana before we left."

"So I've got to get you clothes, too!"

"Again, I can take them with me," insists George. "We have clothing for them at the camps."

"Let's go!" commands the woman, and the Couriel children follow her.

"George, just a minute," says Martín Ling respectfully and taking hold of the sleeve of his impeccable Cuban *guayabera*. "Let me see if the person who's supposed to pick us up is here. Don't leave," and he rapidly skirts the waiting room and returns.

"They're not here."

"Come with me then," concludes George, and asks, "Are any of you headed to the "Hebrew Immigration Society?"

The children shake their heads no.

"I can take you there, or if you're going to the "Children's Service Bureau," or if you're supposed to be picked up by the Methodist church or any other church. Sometimes I take you, or you stay in our camps until they pick you up the next day."

In the airport parking lot, the children get into a van that seems beige to some and white to others, although some have no memory of its color at all. They sit glued to the windows as darkness falls, anxiously searching the Miami landscape, the setting for their new lives. They see little of the city. "So this is Miami?" worry some of the children, comparing the insignificance of what they see with Havana's beauty. "Havana was much bigger and prettier," they conclude, fearing that all of the United States might be like this: a long line of houses with little yards that fade away leaving a long, narrow road lined with pine trees. Ely Vilano remembers some verses by the Cuban patriot, Heredia, that she learned long ago in school. He wrote them during the first part of his political exile to the United States, as he looked at the majesty of Niagara Falls.

> "But, what does my longing gaze seek in you
> with such desperate desire?
> The palms, oh! The beautiful palms
> that on the plains of my passionate island
> are born of smiles and sunshine, and grow
> with the ocean breeze
> as they sway under a pure blue sky."

There aren't any palm trees here," murmurs María del Carmen, and she wonders, "Where have they brought us? This is the boondocks! I can't believe they're taking us to live out in the country! What if I have an asthma attack in the middle of the night, who's going to help me?" she frets with growing trepidation.

The children split their attention between George, who is telling them about Miami, and the echoes of their own thoughts. "Whatever, we're not going to be here long! It doesn't matter if we're out in the country. By next month, Fidel will be gone and I'll be in Cuba dancing with Teresita," Wifredito Chirino reflects. "I wonder if there are boas or racers here?" Juan Ling wonders, as Martín thinks, "What will life be like here? It looks like they're taking us to some sort of camp. I wonder what Father Walsh will be like. At least I know he's a priest." And the new girl who joined the group at the last moment thinks, "If only he'd look back here, I'd smile at him. I have to make a good impression on everyone here. I'm all alone and I need them to help me."

A little light appears in the distance, leading George's van down a path into an area where tall, still trees stand in the darkness of the hot summer night. George stops in front of a silent pavilion, dark except for the entryway. "Here we are at Kendall. Come with me," he tells Wifredito Chirino, opening the van door. The boy follows him and they disappear into the pavilion. Frogs croak and crickets chirp incessantly, further convincing the Cuban children that they have landed at the end of civilization. María del Carmen coughs and Ely covers her chest, trying not to let her see her concern. She gently touches María del Carmen's forehead and draws her head onto her shoulder as she feels her begin crying in the darkness of the van.

"It looks like we're not getting out here," Juan Ling ventures timidly.

"Don't worry, Buddy," Martín reassures him quietly. "George said there were other camps," and he looks again at the silhouette of the last girl who joined the group. "What's your name?" he asks.

"Sol."

He senses that she is smiling at him in the darkness, having put away the little mirror she was trying to see herself in. "What a strange name," thinks Martín. "No one's named that in Cuba. Why would they call her that?" he wonders, although true to the restraint and courtesy of his Chinese heritage he says nothing.

George returns, seemingly tireless, and climbs behind the wheel. The night creeps up on the van like an impatient and mischievous squirrel as they get back onto the narrow road that seems to them nothing more than a footpath. The children listen silently to George's amiable monologue. A while later, they pull up to another camp. "This is Matecumbe," announces George, steering between two pine trees that mark the entrance. A woodsy smell surrounds them as the Ling brothers walk with George, the scorching summer's parched grass crunching beneath their feet. The chorus of chirping crickets and buzzing cicadas reaches a crescendo, and something on the ground rustles as they approach. Juan looks down and recognizes a bullfrog. A sudden breeze rattles the pine boughs and the tents quiver in the silence. The camp is asleep, but a young, slender man, soft-spoken and of medium height emerges from one of the tents. George greets him, "What's up, Sergio? I've got two more Cuban boys for you. They're good boys and won't be any trouble."

"Welcome!" the young man receives them warmly. "I bet you haven't eaten."

"The plane got in very late," George confirms. "They spent the whole day in the Havana airport and they've got to be exhausted."

"Well, we're all friends now," Sergio assures them, giving the new arrivals an affectionate pat on the back. "Let's go get you something to eat," and with his arms resting on their shoulders, he guides the boys to the dining room and turns on the lights.

The sudden brightness brings back a feeling of civilization as it illuminates long tables with wooden benches and window screens that keep out the bugs. The walls are bare except for a small crucifix. The boys take it all in with amazement, and Martín glances at his watch, noticing that it's a quarter after ten. The young man who met them slips the rosary he has been holding into his pocket, opens the refrigerator and takes out a fried chicken. He cuts it in half and serves it to the Ling brothers on two identical plates. Then, he gives them each a big bowl of ice cream and introduces himself, "I'm Sergio García Miró. I'm a teacher here. I'm in charge of three boys' tents. You'll be in one of them, too; but tonight I'm going to set up some cots for you in here. If you ever don't feel well or if anything hurts, let me know. I was a medical student in Havana."

"What year did you get to?" asks Juan Ling, suddenly interested.

"Third"

"So you're going to be a doctor?"

"Yes. I'm going to be a doctor and a priest. What do you think of that?"

"I'm going to be a doctor, too. I'm sure Fidel will be gone soon, and I'm going to study in Havana. We'll be classmates! Give me five!"

"OK, I'm going to take the girls to Florida City." George says good-bye, seeing that they are eating well and that Sergio has begun setting up the cots. "See you tomorrow, boys."

When he gets back to the van, George notes that María del Carmen has stopped crying and she's drying her eyes with the hem of her dress. As he starts the engine, he looks in the rearview mirror at Sol who has fallen asleep. Ely thinks about her cousin Albertico, sixteen years old and sent to prison for fifteen years for distributing anti-Communist flyers. Locked in a damp cell in the brutal prison on Isla de Pinos, a small island to the south of Cuba. Although he is sick with pneumonia, he is denied any medical attention. "He must be looking out at this same night through the bars on his window, burning up with fever. And Mamá, she must be crying! And Papá, I couldn't play *Claire de Lune* for him tonight. Oh, God! What's going to happen to all of us?"

The van stops in front of a chain link fence that surrounds several two story buildings where everything seems to be quiet. "This is the Florida City camp," says George, graciously opening the van door and still showing no sign of fatigue. "Can you wake up Sol?" he asks Ely Vilano. When Ely gently touches her shoulder, Sol awakes with a start. "Don't be frightened. It's just that we're here."

George knocks on door after door in the camp, looking for someplace they can stay. Every housefather who answers explains that they do not have room for the girls. Finally, in the apartment run by the Velascos, they agree to make up the sofa for them. Once they are inside and George has left, they ask the girls if they are hungry. They say no, because they are so tired. Some of the other girls have woken up and the word spreads, "three new ones are here." Two sisters approach them smiling. One is blonde and very fair-skinned; the other has dark hair and dark eyes. They are both chubby, friendly, helpful and very chatty. At the least provocation, they demonstrate their sense of humor, giggling with an openness that refutes any trace of hypocrisy. They quickly befriend Ely and María del Carmen, who asks them where the bathroom is. When the door closes, Ely and María del Carmen hug each other in a dramatic moment of realization.

"I'm scared. What if I have an asthma attack?"

"You heard them say that there's a doctor in this camp. Our 'housefather' is a dentist, so he surely knows first aid," she says, trying out her first words in English. "Don't be afraid. You're not going to have an attack tonight. But if you do, wake me up right away." She dries her sister's tears with the gentleness of a tropical breeze and prepares her toothbrush for her. Then she gets out her pajamas, helps her undress and folds her clothes.

The De la Portilla sisters offer them their beds and they go sleep on the couch after introducing them to all of the girls their age who are currently living in the apartment. Ely and María del Carmen get into one bed together and leave the other one for Sol. There are three sets of bunk beds squeezed together for lack of space. Ely is against the wall and cannot sleep. The image of her mother, crying as she said good-bye, torments her and her sleeping sister's ragged breathing worries her. Knowing that no one can see her in the darkness, she lets herself cry, letting go of the oppressive burden that she has carried since leaving Havana. She cries and prays, prays and cries, bitten up by a swarm of mosquitoes whose buzzing invades the silence of her rest. It is hotter than she' is used to in Cuba, making her sweat and increasing her anxiety about this new situation. Meanwhile, she sees Sol get up from a bed across the room, walk to a mirror and admire herself while she combs her hair. Ely cannot imagine why this girl with blond hair and dark eyes is so taken with herself, and quickly pegs her for a shallow and phony creature, despite her pretty smile. Unconsciously, more of Martí's *Simple Verses* spring to mind:

When I am happy, I recall
like a simple schoolboy
the yellow canary
with a coal-black eye…"

A sudden and intense shaking in the bed next to her startles her. She sits up and looks at the little girl lying at her right. "Oh my God! She's having a seizure! She must be epileptic!" A shaft of light coming from under the bathroom door allows her to see the outline of the girl's face. "She's biting her tongue!" Ely takes her pillow and slips a corner of it into the girl's mouth as she calls out, terrified, "Señora Velasco! Señora Velasco! Hurry! Hurry! Mirta's sick! Mirta's sick!" A flood of people sweeps into the room as lights turn on. "I'm going to get the doctor," says Mr. Velasco on his way out. And again, Ely holds back her tears so as not to frighten her little sister.

CHAPTER 10

Fidel's strident address, as threatening as all his others, is coming to a close and the execution has not been carried out. Sara del Toro stands up, anxious for what she has not yet seen, and as if trying to telepathically hasten this unreal situation she walks toward the screen. "Why hasn't it happened yet?" she wonders, her apprehension growing. "Could they have arrested the people who were going to do it? What if...?" The words that signal the end of all of Fidel's speeches are voiced and echoed by the frenzied crowds that cheer him from the streets surrounding the Presidential Palace.

"Homeland or Death!" "Victory will be ours!"

Sara hears the shouts and sees Fidel wave to the crowd and enter the Palace. She is terrified by the realization that Castro will continue to tear Cuba apart. Although, to her dismay, the feeling is mixed with relief, knowing that the reprisals that would have filled this evening have been averted. Garnering her natural vivaciousness, Sara descends the stone stairs, crosses the entry hall criss-crossed by the shadows of trembling palms, and walks onto the terrace. When the men notice her arrival, they turn toward her expectantly. She tries to disguise her hurried pace and appear calm in front of Rufino, the only remaining servant who is prowling around and from whom they are all trying to conceal the terrible nature of the anticipated situation.

"Fidel just finished his speech," announces Sara, searching for the same tone of voice with which she might say, "I just had a glass of water." The seven men stand, searching her face for some explanation for why the execution was not carried out.

"What happened?" Amador asks her, drawing closer to her, his face grave.

"Nothing! Absolutely nothing happened!" she whispers, before repeating aloud, "Fidel didn't say anything important. He just finished the speech and went inside the Palace."

The ambassadors look at one another silently, and the Brazilian finishes off a glass of wine sitting on the table in front of him. Suddenly, as if giving voice to the alarm that they are all feeling, the telephone rings and Amador hurries to answer it. A fraction of a second later, as he takes the receiver from his ear, he says two words that will be the epitaph of Cuba's freedom: "Martínez left!"

Sara realizes then that Martínez is the name of the man who was to carry out the execution and who, according to whoever just called, fled—by some unknown twist of fate that is pummeling Cuba—without completing his mission. The ambassadors approach Amador, questioning him silently, and Amador repeats the message he has just received, "Martínez left! That's it!"

After a few moments of silence, the ambassadors shake Amador's hand. Before leaving, they kiss Sara's hand, chilled by the devastation of the evening. The echo of the their departing cars tears at the darkness outside, and Amador and Sara stand together wondering what must have happened.

CHAPTER 11

"Two new ones came in from Cuba last night! Look, there are two new ones!"

Martín and Juan Ling awaken, startled and feeling as if they had fallen asleep only moments ago. They struggle to shake the heavy cloud of sleepiness and sit up in their cots, looking out over the tumult of boys gathering around them in the dining room at Matecumbe. Martín remembers having scolded his little brother just before daybreak, trying to make him stop crying, "Go to sleep, and quit being such a baby," he had snapped. Immediately, the other boys start bombarding them with questions that reveal their concern about family members still on the Island and whether or not they will be going back home soon.

"When's Fidel going to fall?"

"Haven't they invaded yet?"

"What's going on in Cuba?"

As they take in the two Chinese brother's monosyllabic answers, the boys begin prodding them with adolescent taunts.

"They train us at this camp so they can send us back to Cuba to fight against Fidel."

"Get ready, 'cause they'll send you guys, too."

"Today they'll show you how to fly airplanes. Didn't you see the airport when you came in?"

Martín clenches his right fist in his left hand and rests them both on his lap, thinking that now would be a good time to let go of his habit of carefully thinking through whatever problem he might face, since this one seems to demand immediate attention. But the self-control that his Chinese upbringing has instilled in him keeps him from showing any sign of fear or worry, and his thoughtful nature convinces him to listen to everything before jumping to any conclusions. In the meantime, he chews his lower lip and begins picking at the index finger of his left hand with his thumb.

"Come on, let me get to the two new boys," says Sergio García Miró, the medical student who took care of the new arrivals the night before. "Let them wake up in peace," he adds in a friendly voice. "Let's go. Everybody to breakfast."

During breakfast, Martín overhears that they are planning an initiation for him and his brother. He crosses his right leg over his left and decides that it would be a good idea for him and Juan to slip away from the group.

"Let's go. They're planning to throw us into the pool with our clothes on," he alerts his brother who is obviously frightened, nervous and completely dependent on him.

With a coolness either learned or inherited from their Oriental ancestors, the two brothers slip outside, moving quietly past the tents and disappearing into the undergrowth of the woods. There, they study the pines that sway in the cool morning breeze and walk across the newly cut grass that seems so dry and brown. They touch the rough bark of the trees, hunting for the mocking birds that rustle in the branches and throw pebbles at them. Some men are installing electrical wires above them, and they walk deeper into the long shadows cast by the pines. In the distance, they see the barracks where soldiers are said to have lived during World War II; and they hide, watching the narrow road that leads to the entrance where some boys already seem to be looking for them. The absence of flowers in this hard, dry soil surprises them as they collect sharp, knotty pine cones to defend themselves from the anticipated initiation. Then, they spot a stinging nettle bush. Just before he died in Cuba, their father had taught them never to touch one since it would cause a painful rash.

"Don't let it touch you, not even your shadow," Martín advises. "You'll swell up."

The brothers turn around, hearing footsteps approach, brandishing the pointy pinecones they intend to use against their attackers. The two are relieved to see Sergio García Miró, who recognizes their attitude of resolved defense against any assault.

"Hey, buddies, I was looking for you two," he says gently. "Come on over to the office so you can give them your information." He guides them, his arms protectively around their shoulders, pretending not to have noticed the pine cones they're clutching or the pebbles they have stowed in their pockets.

"The new guys! The new guys!" shouts another wave of boys who come running toward them as they come out of the thicket. Sergio speaks calmly with them, dissuading them from carrying out the initiation, and takes the two Chinese brothers into the office so they can be registered. Martín, the older brother who has taken on the maturity and composure of an adult, states that he is fourteen years old, and his brother Juan is twelve. He adds that their father was an immigrant from China and had died when he was only seven. Their mother remarried a Cuban, also of Chinese descent. They owned a restaurant in the center of the best commercial district of Havana, but the Revolution confiscated it without paying them a cent. Martín had worked there as a waiter and cashier. When they leave, are swarmed by boys who hurl a basketball at their heads, thus beginning the dreaded hazing.

"You've got to pass initiation!" the boys yell at them, carrying them to the pool.
"If the Catholic kids act like this, I don't want to know what the bad ones are like," thinks Martín, swinging his arms defensively and trying to escape with Juan. He is still swinging when Sergio García Miró arrives and rescues them at the edge of the pool. He takes them aside and delivers surprising and devastating news: they will have to be separated because boys twelve and younger live far away in the Florida City camp. They have never heard of it, but it is near a town called something like "Omestead."

Their good-bye is heart wrenching. It seems to the Ling brothers that this separation confirms their abandonment. Being together was the only thing they had left in their exile, and it was being snatched away from them just as the medallion of the Virgin had been ripped from Juan's neck by the scarred airport soldier before they were allowed to leave. The two Chinese boys embrace, solemnly, unable to voice the words "good-bye" and not knowing when they would see each other again. The possibility of telephone calls is their only hope as Juan boards George's van, filled with a new group of children just picked up from the airport. Martín stands silently, taught by his Oriental family to hide his grief, watching a boy who had gotten out of the van as his brother got in pass by. He is short, with fair skin and dark hair and eyes. His gaze is inquisitive and penetrating. Looking Ling sympathetically, he offers his name: José Frank Aspillaga. Martín turns his back so as not to watch the van leave and begins walking toward the brush to avoid the further hazing. Frank follows him and sits down on a fallen log, setting his suitcase on the ground. He starts tossing pebbles at a Cardinal that has just landed on a branch near them and relates some of the things he has been through in Cuba.

"I'm from Matanzas," he says. "I was an alter boy at the cathedral." His voice is firm and measured, such that no one would ever doubt what he was saying or what he believed. His foot brushes against a worm and he squashes it. "My mother got me out of Cuba because they were going to arrest me for being an alter boy. During the Bay of Pigs invasion last year, they arrested Father Gustavo. I showed up at the cathedral and his secretary told me: 'Two guards just took Father Gustavo prisoner. If you had been here, they would have taken you, too. Go to Juan Hernández's house. He's one of the parishioners. Tell him they've arrested Father Gustavo.' You know, when I got to Juan Hernández's house, I saw his wife crying because they'd arrested him, too. When Fidel defeated the invasion, they took all of the priests who had been arrested to the Bishop's residence and held them there under military guard. Father Gustavo needed medicine for his low blood pressure, so I went to take it to him. A guard with a machine gun asked me, 'Are you from the church, too?' I said, 'No, I'm from the pharmacy.' He thought I was just a delivery boy, so he didn't arrest me. I'm sure it was the Holy Spirit that inspired me to say that. What do you think?"

Impassive, Martín Ling had listened carefully.

"Those Chinese are stone-faced!" thinks Frank, crouching to sneak up on a lizard that slips through his fingers. Just then, a sudden breeze shakes a pine tree, startling them.

CHAPTER 12

As he arrives at the Florida City camp, Juan Ling sees Ely and María del Carmen Vilano in the distance, entering a classroom with a group of girls. At the door of the office where he is to register, Juan sees a girl his age with black braids bouncing on her shoulders. Her dark eyes burn with homesickness.

"What part of Cuba are you from?" the girl asks him.

"Havana."

"What's happening in Cuba?"

"The same."

"What do you mean, 'the same'?" she asks impatiently.

"The soldiers, the marches, the speeches, the firing squads, you can't watch T.V. because there's nothing on except Fidel and talk about what the war's going to be like when the Americans come."

"So the invasion to free Cuba that they say they're working on here and in other countries hasn't happened yet?"

"They're still waiting for it," replies Juan, worried.

"They say that there are lots of Cubans training in military camps in Central America," the girl expresses herself carefully and precisely. "Do you know if a boy from Camagüey came with you?"

"I don't know," says Juan Ling, looking around, frightened by everything and everybody he has seen since yesterday.

The girl starts asking the other boys who have arrived in George's van if any of them is from Camagüey, and suddenly Juan finds himself next to a little girl holding a doll that she has not let go of for a moment. The doll looks like Shirley Temple, the child-actress so famous in Cuba, and is wearing a pink lace sun hat. The new girl is holding on the rag doll for dear life, afraid of losing her last friend in the world. As Juan waits his turn in the office, he overhears the two girls talking:

"Are you from Camagüey?" asks the girl with the shiny black braids.

"No."

"What's your name?"

"Carmencita López."

"How old are you?"

"I just turned six," the new girl responds, holding her doll even more tightly in her right hand, as the little suitcase with its three changes of clothes quivers in her left.

"Did you come with a brother or sister?" the girl with the braids continues inquisitively.

"I don't have any." Her fine, blonde hair falls onto her face like a soft, morning shower.

"Your parents stayed in Cuba alone?"

"Yes," emits a small, trembling voice, her tiny lower lip quivering above her chin like the striker hovering above a percussionist's triangle.

"Does your mother have family there?"

"Her mother died when she was very little," a nun interjects.

Juan watches the girl with the braids take the other by the hand and guide her to a desk where they fill out her registration form and where she asks the adults in charge of the camp if they will let her take the little girl to the house where she'll be staying. Swiftly, she picks up the small suitcase, asks Carmencita if she's tired and gives her a kiss. As she leads her away, carrying her doll as well, it seems to Juan that the two have suddenly become mother and daughter.

In fact, the two leave the office together and the older one proceeds to show the younger one around the camp. She walks her past several two-story apartment buildings, each of which has a married couple that takes care of the girls up to age eighteen. In the middle of the camp, there is a big tent, like you would see at a circus. As she points out everything to Carmencita, a handful of new, English words slip into her speech with the ease of jacks being tossed onto a shiny floor by a child: "Father Walsh," "foster home," "nursery..."

"This is the older girls' house, and that one's for the younger girls. Their housemother is very nice. Her name is Gloria Nodarse," she explains. "But you're going to be with me."

She points at the tent, "Look, that's the daughter of Olga Chorens and Tony Alcares, the singers. Her name is Lisette."

Neither of the girls could know at this moment, that Lisette would grow up to be the wife and soul mate of Wifredito Chirino, who was walking around a different camp, his adolescent head filled with a tumult of music.

Nearby, they see George trying to fix the sole of a shoe belonging to one of the boys who had just arrived from Cuba. Five sisters trail behind this Cuban man who has given his name and his daily labor to this operation. Having housed them for three days in his own home, the girls did not want to leave until his wife promised to come visit and take them out sometimes. The oldest of the sisters is ten, the youngest, two. Behind them is a boy who did not want to leave the airport, convinced that his mother would arrive on the next plane. But his father is a prisoner in Cuba, and his mother was refused permission to leave because she went to the prison to visit her husband. A five-year old boy is in the infirmary with a catheter because he has not gone to the bathroom or spoken in over a month because of the trauma of leaving Cuba. When he sees George through the window, he runs outside. George hugs him and whispers to him, trying to get the boy to break his silence and let out the pain he feels from having been separated from his parents.

A few steps away, surrounded by children, is Dr. Mercedes García Tudurí, a philosophy professor and poet from Cuba who is now directing this school. With her is one of the teachers, María Modesta González. Not far from them, stands a man of average height and delicate features who is talking with one of the nuns who run the camp, plump and jovial Mother María Paz.

"Stay here and work with us, Leopoldo," the girls hear the nun ask sweetly. "You'll be more than a teacher, we need you to be a father to these children. Or do you refuse to suffer with them."

When the two girls are in front of the littlest girls' apartment, they see a slender child, about seven years old, with short, well styled hair standing at the door.

"They say her aunt is Rita Montaner, the artist. Her mother's a doctor and is in prison in Cuba for conspiring against Fidel. Every day she dresses up and combs her hair so the foster parents that come here looking for children to take home with them will pick her," relates the girl with the braids.

"What's your name?" the six year old asks, fighting against her fear and shyness.

"María Magda de Quesada. My cousin is Carlos Manuel de Céspedes y Quesada. He's a hero who started Cuba's war of independence against Spain in 1968. Didn't they tell you about him in school?"

"No."

"Well, now in Cuba they don't talk about heroes, just Fidel, Raúl and Ché. That's why when a mob came into my school to take it over, my mother didn't send me back. I spent a whole year at home learning how to knit and do needlepoint.

Suddenly, Carmencita stops and tells María Magda in a low voice, as if she is confessing a sin, "I have to go potty. But I..." —"You need help wiping?" The little girl nods her head.

"Let's go. Don't worry, I'll help you. Come on."

The two hurry along, again passing Leopoldo Arista, the man who was talking with Mother María Paz a moment ago.

"Hey, are you coming back tomorrow?" ask the little boy with him.

"Yes. I'm going to be your teacher.

"Don't let me down, man! You know that lots of people in Cuba let me down! I'll be waiting for you tomorrow!"

Soon, the camps sponsored by Father Walsh are overrun by an outbreak of childhood illness that spring up at certain times of the year. In Matecumbe, the nurses work eight-hour shifts, taking care of children sick with chicken pox and measles. These women, empathizing with the whole situation, are tireless in their work, visiting the young exiles in the barracks and tents, treating their pox and blisters, giving them medicine and rubbing them with ointments to relieve the itching. Sara Yaballí moves quickly among them, unflagging in her work. In the Florida City camp, these epidemics are joined by sore throats and high fevers brought on by the dust, and boils that emerge from scratching at infected mosquito bites. The doctor and nurse, also immigrants from Cuba, work in endless shifts, barely resting. The nuns, confined to their churches and convents throughout their country in the aftermath of the tragic Bay of Pigs invasion, were expelled by Fidel Castro. They graciously feed the lines of Cuban people who work with Father Walsh's children. Sweet Sister Cristina and Sister María Victoria from an order of Philippine nuns, scholarly Sister María Isabel Lazaga, also Philippine, and all of the sisters from other communities that bring their love and caring to the children of the exodus, are exhausted by caring physically and spiritually for the children in their hour of crisis and homesickness.

Amid the coughs and cries of the sick Cuban children, even more distraught because they miss their mothers as they shiver from fever, the healthy ones and those who are recovering, get up and go to English, Religion and other special classes. Leopoldo Arista, who had been an attorney for *Pan American* in Cuba, now teaches art in a classroom full of empty chairs because of the outbreaks which, fortunately, haven't resulted in deaths. Arista, giving his first lesson, smiles at the boy who had been afraid he would not return. For him, it would have been yet another desertion. Walking around the classroom, Leopoldo approaches the Tang brothers, two Chinese boys nine and eleven years old, to look at their drawings and ask them if they've just recently left Cuba. Later, he is surprised by the two lifeless fish painted by Eugenia Li, also Chinese, who is adding the finishing touches that reveal a true talent for artistic expression.

"Let me see it," he admires. "You paint beautifully."

In the same time, a small, thin boy with lively eyes and fair skin catches his attention. He is sitting on the floor in the corner, as if trying to protect himself from loneliness within the angle formed by the two walls. Leopoldo Arista moves toward him, speaks to him and asks his name. Then, the boy delivers the greatest shock of the morning, responding to him only with howls.

"He doesn't know how to talk, Teacher," explain several students, leaving their seats to come over to them.

"You'll see. He can climb the walls like a monkey."

"Oh, my God!" exclaims Arista, and thinks to himself, "This just shows how bad things are in Cuba! That this boy's mother would rather send him here alone than subject him to the horror of war that Fidel's tyranny incites from one minute to the next!" Arista asks the rest of the students their names and checks the attendance sheet. As it turns out, the handicapped boy's name is Alvaro Artiles and he is five years old. Arista next turns to a mestizo girl who looks very sad. He approaches and asks what's wrong. The little girl does not answer, but one of her classmates does:

"Teacher, yesterday they took us to the movie theater in Homestead and they wouldn't let her in." Their teacher painfully understands that in the neighboring town, they have discriminated against her because of her dark skin, adding to the difficulties she will face in adapting. "Our housemother told us all to leave, so we did."

Suddenly, he feels a breeze in the classroom. When Leopoldo Arista turns around, he sees one of his new students start running toward a woman that none of them recognize. She is overwrought and runs toward the boy until they meet in an embrace, tears streaming down their faces. They remain that way for several moments, until they step back to look at one another. Still wiping their eyes, she greets the teacher and attempts to explain why she is so emotional. She had been diagnosed with breast cancer a few months ago while still in Cuba, and she hid the diagnosis from her son, afraid that he would refuse to go to Miami without her since she did not yet have a visa. The poor woman had postponed the inescapable surgery until she finally saw him off. Now, she had recovered from the surgery and the whole world was a happy and friendly place in her eyes because she was with her son again. All around them the other children clapped until they were interrupted by Alvaro's howling. They turned their heads to see the boy climbing the walls, demonstrating his sad, monkey-like ability.

"What's the matter with him?" asks the newly arrived mother, overwhelmed by the shock of such a pathetic case.

"That's another result of Castroism, Ma'am," affirms the teacher as he walks toward the impaired boy, shaking his head.

CHAPTER 13

"Ms. Sara! The house is surrounded by the G-2!" shouts one of the children's nannies, and Sara looks through the window to see that a swarm of patrol cars has encircled her home in Havana. The knocker on the colonial door echoes thunderously, announcing their sudden appearance. And when one of the servants opens the door, a squad of soldiers storms the house. Eager to fulfill their mission of safeguarding the socialist state in Cuba, they traverse the living and dining rooms, arriving at the terrace where Sara sits knitting, her five youngest children gathered around her.

"Come with us, Ma'am! You're under arrest!" says a short, round soldier as he takes her by the arm.

"Why?" asks Sara, feigning a surprise that she is very far from feeling.

"You must know why," the man assures her.

The others have fanned out through the house, undertaking a meticulous search. Sara sees Amador, wearing his linen guayabera, also apparently under arrest, descending the stairs from the second floor, escorted by two soldiers. Quickly recognizing the advancing threat, the children drop their toys and cling to their mother's dress, screaming at the soldiers not to take her. But they do, and they take Amador as well, forcing them into a G-2 vehicle. The children sob, crying out to them, left with their nannies, the only ones who can assuage their abandonment.

Sara and Amador are escorted into Havana's sinister G-2 headquarters, which occupies a house on the aristocratic Fifth Avenue of the Miramar district. They are separated upon arrival, and Sara sees them take her husband to a wing of the house reserved for the interrogation of political prisoners.

"Good-bye, Amador! I love you!" she manages to tell him, and notes the sad smile with which he says good-bye before disappearing down a hallway. She finds herself faced with a female soldier who pats down her clothes and takes away the jewelry that she is wearing to compliment her lovely dress: the Rolex watch that Fidel noticed in *El Carmelo* and a pearl necklace.

Then, following along as if watching an actress in a movie rather than living the experience herself, she's put into a room that has been converted into a cell with twelve bunks, the last of which she will occupy.

"We're like the Twelve Apostles," a working class woman tells her, coming over to offer her assistance as she adapts to this tragic confinement in which they are deprived of newspapers, television, visitation or even the consolation of a telephone. Disoriented, Sara does not know what to do, nor to whom she should turn. She's accustomed to Amador's leadership and initiative, efficiently resolving any family crisis. Surrounded by eleven women, held like herself for political crimes, Sara wonders which one might be a G-2 agent placed there to learn about her involvement in the charges they'll bring against her. The first thing that occurs to her is to knock on the door to ask for her lawyer. But the guards don't come, and the other women explain that detainees aren't permitted to have an attorney, nor are there any judicial procedures in place by which to defend themselves. Sara circles the small cell, quickly getting to know the other prisoners. Later, she sits to wait and count the hours that eat away at the days like Saturn devouring his children in the bygone days when there were still gods in the world. Now, even gods are forbidden in the construction of this unrelenting socialism.

Sara fights to organize her thoughts. She thinks back on her brief imprisonment after the Bay of Pigs invasion and hopes that maybe they will only keep her here for a few days this time as well. Then, her mind is filled with thoughts of Amador and their five youngest children, protected only by the benevolence of their nannies now that the older ones are in exile and cannot return for them. "Silvia's three children are still so young! She's going to be so worried for us, the poor thing!" she tells herself. "She's suffered so much already! My daughter, the poet; she's going to become so depressed that she won't want to write anymore! Oh, and César! He loves us so much and has always been so worried about us. This is going to be so hard on him, too! And Any Laury, who tells me she loves me more often than any of the others. Who will be the one to tell her that her parents are in prison? My Sarita who's always studying and wants to learn everything. She'll be lost not being able to talk with her father or with me! And without us, Mary Loly is going to feel so all alone, there in Texas on her scholarship."

Sara slips into the routine established by the other prisoners with whom she shares this sad kinship. Before going to bed, they rinse out their undergarments so they can put them back on clean in the morning, since they aren't allowed to receive any clothing from home. And like the others, Amador's wife walks a thin line between solidarity and distrust, not sharing information with anyone, not knowing who might betray her or where there might be a hidden microphone recording words she couldn't deny. This is how she learns to defend herself against spying, and also how tears become her constant companion as she thinks of her husband and their children, the friends who are involved in their cause, in the tragedy that is crushing Cuba, and the Visa Waivers that she can no longer distribute to send children to Miami.

On one of the indolent days that drag on incomprehensibly for the twelve prisoners, the interrogators come for Sara. They take her to an empty office from which every humanizing detail has been swept away, like litter from a wet and windy street.

"Citizen Sara del Toro," the hardened voice of a soldier addresses her with the epithet reserved for traitors undeserving of the title "Comrade." "What do you have to confess?"

"Absolutely nothing," she responds with an immediacy granted by her dignity and the strength of her deep convictions. She has forced away her tears and faces them with unshakeable confidence.

"We have Amador, your husband, in the chapel. We'll shoot him if you don't talk."

"They're not going to shoot him. They want to frighten me into talking," she thinks quickly then states bluntly, "Well, you'll just have to shoot him because I don't know anything!"

Several days later, they enter the cell the twelve women share and demand, "Come down to watch the television. Pedro Jiménez is going to speak."

Sara recognizes the name of the man known in her house by the codename "Juan." He is the one who took over the national leadership of the People's Revolutionary Movement after Manolo

Ray and "Eugenio." Only a few days earlier, Pedro Jiménez y Martínez, had planned the mission with the bazooka in front of the Presidential Palace that was to have executed Fidel. Dr. Alberto Cruz, a former minister in the democratic government and the current national leader of *Rescate*, a clandestine anti-Castro movement, had collaborated with them as well. They had arrested Pedro Jiménez at Amador and Sara's estate the night he was to leave for Miami, shortly after the failed attempt. Amador had driven Pedro's mother-in-law to his house in the middle of the night and on the way instructed her to destroy the incriminating documents she carried in her purse. Amador had then hidden in one of the Venezuelan embassy's residences, from which he emerged a few days later believing that if he stayed it would confirm his participation in anti-Castrist activities and further compromise the imprisoned Pedro.

"I can't come down. I'm not feeling well," says Sara as she watches the others leave. She stays behind thinking that if Pedro Jiménez was going to speak on television, he must have something to say that is of benefit to the Revolutionary Government. If not, they would never allow him this, or any other, opportunity to appear.

"Sara, Pedro just ratted out priests, diplomats…" one of the prisoners tells her when she returns. "Damn him!"

The next day, Tuesday, November 7th, 1961, the official newspaper of the Castro regime, *Revolución!* publishes detailed information about the Presidential Palace attack. Amador Odio is accused of aiding political refugees, and Sara is named as an accomplice. Their estate is identified as a headquarters for anti-Castro conspirators.

The leaden resignation of being condemned falls on Sara del Toro like a mountain on a grain of sand. Once again, Amador, their children, the Visa Waiver children and all of Cuba flood her emotions. Sara takes refuge in her tears when the guards are not looking, as if her suffering alone could extinguish the social and political firestorm that is consuming her country.

CHAPTER 14

Silvia and Juan Couriel are cruelly insulted and mocked by the oldest son of the family that so begrudgingly received them. Their heads drop with the devastating sadness of a child's humiliation and they desert the miserable cup of coffee with milk that has been arrogantly set before them, like coins cast at a beggar. This intolerable situation has carried on since the day they were retrieved from the airport by the scowling woman irritated at having to waste her time waiting for them.

The family consists of a couple and several adolescent children. They immigrated from Cuba a few months earlier, frightened by the winds of revolution, and settled in Miami, where they work as their older children begin to develop asocial behaviors. In addition to being away from their family, Silvia and Juan suffer these people's lack of affection, aggressive distain and psychological bullying.

Silvia and Juan knew them well in Cuba because their grandparents had taken care of the mother years ago. When her parents died, they took her in and raised her as a daughter. They sent her to private schools, offered her the same opportunities as their own children, and facilitated a marriage to a wonderful man. Divorced shortly thereafter, this woman on whom Silvia and Juan now depend, remarried and raised the family that now mistreats them, ungratefully repaying kindness with antagonism and hatred.

"Let's go, Juan," says Silvia who has just turned twelve, pushing away the untouched coffee and taking her ten-year old brother's hand protectively. The unwarranted insults continue to rain down on them like stones thrown at a kitten by cruel children. They have tried to intimidate them with verbal abuse and, it is sorry to say, hunger. This sadistic family has gone so far as to feed themselves with the food given to support Silvia and Juan in their American asylum. Under a cascade of insults, Silvia picks up their book bags, hands one to Juan and finds the pencil he's lost, slipping it into the front pocket of his shirt that she herself has washed and ironed. When they reach the street, the children begin walking toward their school.

Thirty years later, Silvia would refuse to discuss this abominable situation. And as Juan recounts it, the pain of experiencing it would leave him at a loss for words.

"Juan," Silvia speaks with the decisiveness that she has developed during their exile, "you know we can't stay in that house anymore."

"I know," he responds, choking back a sob that threatens to escape.

"As if it weren't bad enough, those boys are in a gang, and from what I can see it's just going to get worse if we stay."

Juan looks at her, and thirty years later, would remember how he felt at that moment, realizing that Silvia had made a decision that would affect them both—to strike out with him into the unknown which, if the months they'd spent in an unstable and dishonest home were any indication, could be worse or at least just as bad as that disastrous experience.

"Look, Juan," she says, seeming to grow up before his eyes, her child's appearance becoming increasingly protective and maternal, "I talked to the counselor yesterday at school." The English words are pronounced with increasing assurance, "and I told her what's happening to us."

Juan looks at her again, afraid of a situation fraught with dangers that seem beyond his child's ability to confront.

"The counselor believed me, because she knows I'm not a liar." The self-respect of her statement, countering the magnitude of past humiliations, surprises Juan. "The counselor is going to help us."

"How?" asks the boy, stopping in front of Silvia, in a moment of abject confusion.

"She spoke to a Cuban couple she knows. They're nice people and today after school she's going to take us to their house. Then, they're going to take us to live in a camp run by the Catholic Church. Lots of Cuban children that came here alone, like us, are there."

"Do you think they'll treat us better?" asks Juan with the doubt that befalls those who have suffered greatly and fear they will never see the end of their misfortune.

"Yes. It'll be alright. You'll see." Hope penetrates her brother's heart like an unexpected arrow.

Juan walks into the school amazed by his sister's courage and sets aside the uncertainty he feels about the change that awaits them, abandoning himself to the activity of the day. In the classroom he tries his best to learn as many English words and phrases as possible, anxious to master the language that will let him be accepted by his peers, native to this country that on a map looks as big as a snow-covered mountain that he's just begun to climb, sinking into its fluffy whiteness and slipping on it frozen surface.

When class is over, Juan sees Silvia in the doorway with the counselor and again admiration for his sister's strength fills his heart. Walking toward her, he lovingly takes stock of her: She is chubby and olive-skinned with dark eyes and short, dark hair. She seems so strong and self-assured that he will trust her forever.

Thirty years later, Juan would remember how it felt, after months of hunger, to eat his fill at the Rodrígucz's house. This Cuban couple graciously takes them in and drives them the next day to the Florida City camp. When they arrive, the boy sees a tall, muscular priest outside. He is smiling, surrounded by Cuban boys, and playing basketball with them.

"Father Walsh, throw it to me."

"Me, Father Walsh, to me," the children vie for the ball.

"That's the priest who runs these camps," Silvia whispers to Juan before they say good-bye to the Rodríguezes. The priest, noting their arrival, comes forward and greets them in Spanish, tinged with an Irish accent. His smile is like a cool drink on a hot, summer day as he tells them how to find the office where they will fill out their registration cards. The priest's blue eyes dance happily beneath bushy, blonde eyebrows, like lights at a children's carnival. Still smiling, he asks the Couriels where they are from, since George is not back from the airport. When Mother María Paz comes to take Silvia to meet her house parents, Juan begins to think that this warm and athletic priest will forever be a father figure to him.

When she arrives at the Velasco's apartment, Silvia counts fifteen girls between the ages of twelve and fourteen who are busily washing windows, dusting furniture and sweeping floors. After Mrs. Velasco gives her some hand-me-down clothes to replace the three outfits she had left at her mother's friend's house, Silvia sees two sets of girls hugging each other and crying.

"Write to us, Ely! Write to us María del Carmen!"
"Good-bye, Raquel! Good-bye, Marta!"
"Don't forget us!"
"No, no. Never, ever!"

Awash in tears, Ely and María del Carmen leave after kissing their houseparents and the fifteen girls who have stopped their cleaning. Sol, who was cleaning a window and furtively looking at her reflection in the glass, is the last one they hug and kiss good-bye.

As Ely and María del Carmen leave, tears begin to flow in the girls' shared sadness. Walking from the apartment back to their classrooms, Raquel de la Portilla is frightened by a black snake hanging in a tree.

"Ayy, watch out, Marta!" she screams. "We only had boas and racers in Cuba. Who knows if that one's poisonous!"

Back in the classroom, the absence of their friends, the Vilanos, falls on Marta and Raquel like a leaden guillotine on a startled bird. The two remember their last days in Cuba, their tears falling on their littlest brother's diaper as they changed him, overwhelmed with sadness at the thought of leaving without their parents. Raquel dries her eyes with a hanky and writes a note to Marta, tossing it onto her desk when Mother María Paz turns to the blackboard to write the Ten Commandments. Marta thinks, "Now Raquel's sad because she's missing the Vilanos as bad as she's missing her boyfriend in Cuba." She hides the note in her book so she can read it: *We were finally getting use to this camp. We were happy here. But now, girls leave every day for foster homes and new ones we don't know come in from Cuba.* Marta nods in agreement and tears a sheet of paper out of her notebook to write a letter to Ely and María del Carmen Vilano's mother:

> ***Dear Mrs. Vilano,***
>
> *I hope this letter finds you well. My sister and I are fine. You know us from your daughters' letters.*
>
> *Today, Ely and Mary went to a foster home in Buffalo, a city they say is near New York that must have a lot of buffalos. My sister and I are very sad. We'll never have friends like them again.*
>
> *I'm sending you my parents' address in Matanzas. Write to them for us. I hope that you and your husband can meet them. That way, when they cry because we're not there, they won't be all alone like they are now.*
>
> *My sister and I want to meet you very much.*
> *Hugs and kisses,*
> ***Marta de la Portilla***

When the two sisters leave the classroom, they see George helping a handicapped boy from the van. He has to carry him because they took his wheelchair away in the Havana airport right before he got on the plane.

"Poor thing!" they say and run to give him a candy, scarce in Cuba now that all of the sugar needed to make it is being exported to pay for tanks and fighter planes to defend Fidel's "Direct Democracy" and his right to establish relentless State Capitalism throughout the country, under the promising name of Socialism.

CHAPTER 15

The airplane carrying Ely and María del Carmen Vilano to Buffalo lifts off as winter is already departing. Traveling with them are two other girls, from among the hundreds who lived at the Florida City, whom they have never met. The four prepare for the seven-hour trip and many stopovers in unknown cities. They are headed to a home in Buffalo to live with a Catholic family that has sent for them; and that is all they know.

"Ely," says María del Carmen, shaken by this second upheaval, "maybe we should have stayed in Florida City. We were happy there."

"Trust in God. You'll see. The new family will be nice." She naively imagines Buffalo as a wild, snow covered prairie where quadrupeds of the same name roam freely.

The plane banks above the clouds and casts its shadow over Miami and Florida's dry land covered in pines and mangroves. The four girls remember leaving Cuba and relive the uncertainty of facing the impending unknown. Leaving behind the security and affection they had found in Florida City, Ely looks at the wing of the plane, shining like a silver bar, and sees her life flash across it in ever-changing memories intermittently joined together as if by a paper ribbon. Her big house in Guanabacoa, near Havana, with its high, wooden ceilings. Her father's hunting dogs, dragging their long ears through the rooms. Her piano and her studies interrupted a month before graduation by her departure. The jewelry and furniture stores her father had opened nearby. *Saint Theresa of Avila*, the school two blocks away that Fidel Castro sent his street mobs, armed with sticks and stones to take over for the State. Ely and María del Carmen's grandparents had come to Cuba as immigrants from the Canary Islands, where their grandmother was unable to take her vows as a novitiate because of a serious pneumonia that spirited her away from the convent's lattice covered windows. Her grandmother's sister, whom Ely and Mary had always wanted to meet, stayed in Granada as the Mother Superior of that region's Sisters of Charity. Ely had frequently gone hunting with her father, the leather saddle creaking as she trotted beside him on a palomino horse. Cuba's beloved countryside leaps to her memory with its fanned palms, and rivers stirred by her horse's hooves. She was happy there among the peasants' children who invited them to share their bitter, roadside coffee, steaming like newly burned cane fields hastening the sugar production that was the nation's wealth. Ely remembers her fear when rumors coursed throughout the country in the last days of the Batista regime and the hopefulness of the first days after Fidel Castro's victory, when his bushy beard filled television screens, adding to his charisma as a romantic freedom fighter. Camilo Cienfuegos, Ely's first love, was beside him during his long, political speeches, a watchful, machine-gun carrying bodyguard on the lookout for anyone who posed a threat to the Maximum Leader. "Look how much that romantic image cost us!" Ely thinks to herself. But one detail of the memory remains sacred to her: Camilo's handsome silhouette holding out his hand to help her mount her young palomino at the aquaculture festival in Guanabacoa where she was the Queen of the Blue Brigade at the horse races. Camilo, riding next to her, under the envious gaze of all the other girls, and his charming demeanor, as blissful as a sleeping child. The image of her mother, as sweet and gentle as herself, surprising big eyed, dark haired Ely when she leaned in to ask her what she thought of Commander Cienfuegos.

"Oh, he's wonderful, Mamá. So kind and so good!" replied Ely.

"Ely, he's asked your father for permission to call on you."

"Oh, Mamá! He did?"

"He did, but your father told him absolutely not, because you're still just a girl and he doesn't want you to have your heart broken by a man every woman falls in love with," was her mother's conclusion. Later, Camilo's strange disappearance shocked Ely into a devastating political realization: Fidel killed him because he was afraid of him. "The people loved Camilo more than they did Fidel. They said that Camilo wasn't a Communist and that he was going to stand up to Fidel so he couldn't become a dictator," Ely remembers having heard many Cubans comment.

The day drags past the airplane like a slow, plodding horse, and when the heartache of nightfall looms over the last arc of afternoon, the houses of Buffalo appear; a mix between the allure of what's new, and the bitter uncertainty of the unknown.

"Look at how pretty the houses are, Mary!" They look like Hansel and Gretel's!" exclaims Ely, squeezing her sister's hands and surprised to see a city where she expected a prairie covered with buffalo.

They are met with a smile at the airport. It's Miss Murphy, the American social worker who will take them to the home were they will stay, one of these pleasant two-story houses tucked away in a quiet suburb. The woman who greets them is Guatemalan, a little reserved, and still mourning the recent loss of her husband, an Australian immigrant. The two new girls are situated on the first floor and Ely and her little sister on the second. Exhaustion threatens to overtake Ely as they are all getting to know one another, and this unexpected complication makes the situation even more difficult.

"I don't feel good," she thinks, calling on God, who has always been her greatest ally. "But I don't want to say anything or be a bother to anyone. What if they get fed up with me?" With superhuman effort, Ely smiles and takes a seat at the table sternly presided over by the Guatemalan woman. Ely looks at a platter of roasted meat that she does not recognize and gently nudges the girl next to her, asking in a low voice, "What is that?"

"It's tongue," rings the woman's authoritarian voice. "I made it for you. It's very nutritious.

"It must be a Guatemalan dish," thinks Ely. "I never ate that in Cuba." Obliged by the woman's insistent tone, Ely tries to take a bite of this strange meat, but she gags from nausea. The woman, shocked, sees her cover her mouth with a napkin and go pale with shame.

"Try to eat it. It's very good."

But Ely can't swallow a single bite of the tongue, and ashamed, she silently reproaches herself for her inability to carry out this one act of courtesy toward the woman.

When she finally enters the bedroom she will share with her little sister, she's afraid María del Carmen might suffer an asthma attack brought on by the stress of the long trip and the new situation they're facing. Ely rests her warm head on the pillow and thinks of the Moorish mosaics in her house in Cuba. "I need to get up and write to Mamá and Papá," she thinks, battling intense exhaustion. But a mountain of sleep descends on her, settling over her eyes.

In the morning, Ely can barely get up. But she's afraid of alarming the woman who has taken her in, or missing a day of school where she and her sister are attending on scholarship. Also, panic about making the Guatemalan woman feel like she's going to turn out to be a bother because she's sick forces her out of bed, like one of those wounded soldiers who in the heat of battle struggle to their feet, pick up a gun and fight.

"Bundle up, girls. It's still cold here," warns the woman firmly.

Ely walks with Mary to the sidewalk to wait for the bus that will pick them up, feeling like her little heart might explode in her chest. In the classroom, a wave of nausea passes over her, and she nearly collapses onto her desk. "I know I've got a fever, but I'm not going to tell anyone," her worry increasing; and she touches her right cheek. "Yes, I'm burning up, but I don't want the Guatemalan woman to get tired of me!" and gently, as is her nature, she rests her precious face on a delicate and feminine hand, unable to concentrate on understanding the American nun's explanations, or even answer her when she asks rapidly in English if she has understood the lesson. "Mamá, Papá," thinks Ely, "I miss you so much. I love you! I wish you were here! I wish Fidel would fall today so Mary and I could go back to Cuba tomorrow!"

Ely suffers through the week, like a nomad crossing the desert on foot, enduring the scorching sun by day and the unspeakable cold of night, rationing out his water drop by drop until the last one signals his death. On Saturday, the Guatemalan woman's daughter comes to meet the four girls. Like an acrobat falling dizzily from a trapeze after her last somersault when they have already removed the net, Ely steps forward to shake her hand.

"Do you feel sick?" she asks the new arrival in her americanized Spanish, looking at her sweet face and gently holding the hand Ely had extended so she can take her pulse.

"Yes," the girl admits weakly, surrendering like a butterfly to a gardener who is trying to protect it from a sudden storm.

"I'm a medical student," Ely hears the visitor say. "Come with me. I'm going to check you over."

After examining her, the young woman hurries to the phone. "Mom! Ely's very sick! I'm calling the hospital!" In a few minutes, the ambulance arrives in front of the house. A doctor examines Ely quickly and announces that she has the measles, complicated by double pneumonia. Immediately, they give her shot in the left arm and two orderlies come into the bedroom to carry her out. Realizing that they are carrying her on a stretcher down the stairway to the first floor, she lies there, subdued by fear and exhaustion. Ely hears her little sister crying desperately and the Guatemalan woman shrieking, "The girl's going to die! She's going to die! What a disaster!"

Ely's fatigue overcomes her fear, and she closes her eyes. When she arrives at the hospital, she becomes aware that she is on an exam table, that they're undressing her and that they're putting a thermometer in her mouth. "Oh, how strange! In Cuba, my mother used to put it under my arm," she recalls. And then she realizes that in her feverish state she's bitten the fragile glass because she thought it was ice. She spits it out, half choking, startled and shivering with chills under the white sheet, surrounded by desolate, white walls adorned only by a crucifix. When they take her to a bed in the intensive care unit, Miss Murphy, the social worker, comes to see her. The tears she tries to hide reveal that, indeed, Ely is fighting for her life.

"Miss Murphy, I'm going to die," says Ely, her voice breaking.

"Ely, you are not going to die."

Not knowing how to express her dying wish in English, the little girl manages to say it in Spanish, which Miss Murphy doesn't understand, but intuits. "I don't want them to bury me in the snow."

The sores that had erupted on Ely's chest and back the day before spread over her whole body like a brilliant, purple shroud.

From within the haze of I.V.s and antibiotics tormenting her veins, Ely imagines Camilo's smile, her mother's magical hands and her father's serene gaze. No one around her speaks

Spanish, so as a member of the generation raised on José Martí in Cuba, she recalls his "Simple Verses:"

> "When I to death succumb
> nationless, but free,
> place on my tomb
> a clutch of flowers and a flag."

"I wish I were in Cuba with Mamá and Papá, even if I had to be a slave to Fidel who killed my Camilo... Oh, if I die, who will take care of my little sister. Oh, God! Please don't let me die, even just for María del Carmen's sake, and so my parents don't have to suffer!"

"Hello, my child. How are you?" Ely opens her eyes and sees a priest by her side.

"Oh my God! I'm going to die!" she thinks, looking for the sacred oils he must be carrying.

Speaking very slowly, so she can understand him in English, the priest asks if she wants to confess her sins. She recounts them in her hastily acquired English, riddled with grammar and syntax errors but understandable nonetheless.

"Father, I've said bad words, but I've never wished anything bad for anyone," she says, scouring her memory for any shadow of sin, which she communicates as naively as a kitten frightened by a crystal statuette of a dog. "I've told my parents a lot of lies since I've been here," she considers, "but I'm not going to confess those, because I told them so they wouldn't worry about Mary and me." As she closes her eyes again, she asks God to protect her, and the paroquets and finches that flutter in their cages at her house in Cuba seem to surround her, bringing her well-wishes from home.

"Father, I don't want them to bury me in the snow," she murmurs in Spanish. "I want to be buried in the warm earth of my country."

CHAPTER 16

"**M**y cousin had his fifteenth birthday party and I didn't get to dance with Teresita," thinks Wifredito Chirino as he moves into *Casa Carrión*, where twenty boys who emigrated alone from Cuba live. The old mansion situated on Biscayne Boulevard is where Sara del Toro and Father Walsh first met and began sending Visa Waivers to Cuba, more than a year ago.

Entering the spacious living room, well-decorated with clean but somewhat worn furnishings, Wifredito is flanked by Juan Couriel, whose sister Silvia has been taken to the Florida City camp.

"Hello! Welcome!" Father Walsh greets them, smiling. His Spanish tinged with a Celtic accent. He is the Irish priest who now cares for thousands of Cuban children housed in camps he has founded for them. He is tall, and his sturdy frame shows that he is a man accustomed to sports. Anyone who sees him feels the kindness and compassion of his immutable smile, balanced with his ability to say no when necessary. This balance is but one cause of the respect he garners from those who work with him. He projects limitless energy, joined with contagious enthusiasm. He is never overwhelmed by his many responsibilities, confident that time is on his side, even offering him the opportunity to escape to his sailboat or his plane, which like so many extroverts he enjoys with the company of others. He seems able to fight tirelessly for any cause he deems worthy. This obviously modern priest is at once open and contemplative. Although he makes a first impression with jokes and kind gestures, the strength and determination of his personality never go unnoticed. Intuitive individuals recognize that Father Walsh is deeply practical and objective, given his astute perception of the present situation; they also understand that beneath his good-natured exterior beat a frankness and decisiveness able to immediately disarm a Pharisee's hypocrisy. He is a realist, given to finding solutions and convinced that problems can always be solved. He is as perceptive as a psychologist and anyone who speaks with him feels that his piercing eyes see through them, as if he were photographing the depths of their soul. He understands humanity and possesses the miraculous gift of empathy. He works for mankind, faithful that the attention and support he offers in each casual encounter will produce spectacular results. Due to experience, a rational conclusion, or maybe both, he never expects to be thanked or remembered. The realization does not leave him bitter, nor does it weaken his resolve. He accepts that the rules that govern human existence determine that he will be overlooked. He seems to have rejected long ago any deep emotional attachment to others, since logic dictates that those he supports today will leave him soon to go their own way and live their own lives. He sees himself as just a momentary part of their lives, trying to transmit a tiny bit of the Christian mindset that guides him. His love for them, when they depart, will transform into love for the others who will arrive, in need of his care. This open and healthy attitude has freed his spirit without robbing him of his ability to feel and express love for all. To him, the most important thing is to act on his conscience, which should always be in harmony with God. He is like a warrior for righteousness, something that comes to him spontaneously and naturally. Behind his strength and vitality there is a deep, spiritual vocation that compels him to serve with priestly humility. His presence radiates a peace that undoubtedly comes from the Christian conviction in which his spirit is deeply rooted.

Juan had seen Father Walsh in passing, when he arrived at the Florida City camp, and Wifredito, who did not know him, sees him step away from a group of boys that surrounded him to come greet them.

"What part of Cuba are you two from?" he asks them, putting his arms around their shoulders like a member of a close-knit team and taking them on a tour of the house.

"Father Walsh, this boy is a relative of mine that I asked to have sent here," says a friendly and distinguished looking lady with a nod toward Wifredito. She has just emerged from the patio where she was sitting on a bench and is carrying a shirt that she was sewing a button onto. The twelve-year-old boy it belongs to trails behind, calling her "Mamá Nina." She is the housemother, and it is her husband's name, which she took when she emigrated from Cuba a few months ago, that identifies the old mansion where they live as *Casa Carrión*. Nina kisses Juan and Wifredito, giving them some gum and explaining to Wifredito that she wanted to bring him to live with her so he would feel closer to his sister, Marilé, who is married to Nina's son and has just given birth to their first child.

"She will come to see you soon. She sent these letters from your parents for you.

They just arrived yesterday," says the woman, sitting down to continue sewing on the button. Two charming dimples appear in her cheeks as she smiles, her dark eyes survey the room, watching the children at play to see if they need anything from her.

Wifredito thanks her and follows Father Walsh to the patio where they sit down on a bench with Juan Couriel. The priest asks them how their English lessons are coming along, and tells them that they will be attending the school next door. Sometimes he speaks to them in his Irish-accented Spanish, other times in English so they can practice this new language that he pronounces clearly and slowly so they can understand. Soon, he is talking to the two boys about their interests, winning their friendship and confidence. Father Walsh learns that music is Wifredito's passion but that he was never able to study it because his father wanted him to be a doctor or lawyer, reflecting the social prejudices of the day that placed artists beneath college educated professionals. His father, demonstrating another of the time's prejudices, feared that playing the piano would diminish his only son's manliness. Wifredito, in spite of his homesickness, is happy and self-assured. His inherent confidence wraps him in contentment. He does not let challenges defeat him and he knows what he wants to do in the future; he wants to be a musician. Father Walsh notes in Juan Couriel a passion for adventure and novelty, a desire to grab life with both hands and feel the thrill of the unknown. Father Walsh invites both boys to join his Boy Scout troop and promises to take them to the ocean to sail on his boat around Miami Bay on Sunday.

When the conversation ends, the priest calls all of the exiled Cuban boys to tell them that he will be out of the city—something that almost never happens—because he is taking Mr. Carrión on a trip in his airplane to see a car race in Sebring.

"I hope you will all behave yourselves and help Mrs. Carrión around the house," he tells them, presenting a good-natured challenge as he rests his fingertips on the table. "I don't want her complaining about you when I get home tonight."

"Father Walsh," Juan Couriel appears, out of breath, in the doorway where he has been looking out onto the street trying to get a glimpse of Miami, which to a boy his age equals the thrill of exploring the world for the first time.

"Father Walsh, can I go out for a walk?"

"Where to, son?" the priest adds the term of endearment common in Cuban conversations as he puts his hands in his pockets.

"Just around here—on this street— and just to look around."

"Are you going alone?" the priest asks, his palms resting on the tabletop.

"One those boys over there will go with me," he answers assuredly as Father Walsh scratches his head.

"Do you promise to come back soon? You know I'll be gone and I don't want you worrying Mrs. Carrión," he responds quietly, in a deep voice.

"Sure, sure, Father. Really soon."

Juan Couriel hurries past Wifredito Chirino who is playing dominoes with another boy and takes to the street with a boy from the house whom he has just met and with whom he has discussed his curiosity. Stepping out onto the wide sidewalk, Juan feels the rush of adventure as he gears up to explore Miami. By the time he reaches the corner, he has forgotten that he should turn back. The whole universe now consists of this wide street, lined with buildings and mansions, where he can walk where he likes, run, jump, shout and do as he pleases. The giddiness brought on by this freedom soars as he passes the glass doors that mark the entrance of a gigantic store.

"It's Sears, man!" he tells his new friend. "In Havana, the Sears have elevators and escalators. Let's go ride them!"

The store is overflowing with delights—everything Juan lost when he left Cuba: bicycles, skates, lifejackets, plastic boats, tents ... endless pleasures to be enjoyed as he wishes.

The two boys walk along the store's wide aisles, tempted unrelentlessly by the marvelous things they see. But the highpoint of the afternoon is marked by their discovery of a fabulous pool table. Juan and his friend stop in front of the sea of green. Taking advantage of the salesman's absence, they pick up the cues and start shooting balls, which roll across the alluring velvet surface with amazing speed and clatter as they hit one another.

"Children are not allowed to touch the displays!" the salesman's angry voice paralyzes them as he takes away the cues and balls. Juan's resourcefulness does not wane, however, and a moment later he proposes a solution to his friend.

"Let's hide under the table. Look, it has a cover that goes down to the floor. They'll never see us. When everyone leaves for the night, we can come out and play."

"What if they catch us?"

"They're not going to catch us."

The first time the salesman turns his back the two mischievous boys climb under the pool table and hide, waiting for nighttime to offer up the joy of indulging their desires as if at a banquet of forbidden fruits.

Meanwhile, Nina Carrión watches the evening approach, worried that the two boys have gotten lost. The poor woman sends out three of the older boys to search the nearby streets, but they return without finding them. Once more, Nina paces through the entryway, the living room, and the small den-turned-bedroom filled with cots, the dining room, the kitchen, and the cement patio that separates the house from the apartment occupied by Father Walsh. A shadow has fallen over her easy smile and pearly teeth, and she has abandoned her usual pose of resting a finger against her right cheek as she props her elbow on the arm of her chair. Her thick, black bun trembles against her neck as she climbs the stairs and walks through the two large bedrooms with cots for ten boys. At bedtime, she watches them turn in and is left worrying about the missing boys and also about her husband and Father Walsh whom she fears could have had an accident in the fragile little plane the latter so loves to fly.

The doors at Sears close, and Juan peeks out from beneath the cover to ensure that everyone has left. Then he invites his friend to come out and they run together through the aisles that separate the merchandise. Juan gets a bicycle for himself and another for his partner and they ride around the store. Later, they put on skates and glide across the floor. They try on the mannequins' clothes and the shoes on display. They run up and down the immobile escalator and become engrossed in a billiard game of their own invention, since they do not know the rules. In the intoxicating excitement of their adventure—the first all-night adventure of their lives—they feel neither tired nor sleepy.

At the same time, Nina Carrión is relieved to see her husband and Father Walsh, who limps slightly because of an ankle he had fractured long ago in a skiing accident, walk safe-and-sound into the living room of the large house they share.

"Thank God you're home safe!" she exclaims.

"What's the matter?" they ask, seeing her so concerned. They look toward the stairs where they hear a relentless drum solo played on some piece of wooden furniture upstairs echoing along the handrail.

"What is that?" Father Walsh asks, confused by the musical hullabaloo that has broken the home's nocturnal silence.

"It's Wifredito. He's playing his music," Nina answers, slightly relieved, as she places her finger against her right cheek and resting her elbow on the table.

"He's not sleeping?"

"Poor thing, he can't get to sleep. He must be missing his family."

"I'll go up and tell him to stop," concludes the priest. "But tell me, Ms. Nina, what's wrong?"

"Juan Couriel and Luisito never came back from their walk. I sent some of the boys to look for them, but they couldn't find them."

"We'll go look for them," determines the priest. "Don't worry, Ms. Nina. You'll see, we'll find them. But right now I've got to tell Wifredito to stop that drumming."

Father Walsh and Mr. Carrión get into the Mercedes Benz the priest brought back from his home in Ireland on one of his frequent visits. They drive the black car up and down the streets in search of Juan and Luis. Soon, Wifredito resumes his homesick concert. As the drumsticks echo in desperate catharsis, he remembers Teresita's blue eyes. He sees his sisters Ana Lourdes and Fefita, who stayed in Cuba with his parents, and he fortifies himself once again with memories of his childhood escapades in his family's home. He remembers, too, episodes of "The Three Villalobos" that he listened to on the radio at exactly noon. The three young heroes galloped tirelessly throughout the world fighting injustice. A taxi comes to mind, and him riding reluctantly to the LaSalle School in Pinar del Río. Wifredito watches the morning sun creep across his cot as he thinks about his life in Cuba. The other boys have given up complaining about the rhythm that has kept them awake, and have resigned themselves to lying sleepless in their cots, listening to it. It is at this point that Father Walsh's smiling face appears among them once more.

"Wifredito," he says gently. "Give me those drumsticks, and let's see if the boys can get some sleep before I say Mass."

Limping on his sore ankle, Father Walsh heads to the dining room where Nina Carrión bustles about. She will prepare the tea he normally drinks after Mass in the silver teapot he brought from Ireland as a cherished family memento.

"Where could Juan and Luis be?" Mr. Carrión asks himself, worried. "Father Walsh and I didn't sleep all night. We went to every hospital in the city looking for them. We went to the parks, the movie theaters, and the police stations. Nothing! We couldn't find them anywhere!"

Father Walsh picks up his rosary and heads to the chapel to say Mass, which many of the boys attend voluntarily. The Brickell Church bells ring out, proclaiming the morning. But only as the Church of the Assumption's bells strike eleven; echoing along the broad avenue, do Juan and Luis appear at the door of *Casa Carrión*. Father Walsh's smile disappears as he approaches them, holding the leather strap with which he punishes the boys under his care if he sees that they have misbehaved.

"Come here!" he calls, holding up the leather strap as announcement of their immediate punishment. "And, of course, you know that you won't be going to sail in the Bay with me on Sunday."

Just then, Nina Carrión hands Juan Couriel a letter from Cuba. Spurred on by his homesickness, the boy opens it quickly and sees his mother's signature at the bottom. His emotions keep him from reading the letter in order, and the first words that he stumbles across stop his heart: 'Your father is in prison here in Cuba. They've accused him of conspiring against Fidel.' Father Walsh's anger subsides as he sees the color drain from Juan's face. He steps closer and asks him what is wrong, feeling that yet again the misfortune brought about by Castro's tyranny has wounded another one of his boys.

THE CHILDREN'S PRIEST

I

When Bryan Walsh was about to be born, the firstborn son of a wealthy family living in an old house at the edge of a white road in Ireland, the old doctor attending the distressed household announced that he would have to sacrifice the child to save the life of the mother, a strong and robust woman, intelligent, liberal and refined, who spent her time reading so as to remain current with the world's progress. Hearing this pronouncement, Bryan's father ran in search of a young doctor who expressed hope of saving the child through the use of a new instrument called forceps. Immediately, the old doctor, who had accompanied the Walsh family through their medical travails for years, stormed out of the house, indignant at having been supplanted by a member of a better informed generation.

This fortunate boy's childhood played out in a truly blessed house, cavorting with his four brothers under their mother's watchful eye. Bryan's father was an established businessman in Portarlington, a small enclave thirty miles south of blustery Dublin. They lived together in a large house belonging to the maternal grandfather, constructed by French Huguenot refugees at the beginning of the Eighteenth Century. Frolicking in the enormous gardens and ice-skating during the long winters, Bryan dreamed of traveling around the word on a merchant ship, dressed as a sailor.

After his family moved to the quiet town of Limerick, his maternal grandfather passed away and the large house where he spent his childhood was sold along with the surrounding grounds that had for so long ensured the children's glorious freedom. His paternal grandfather, faithful to the markedly Anglo-family tradition, died while serving in the English army during the war in South Africa.

II

At eighteen, Bryan finished his studies at a rigorous, Jesuit high school and felt the providential call to the priesthood. He imagined himself a missionary in Africa, and when his friends informed him that he would never be able to preach because of a speech-impediment, Bryan applied his faith and prayers to help himself overcome it.

Bryan had become an enthusiastic pilot before leaving Ireland. In 1950, in Florida's warmth, he became a seminarian. His bishop decided to send him to Rome for his preliminary studies. But Providence had another route in mind, and when war broke out in Korea, threatening a world wide military conflict, Bryan joined a seminary in Maryland. His preconceived notion of the United States was shattered by a different reality, realizing that not all North Americans were rich; and that even at the end of the Sixties, they were mired in racial discrimination, at times unthinkably cruel in its fanaticism. He celebrated his ordination, after an abbreviated period of intense study, in a charming ceremony in the city of San Agustín, cloaked in its inviting climate and atmosphere of Spanish tradition. During those youthful days, when his high school friends set out into the world to sow their destinies amid the sugar cane and kangaroos of Australia, or among the wooly sheep of New Zealand, Father Walsh was sent to practice his ministry at a southern church in the United States where the privileged white parishioners received the Sacrament before the long-suffering blacks in the congregation. Once, the young priest dared to give Communion to a dark-skinned woman before the last white man had received the Host. His parishioners criticized him bitterly, even as he renounced the practice of discrimination as a Christian. During those days of intense spiritual refection, his first sermons proved that his determination had overcome his speech-impediment and he threw himself into preaching and acting on the message of Christianity.

Finally, the twists and turns of Fate brought Father Walsh to the heat of Miami, where he fell in love with the ocean and the breeze. There, he bought a sailboat and a small airplane so he could immerse himself in nature during the few moments of freedom that the confessional allowed him.

III

Father Walsh settled into Miami, fully committed to his ministry. It was Christmas Eve, 1960, when communism so tragically crept into Cuba, clawing into its heart. Father Walsh held his rosary, saying his evening prayers after he had finished his work at the Catholic Welfare Bureau, when the telephone jolted him awake with its anxious ringing. It was Frank Auerbach, an agent with the U.S. Department of State. He informed him that as a result of the upheaval in Cuba, the U.S. Embassy in Havana had received two hundred visa applications for children to enter Miami. The idea that the Communist State could take control of the lives of these children and that Fidel Castro could turn them into mercenary soldiers to fight throughout the world in wars of his own creation, enslaving their minds in the irrational web of Marxism weighed on Father Walsh's conscience. He was equally struck by the certainty that very soon these children would be deprived of any knowledge of or faith in God. That is why he took on the responsibility of this caravan of children in transit. And thus began the exodus of fourteen thousand children across the sea, like tragic, human dolphins who became the living image of an era.

CHAPTER 17

Sara del Toro is lying in the cell she shares with the other female prisoners. The structure that outlines her desolation is the gloomy Women's Prison in Guanabacoa, near the capital of Havana. The political prisoners who overflow it have initiated a hunger strike. They are protesting the inhuman conditions heaped upon them in this old building, the obviously insufficient food they are given, and the many other things that make this prison a living hell.

Lying down with the intention of conserving her energy for the coming days that the strike may last, the searing memory of the trial in which she and Amador were summarily condemned passes through her mind. They had asked for the death penalty for Amador, but he was sentenced to twelve years of forced labor instead. It was rumored that they did not send him to the firing squad only because the Cuban representatives to the U.N. made it clear how counter-productive such executions were, causing international repercussions for the Revolution that was governing their country. Sara and her husband sat side by side in front of the soldiers who judged them. They were never allowed to testify since theirs, like every other political trial, was a farce. Sara and Amador cried together for their exiled children, and for the younger ones where remained at their home in Havana, cared for by one of the family's maids who overcame the fear of political ostracization for living in the home of two imprisoned conspirators. Sara envisions Amador's face and his hands cradling hers. She sees him depart, this time to carry out his twelve-year sentence in the prisons on Isla de Pinos and the fortress of *La Cabaña*, not knowing if he will survive. His attempts to console her dissolved into tears. At the trial, the women implicated with them spat and hurled insults at one of the prisoners who was condemned with them as he passed by. They were certain that he had given them up to the G-2 interrogators, and they reproached him angrily. Only Sara greeted him and asked about his wife, who had sat with her at the table at *Hurra!* so many times, sharing the worry of knowing that their husbands were involved in conspiracies.

The sores that have covered Sara's withered body for months ooze fetid pus onto the sheet. A cockroach drops from the wall and scurries across her chest. In the midst of her tribulation, she sees two female soldiers arrive to take her to the warden's office. One of them, gray faced and wearing an olive green uniform, speaks to her in an authoritative tone.

"Citizen Sara del Toro, the ambassadors of Mexico and Germany are in the prison yard. The have come with your lawyer and have requested that you be allowed to see your children. They have brought them along so that you can say good-bye since they are sending them out of Cuba alone. In spite of the current situation at the prison, the Revolution, in its infinite generosity, will allow you to see your children."

The five young children appear, clustered together as if to protect themselves from this depressing place. Seeing their mother, they cling to her neck, her waist, and her knees. Sara does not mind that they inadvertently brush against her sores, which flash with pain and weep pus onto her skin. She is not bothered by the weakness brought on by the hunger strike that she has supported. She only knows that she is kissing her children, and that they are crying because they are going to be sent far away from her love and support. The five little ones climb onto her knees and stroke her un-styled hair, which they barely recognize, begging her to let them stay, even here where they would be happy just to be with her. Sara is stunned to see Freddy, the most unassuming of her children, who in the months that she has not seen him has become as bald as an old man. In fact, he has lost all of his dark hair and eyebrows. Sara, with devoted mother's concern, asks him what has happened in the six months since the trial when the G-2 imprisoned her and Amador.

"The doctor said it's nerves," answers his brother, Amador, in tears. He is the oldest of the five and has matured beyond his ten years. His blond hair has darkened a bit and his young face has grown sad.

Sara caresses Freddy's bald head and the ridges where his restless eyebrows used to quiver. Silent tears, as cool and fine as an autumn mist in Paris, spill from his almond shaped eyes.

"Freddy, have you quit misbehaving? You haven't kidnapped Marianne again, have you?" Sara asks him, desperate to cheer him up.

"He's being good," affirms Javier, who has grown very thin. Sara touches his beautiful, black hair, which pokes out here and there since he is left to comb it by himself.

"And you, Javier, tell me how are you?" Sara asks.

"Javier can't sleep at night since they took you away. And when he does sleep a little bit, he wakes up screaming," offers Jorge Carlos, the precious boy who was a ring-bearer at the wedding of Fidel Castro's sister.

"Jorge Carlos won't kiss anyone anymore. He said he wasn't going to kiss anybody until he could kiss you, Mamá," tells Javier.

"And you, my little Marianne, who tells you your bedtime stories?" Sara, in tears like her children, asks her youngest. They are all overwhelmed by their misfortune.

It is time to say good-bye, the time allowed for the brief visit having expired. Sara manages to tell her children to relay a message to the older ones in exile. "Tell César and Silvia that I will always be grateful to them for taking care of you. Tell Sarita to keep studying. And tell Any Laury that I will give her a *Crèche* when I see her again, someday. And Mary Loly, tell her I remember her playing teacher with her dolls..."

Suddenly, Amador, the oldest of the five siblings says something that surprises her. Not knowing if she imagined it or not, she heard him say, "Mamá, Communist regimes don't fall because of little hunger strikes!"

The children cry out as they are pulled away from Sara and taken away, dampened by the oozing of her sores. She watches them disappear into a maze of gates and hallways, like she watched Amador fade away at the G-2 and at the trial in *La Cabaña*. When they return Sara to her cell, the other prisoners embrace her in tears, touched by this heartbreaking good-bye. The women who guard them cry as well since they, too, are mothers. The warden of the women's prison resigns because she can no longer bear the emotional toll of these cases.

"They're going away, just like I saw all those children I gave Visa Waivers to. Amador and Javier will be in one of Father Walsh's camps. The little ones will go with their older brother and sister." She, her ten children and Amador are enveloped in a veil of uncertainty, as if held in a womb of tears.

Suddenly, as if forced onto them by surprise, soldiers armed with enormous hoses arrive. Determined to end the hunger strike, they unleash torrents of water at the women, knocking them off their feet. The women shield their chests with pillows and huddle together for protection until other guards come in and drag away the majority of the prisoners to the prison in Baracoa in the remote eastern province at the other end of the Island. Sara is among those who remain. The hunger strike has been broken; but the dignity of enduring this inexorable imprisonment sustains the prisoners who were taken East, and those who remain in Guanabacoa. It strengthens their resolve to uphold their principles and the hope that their sacrifices will move Cuba closer to liberty, deepening their conviction to never regret any action taken against communism.

One morning as Sara stands near the bars of her cell, a female guard approaches. She is carrying an infant who is wailing, perhaps because of the dreary influence of this frightening Guanabacoa prison.

"My daughter won't take her bottle," she says. "And I don't have anyone to care for her while I'm at work."

"Let me take care of her," Sara says, making one of her irrevocable and fully justified decisions.

The woman gives her the child that day, and the next, and on the countless others that turn into months on the map of time. Sara, with her maternal touch, cares for the baby, feeding her, bathing her and singing to her the songs she used to sing to her own children; and she is touched by the love that only innocence can awaken. If another prisoner asks her why she is caring for a Communist's baby, Sara replies, with her unquestionable decisiveness, "It's not the baby's fault her mother's a Communist. And I'm not going to sully my soul with bitterness."

So, she prays that God will watch over her children, whose letters are intercepted at the prison and never delivered to her as punishment for her participation in the hunger strike. She prays for the Visa Waiver children, from whom she has also heard nothing. Everything has been taken away from her: the shipping business that Amador build with his tireless work, the apartments and garages in the beautiful *Foxa* building, the country estate, *Hurra!*, the lavish bank accounts, the cars; and now, with the departure of her children, the beautiful house in Havana.

The months weigh heavily on the prisoners, who are being punished for their rebellion with one year of not being allowed visitors or letters. Sara does not know if Amador and their children are alive or dead, sick or well, or even if the younger ones arrived in Miami. Worry and uncertainty feed the sores that go unhealed.

One morning, a female soldier she knew from before loiters near her in the cell. Sara watches her approach indifferently, as if she is going to walk right by. Unexpectedly, she hears her whisper, "Don't look at me. Your daughter Silvia gave birth to a boy. All of your children are well and Amador is alive. He's still a prisoner at *La Cabaña*. Don't look at me." The woman passes by, like a miracle granted; and Sara, without looking at her, blesses her and thanks God for this news that has revived in her the priceless gift of hope.

Chapter 18

Released from the hospital, Ely returned to her foster home in Buffalo with cold, trembling hands and a feeling of immense gratitude to God for giving her back her life. Several months pass peacefully, punctuated by crises of perpetual homesickness, until one unexpected day in October 1962 when a wave of terror washes over the world.

"Oh, the rockets! They're going to bomb Cuba! They're going to blow it off the map!" the Guatamalan woman tells Ely, looking at her sympathetically.

"Why? What's happened?" asks Ely, terrified as she thinks of her parents and her island, suddenly imagining them torn to pieces and flying through space. María del Carmen runs to her and hugs her tightly.

Ely needs to sit down as she absorbs this shocking news.

"We have to call Mamá and Papá!" she insists, never losing her characteristically calm demeanor.

"We tried, but they've cut off communications with Cuba," her sister replies, nearing a state of desperation.

Ely could never have imagined that after fighting off her illness, looks of pity would again fall on her like knives anointed with a bit of honey, this time motivated by something other than her state of health. Setting aside her school-books and pencils, the girl begins to reflect on her country's situation. "What a nasty trick! Look how easily we gave in to Fidel when we left Cuba! We should have stayed to fight for our country! It worked out better for Fidel that we left. We were rebellious children and we were going to go out into the streets to protest against him." Ely stands and walks to a window laced with the autumn cold. "I can't believe that the world might end because of someplace as idyllic place as my country. The last generation ruined it all for us with their corruption. Fidel is a maniac. And we all sat there waiting for the marines to come save us from Fidel. You can't depend on anyone. We should have done it ourselves! And now, oh my God, what a mess! My country is going to cause the end of the world!"

The Polish nuns and American students look sadly at Marta and Raquel de la Portilla in their school in Danville, Pennsylvania where they have been relocated . The new arrivals look around, searching for someone who speaks Spanish. On the television, they see President Kennedy and hear him say "Cuba," suspecting that something important is happening in their country. Thirty years later, they would not remember how they found out that there was a Puerto Rican girl in one of the classrooms on the other side of the playground, nor at what point she was called in to explain to them what was happening since they could not understand the English spoken by those around them or on the newscasts that explained the events of that day.

"They are going to bomb Cuba and wipe it off the map!" the Puerto Rican girl blurts out with the irresponsible bluntness of adolescence mixed with a heady feeling of self-importance as the only one able to communicate with the girls.

"That's terrible!"

"That can't happen!" the De la Portilla sisters look at each other, terrified, exchanging the cheerfulness they had begun to regain for a tense shadow of uncertainty. Raquel has turned as red as the fleshy interior of a watermelon.

The sisters' first reaction is to try to call Cuba and talk to their parents, but their beloved island, held hostage by Fidel Castro has cut all communication with the Free World.

Seated at their desks, not understanding the math lesson being given in English, Raquel and Marta think of their family in Cuba and their beautiful and elegant hometown, Matanzas, settled at the edge of the calm, blue sea like a sapphire set in an ivory anchor. Their father, a lawyer, had once given Ernest Hemingway the keys to the city when he visited at the height of his celebrity. The novelist had arrived by chance, a passenger on the *Ile de France*, sent unexpectedly to that city's port because it was deeper than the one in Havana where the large ship would have run aground. During the last War of Independence, declared in 1895 against the colonial Spanish power, their family had supported independence and Spanish soldiers had burned down the house on their estate. Clarita, their great aunt who was still a child, lost a shoe as she fled after her parents' death. The trauma of the event had left her in an irrational and irrepressible panic whenever she found herself barefoot. Later, their grandmother and Clarita emigrated to the United States. When the war was over, only their grandmother returned to Cuba. Clarita stayed behind in Philadelphia and married an American. "We have a great aunt here," the girls think simultaneously, as if joined together by some telepathic thread, "but here we are living in a foster home where we feel miserable."

The classroom door opens and the students stand. The Mother Superior steps in and calls the two Cuban girls, who follow her to her office. There, they sit in front of her and begin reading a book in English. Raquel and Marta read, mispronouncing the words as the principal corrects them. They understand nothing of the text and when they look up, they see that the revered Mother Superior has fallen into a deep sleep.

Raquel and Marta elbow one another mischievously. They smile, dimples emerging from their sadness, complicit in their discovery of a weakness in the severe headmistress. They continue reading, but their minds drift back to Cuba, terrified that their father will again be arrested as he was in the days surrounding the Bay of Pigs invasion of April 1961 when soldiers came to search their house. Many of the family's belongings disappeared during that search, and their father was taken prisoner to a far away estate that had been confiscated by Castrist government. They blindfolded him during the trip so he would not know were they were taking him. He ended up in a country school, and they ordered him to sit in a classroom filled with desks. He and other prisoners were guarded with machine guns. They were not allowed to speak, and they were forced to stare at a chalkboard on which were drawn a hammer and sickle, the international symbols of communism. Seven hours later, when Mr. De la Portilla asked to be taken to the bathroom, the soldier guarding him left the door ajar.

"Aren't you ashamed, guarding me like this?" he asked, irritated; and the soldier backed away a little. Later, he and the other prisoners were locked in closets for several hours. There was a pregnant women in the pathetic group, and when the soldiers saw a man caress her cheek, they realized that the two were married so they separated them. Then, a young man suffered an attack of appendicitis. The prisoners demanded a doctor for him, who came and ordered that he be hospitalized, under guard. They operated on him and he recovered. Then they tried him and shot him. Three days later, they put Mr. De la Portilla into a vehicle and took him away from the school. They opened the door in the middle of a field and said, "You're free to go." As he began walking, he expected them to shoot him in the back. "What did I do to be locked up?" he asked. Their reply was, "Don't ask questions. Just get out of here." Mr. De la Portilla was not a conspirator, but at his practice he did process passports for people planning to leave the country. That professional activity was enough for him to be considered an enemy of the Revolution. Another reason for his arrest was that he had sent his oldest son, a fifteen-year-old member of the Catholic Youth, out of Cuba. Before the Bay of Pigs invasion, Raquel and Marta were leaving school and ran across a mob that was shouting terrible insults and harassing someone they could not see. Suddenly, a chorus of voices rang out, demanding the firing squad, a common occurrence at the time. "Portilla to the wall! —Portilla to the wall! —Portilla to the wall!" As they got closer, the girls realized that the victim was their own brother.

The Mother Superior awakens, looks at the time and lets them leave. The sisters are miserable as they cross the threshold of their foster home. The housemother, who is so tall and fat that they jokingly calculate her to be twelve feet square, has taken them in solely for the economic assistance that the Catholic Church provides for the girl's care. She does not like that her husband, an elementary school teacher, tells them jokes. Raquel and Marta are horrified to see that their houseparents punish two other little girls by roughly scrubbing their heads if they are caught in any childish mischief. The other two come from troubled families and are being raised without affection, only for the financial benefits paid by the federal government. Seeing them, the De la Portilla sisters are reminded of their three-year-old brother, whom they carried around lovingly and whose childish antics they miss terribly.

The foster home is a poor, wooden construction without carpeting. The mother supports her own children with the monthly allowance the Church sends on behalf of Raquel and Marta. Meanwhile, both girls suffer this painful situation, unjustified by the distance that separates them from their parents.

"Marta, if this threat of war passes and we can call Cuba again, we're going to tell Mamá and Papá that we want to come back home with them." The two girls, who laughed constantly in their country, enjoying their carefree happiness, hug each other crying, their happiness buried since the moment their mother told them that they were leaving Cuba alone.

CHAPTER 19

"Father, let me take this little girl with me to the school in Colorado," María Magda de Quesada asks the Mexican priest who has come to the Florida City camp to accompany a group of seventy-five children who are being relocated to the western United States. This is the beginning of the relocalization of the young exiles who came alone from Cuba to Father Walsh's camps in the United States.

Hearing the girl with the trembling, black braids, the priest turns to Carmencita, all of six years old and clutching her doll as she stands beside María Magda, under whose tender, maternal protection she has taken on the role of daughter.

"Yes, take her with you," he responds, guessing that caring for the little girl serves as therapy for the older one, suffering an abandonment complex. These feelings took hold when her parents sent her into exile and stayed in Cuba, although she understand that they did so only because it was impossible for them to obtain a visa to any country that would permit them to accompany her, or even to be reunited with her later.

The next day, the seventy-five children who are leaving nearly fill the cabin of the airplane destined for the Pueblo region in Colorado. María Magda, holding Carmencita's hand and taking care to keep her bundled up, clean and well fed, tells her again about her life in Cuba.

"One of my uncles attacked General Batista in the mountains. In my family, we were all behind Fidel. I wasn't afraid of the Revolution. Everything was happening a long way away from my house. When Fidel took over Cuba, we were thrilled. My parents said there were going to be big changes. But soon, they said what he was doing was communism. I was scared to death the day one of the nuns who taught at my school called my mother to tell her that a mob of people were sacking the school. Mamá and I ran there and saw the mob moving through the classrooms and the hallways, taking religious icons out of the chapel to smash them in the street. It was crazy in the school and Mamá told me, 'Don't leave my side,' and she took two boxes of religious histories from the library so the mob wouldn't burn them. I went to find my embroidery in the sewing room and took it with me. The school belonged to Fidel after that, and he forced our dear nuns out of Cuba, and I couldn't go to school anymore because Mamá said they would turn me into a Communist. For more than a year, Mamá had a teacher come to the house, until she got me a Visa Waiver from Polita Grau. I'm an only child, and Mamá told me, 'You're in danger here in Cuba and we have to get you out of here. If you go first, your father and I will come soon.' I saw that everyone was leaving Cuba and I told Mamá, yes, I would go. I left with my cousin. Until they closed me into the "fishbowl", I didn't realize completely that I was leaving and parents were staying!" María Magda lets a sob escape and feels Carmencita's hand slip out of hers. She stops talking and looks at the intense little face and the doll wearing a pink sunhat that has slid onto her lap. Sadly, she sees that the little girl has fallen asleep.

María Madga looks at her cousin, Fefita, who is seated at her left and seems to be embarking on this journey as if on a great adventure. Then, the girl with the black braids thinks back on her own arrival in Miami, where some relatives picked her up and took her to live in their apartment in the Southwest. Fifteen new arrivals from Cuba lived there, taking turns sleeping in the scarce beds available. María Magda, feeling that they have neither the time nor the resources for her—overwhelmed as they are by the basic need to survive—asks them to take her to the Florida City camp. Her twelve-year-old cousin Fefita is already there. That whole period was terribly traumatic for María Magda. She feels that her parents have betrayed her by sending her alone to the United States to face the horrible uncertainty of spending every minute afraid of what might happen to her next.

Their arrival in Colorado holds a surprise for the Cuban children, shuttled in busses to an enormous, brick building five or six stories tall. María Magda reads nine letters above the door that spell out the heartrending word "Orphanage" that stings like a slap in the face.

"I'm not going in there," she announces bluntly in a fit of rebellion toward the priest who had promised to bring her to a school. "You lied to me, Father! You told me you were bringing us to a school and you brought us to an orphanage." She sits on the bus with Carmencita, feeling her black braids tremble as the other children get off.

With loving patience, the priest convinces her to come out as well. And when she enters the immense building, holding out her frozen hand to Carmencita, her heart breaks anew as she walks down the long hallways, the echo of her worn-out shoes sounding against the cold, wooden floors. She looks sadly out the windows that open onto a central courtyard and unexpectedly bumps into a group of American girls, some orphans and others from troubled homes under the protection of Catholic services, who scowl at her. At that moment, María Magda de Quesada feels more deeply than ever the tragic magnitude of exile.

The nuns take away the three outfits brought from Cuba by the girl with the trembling braids. They give her the uniform she is to wear from here on out, and also a red nightgown. They tell her that she cannot speak Spanish. So she takes refuge in silence, unable to express herself in English. They require her to gather her hair into a bun when she sleeps. The only allowance granted is her petition not to take Carmencita to the dormitory where the younger girls sleep, which consoles María Magda greatly. She prepares a little bed for her next to hers. Before bed, she bathes her, helps her into the red nightgown, brushes her hair and wraps it into the uncomfortable bun. She holds her hand and helps her to sign her name to the letter written to her mother Isabel, in Cuba. She says her prayers with her and tucks her in.

"Carmencita, you're still not eating much," she says. "It's been months now that you only eat cornflakes and milk. Is it because you miss your mother?"

"Yes, and my father. Do you know when they are coming?"

"Soon, you'll see."

"Write another letter to my mother and ask her. O.K.?"

The upheaval of the past days inflicts on Carmen the fever and scorching rash of chicken pox. Dazed by the itching that keeps her awake in the infirmary alongside María Magda who is suffering from the same malady, she pulls from inside her pillowcase the passport photo of her mother, Isabel, the only token of hers she has brought with her into exile.

"A little piece tore off. Fix it for me. My picture of Mamá got torn," she mutters, racked with fever.

María Magda finds a band-aid and fixes the torn corner of the photo before she tucks her friend into bed. Then, overcoming her own discomfort and the nausea that hovers over her, she tries to disperse the cloud of homesickness for the little girl, opening the frost covered window a tiny bit and telling her, "Catch the snowflakes, Carmencita. You've never seen snow before."

"I'm thirsty. Can I eat a little bit of it?"

"Yeah, take some off the windowsill."

Carmen eats some, and it is just like the cotton candy she used to eat at the circus that melted away in her mouth, like a dream does when touched.

After they have recovered and returned to the big dormitory, their emotions eaten away by homesickness and the weight of the orphanage crushing their hopes like a hurricane bearing down on a canefield, María Magda remains sleepless, feeling more than ever that her parents have betrayed her by sending her alone into this generous and welcoming world, which in her desperate loneliness seems distant and desolate. She has just fallen asleep at dawn, when she is awakened by frantic screams coming from the bed opposite her own where Carmencita sleeps. María Magda, guided by the faint light coming from the hallway, runs, terrified, to see what is happening to the little girl and wakes her up. A moment later, she is sitting up in her bed, sobbing, and she listens as she recounts her own story in her Mexican inflected Spanish.

"I saw my father kill my mother with a knife! I wanted to take it away from him, but I couldn't! I couldn't! I couldn't!"

María Magda, guided by the instinctive kindness possessed by children, hugs her, sharing her body heat in the darkness. She has barely lied back down when the wake-up call comes. It is four-thirty in the morning and the girls must bathe and dress in order to help clean the orphanage before they go to Mass at six. Praying, she calls to mind her frustration at having to repeat the sixth grade, since there is no middle school or high school at the orphanage. Awash in desolation, acting as a mother to Carmencita keeps her going. In her letters to the girl's parents and to her own, she tells them that the two of them are doing well, that they are happy and that they need not worry about them. The responsibility of caring for the mental welfare of their parents who remained in Cuba is common among the children who have left their beautiful island alone, pushed away by the wind of a revolution that calls itself egalitarian and communist, and whose most recognized symbols are a red and black flag emblazoned with a hammer and sickle. The feelings of tragedy derived from all that has imprisoned María Magda de Quesada's young soul by a level of suffering much greater than her frail twelve years, overflow at lunchtime when she sees a horrifying story about the Missile Crisis on the television.

"Oh, my God! My parents! My country! It's all going to disappear! I can't believe it!" But a moment later, she chokes back her desperation so that Carmencita will not notice.

Over the course of these same days, at the other end of the country, Teresita Ayo, a fourteen-year-old Cuban girl walks in one of two lines of children headed to their orphanage on their way back from the movie theater. Teresita is conscious of being taller than all of the other girls. The winter coat she has been give to wear is tight across her shoulders, but she is relieved that the nuns have bought her some shoes big enough for her growing feet; although her feminine vanity finds them as ugly as those worn by the nuns who care for her—black, bulky and thick laced. In fact, when they could not find shoes for her in the quiet town of New Bedford, Massachusetts, where they live, the nuns took Teresita to Boston to get her some there. Together, they made the pleasant drive to purchase fabric for their habits and they took her out to eat in a restaurant. "Now, we won't get to go out again until Sunday, when the ladies from the church come to take us out for the day," thinks Teresita, flirtatiously looking at the line of boys. Downtown New Bedford stretches out behind them as does the port with its quiet whaling boats under the evening sky, which descends by five o'clock in the afternoon. "Oh, at this time it's still daylight in Cuba, even if it is winter!" mutters Teresita, thinking of her parents who remain on her beloved island. The children turn onto Keelton street and enter *Mary's Home*, a three-story, brick building where they are greeted by Father Hogan, a priest from a well-to-do family who abandoned his privileged life in a comfortable home to go out to serve others in this refuge for American orphans and Cuban children who came alone to Miami.

Father Hogan is of average height and a bit chubby under his black cassock. From the hug he gives each child, they know that he his good and kind. Teresita's brother, who is fifteen years old, lives in this same orphanage and considers Father Hogan to be a fantastic friend.

The heat that envelops her body, chilled by the cold of the street, the inadequacy of her coat and the lack of boots or gloves, comforts Teresita Ayo, who is hoping to see snow tonight for the first time in her life. Her embarrassment at not dressing fashionably diminishes inside these tall, protective walls. "They don't let us wear make-up here," she laments, casting another flirtatious gaze at the line of boys. "They don't even let us paint our nails," she mutters, missing such freedoms.

Father Hogan has mercifully ordered that the televisions be turned off for the past few days so that the Cuban children do not learn of the terrible crisis in the Caribbean. Daily life carries on at the orphanage as if the world were not threatened with annihilation.

In the dining room at dinnertime, something happens that catches all of the children's attention. The mischievous ones who played tricks behind the nun's backs as well as the well-behaved ones all turn to look at a boy who refuses to eat the egg that is served. They wait expectantly as they see a nun with a reputation for being strict and harsh comes to make him eat it. The boy makes a Herculean effort to eat the egg, but a moment later vomits it back up. The nun, unyielding beneath her black habit, demands that he eat the vomited egg. The boy, desperate because this order seems so cruel, stands up and slaps her. Suddenly, it seems to all of them that the world order has been turned upside-down. The nuns run, and the boy does, too. Father Hogan is called to reestablish the order that this little insurrection has disrupted. Teresita watches the whole thing, feeling sorry for the boy and contemplating mirthfully the scene she had not expected to see in her whole life: somebody slapping a nun.

Later, when their homework hour draws to an end, Teresita has not finished memorizing all of her English vocabulary words, nor does she understand the math problems since they hinge on a few words she ought to look up in her ever-present dictionary.

In the dormitory, Teresita pretends not to see the black American girls who stick their tongues out at her and insult her under their breath with words she does not understand. They maintain a dismissive attitude toward all the Cuban children.

Suddenly, joyful sounds from the street approach the orphanage. Teresita is stirred by a desire to escape and lose herself among the children carrying flashlights and bags. The Cuban children gather to see what is happening outside.

"Halloween! Halloween!" shout the black children enthusiastically while the Cuban children wonder what sort of holiday is this 'Hello-ween' that has brought such joy to the city.

"Don't get too close to that little black girl," Teresita whispers into the ear of one of her Cuban friends, referring to a little American girl who goes to visit her troubled parents from time to time. When she comes back, her hair is overflowing with lice. "I saw one crawling on her. The nuns will get them out tomorrow; but in the meantime be careful!"

At the required bedtime, the girls lie down. The Cubans gather at one end of the dormitory to protect themselves from the hostility of the American girls gathered at the other end. "Oh, if only we could have been at the Hello-ween party," whispers Teresita Ayo, watching the neighborhood children knock on door after door. Her homesickness mounts as she sees them, separated from her only by the glass of the window. But her inescapable reality reminds her that she still does not know the English vocabulary needed for tomorrow's classes. When one of the nuns turns off the dormitory light, Teresita gets out of bed and walks toward the bathroom, carrying her English notebook and guided by a faint glow coming from the hallway. She silently walks past the white beds, each with a crucifix hanging above it. Before she enters the bathroom, she turns, afraid to see the silhouette of the nun on duty, wrapped in her white habit and veil. Careful not to make a sound, she sits in the bathroom to study. The white, oilcloth shower-curtains seem to watch her, as do the wooden walls and the line of impeccable sinks. Teresita closes the little door that opens to the hallway, wraps herself in her long robe and sits down on a little bench, tucking her feet up so that the nun will not notice her when she walks by with her little light and looks under the door. Outside, the happiness of Halloween echoes, increasingly muted by a light snow that has begun to fall. Teresita falls asleep for a while. When she awakens, she looks in the large mirror and smiles compassionately at herself, opens the door and goes to the window to watch the snowfall, something she had never witnessed in Cuba. "Tomorrow, I'm going to touch it in the courtyard," she tells herself, excited by the novelty. "Tomorrow, I'm going to eat snow. When will Mamá and Papá be able to see it? When will they be able to leave Cuba?" Teresita looks out at the night, that becomes gradually lighter. "Dear God, bring my parents and my brothers and sister soon! Bring them so they can see the snow, God! So they can touch it! So we can make snowmen together! Please, God, do this miracle for me!"

CHAPTER 20

The horrifically dangerous Caribbean crisis has the world awaiting the decision of one man: Nikita Kruschov, the Soviet Dictator. The situation is rooted in Kruschov's installation of long-range missiles capable of devastating much of the North American territory in Cuba to defend Fidel Castro's Communist government from a possible attack by the United States. John Kennedy, President of the United States, orders the Kremlin Czar to take the missiles back to the U.S.S.R. Faced with the tyrant's adamant refusal, which places the planet on the brink of a thermonuclear war between two rival superpowers, hundreds of Cuban immigrants rally to enlist in the United States army. Among them is José Frank Aspillaga, the boy who had arrived at the Matecumbe camp and hidden in a thicket with Martín Ling to escape the hazing endured by newcomers at the hands of boys who had arrived from Cuba before them.

Frank has just turned eighteen and is motivated by the patriotic call to defend the freedom of the Western World against the brutal armies of fierce, Soviet Communism. He is happy to have passed the physical exam to be accepted into the armed forces, but now he curls his strong, tanned body into a ball against the shocking Kentucky cold on an enormous military base that houses more combat tanks than anywhere else in the United States. "Dear God, I'm happy to freeze here, as a sacrifice to You, if it will help bring freedom to the world," he prays silently with the devotion of one who is certain his prayers will be answered. Suddenly, a gruff voice calls out before the bugle sounds *reveille*, waking the recruits. It is their Sergeant, whom the young men have nicknamed "Lock" because he was always after them to line up their footlockers. The numerous Cubans in the battalion did not know what he was talking about until they realized he was referring to their storage trunks, a common fixture in their grandparents' homes but called something different. "Poor guy, we started calling him 'Lock' because we thought he was a jerk, but now we like the guy. He's Mexican, a Latino, like us. He's a good guy," thinks Frank shivering even more from the cold.

Frank jumps from his bunk in a flash and smoothes the sheets and blankets, leaving it in perfect shape for the inspection that could come at any moment. He slips his fatigues over his underwear and hurries to the bathroom to shave. As he glides the razor over his cheeks, he thinks to himself, "Mamá's in Cuba, and she's all I've got left in the world. What if the army invades my island to liberate it and one of my stray bullets kills my mother, or Father Felix who used to be my confessor, or anyone I know! Jesus Christ, my Lord and Savior, don't let one of my bullets kill anybody I love! Please God, Just let them hit the enemies of freedom!"

Trying to control the shivering brought on by this never-before-felt cold, Frank takes his place in formation for the morning inspection. The day's hours will unwind in a routine series of events, to which is added the fear that at any moment the world might erupt in nuclear war and not allowing time to properly prepare your soul to meet God in the event that it is your turn to die.

Lengthy training operations begin, having barely allowed sufficient time for the men to brush their teeth, throw on their packs, pick up their m9 Garand .30-caliber rifles and clamp their helmets over their ears.

The day slips by, like a snake through a field, for the thousands of men training to defend liberty. They eat a hurried lunch during a break in their intense drills; and in the afternoon when they have returned to the barracks, Frank cleans his rifle, which must be ever-ready for inspection. "I'm tired," he thinks. "But I need to write to Mamá. I can't tell her that this might be the last letter I ever write—that I might never see her again. Dear God, don't let that be the case."

Once he has showered and eaten, Frank sits down to write his mother. He does not mention that he is in the American army, because that would cause problems for her in Cuba, already suffering under Fidel's repression. "So long as I get to see her again," he thinks, with the same uncertainty that weighs on the five hundred Cubans who have enlisted in Cuban Volunteer companies, ready for deployment to Cuba. He fiddles with his dog tags on which his name is engraved, and hears Sergeant "Lock" bark out the order for an inspection of the barracks. "Make sure your footlockers are lined up straight," he orders. "He yells at us, but I know he's come to like us," Frank thinks, responding to the order. Suddenly, he hears whispering that brings the magic of hope to his heart.

"Nikita Kruschov has agreed to send the missiles back to the U.S.S.R. The Soviet President, Mikoyan, has gone to Cuba to demand that Fidel accept the decision.

"There won't be a nuclear war!" shouts Frank, overjoyed. "Thank you, God! The human race is saved! Without those missiles we can defeat Fidel! Soon, Cuba—my country, will be free!"

CHAPTER 21

Rewinding the story of these trying times, we return to the moment when Isabel, Carmencita López's mother, leaves the Havana airport terrace where devastated family members said good-bye to those leaving the country forever. This tragic rectangle is invisibly impermeated with the tears of departing passengers, and the resignation of hundreds of thousands who could not escape to freedom because they could not obtain a visa to any other country in the world, or they could not leave behind an aged mother, or a son imprisoned by Castro, or a spouse taken in by communism. When the airplane pierces the sky and disappears into the horizon, those who remain behind in Cuba disperse in every direction, like armies invading a city.

Isabel's legs are two rigid pillars of ice, and her husband has to hold her up as they descend the terrace stairs. In her purse, Isabel carries the last bottle she gave to her beloved Carmen before she watched her tiny frame walk, alone, into the "fishbowl" and disappear, as if swallowed up amid the adults waiting to leave. "What if she forgets George's name? What if someone kidnaps her before George finds her in that foreign airport? What if my little girl gets lost among all those people?

"Calm down, Isabel. Not one child has gotten lost," her husband tells her, sensing her frantic worry.

"We don't even know who George is, or where the camps are where they say they take care of the children."

Isabel, overwhelmed by uncertainty, remembers Carmencita reappearing among the people in the "fishbowl," tripping and falling, and beginning to cry.

"She looked at me through the glass, knowing that she had to be quiet. And I saw her grow up that very moment," this mother, who has spent months preparing her daughter psychologically for this separation, tells her husband. She trained her not to cry in the airport, or to cling to her when they were there because either behavior would cause the Emigration officials to permanently deny her departure from Cuba. The image that most pains Isabel's memory is that of her daughter who has just turned five years old standing on her tiptoes, hugging her doll with the pink sunhat and taking her travel documents out of her little purse and placing them on the corner of the desk for inspection by the harsh official seated there.

Havana becomes an unbearable curtain of smoke for Isabel. Life is reduced to one word: Carmencita. Her soul shrinks, becoming a tunnel of fear that her daughter will disappear on her journey and she will never know what happened to her. "But I had to send her away, what was I going to do? There's a war coming, with bombings and who knows what horrors. Fidel has blown up the factories and the docks, and anything else that could be blown up in case he loses. I couldn't even feed my daughter since she wouldn't eat rice or beans or any of the few things they give us now with the ration booklets. She was so upset that she would only eat ham, compotes and Corn Flakes, things you can't find in Cuba anymore," Isabel tells herself, sure that she had no choice but to send her daughter away like so many other mothers who have let go for the first time of their overprotection and an attachment to their children that other cultures consider excessive.

Day after day passes over the sharp edge of her desperate hope, each one as long and black as a vulture disappearing into the horizon. The first week goes by, and the second, with no news of Carmencita. When Isabel manages to find, in the secretive silence of Havana, a telephone number for one of the camps in Miami where they say they are keeping the exiled children, she is unable to call because the enigmatic G-2 has blocked the number at the state-run telephone company. "She's disappeared. Someone took her at the airport. She didn't find George. My God, what could have happened to her? Give me some clue, God! Send me some sign that my daughter is alive!" An insult from the police captain who signed one of the many necessary documents she had to present at the station for permission to leave Cuba strikes her like a pendulum slicing through the wind and hollowing her out: "You know that your daughter will become a prostitute in Miami, right?" Isabel had to bow her head in humiliation in order to obtain the signature and avoid being sent to jail because the people have lost the right to speak out, and every element of life has been bottled up by Fidel Castro's socio-political agenda.

Finally, Isabel manages to call a camp where a pleasant female voice responds.

"Caremencita is fine," she says. "Since she got here a month ago, she hasn't wanted to eat anything but Corn Flakes and milk. I can't put her on the telephone because she's still in shock, missing you. She would want to go back to Cuba if she heard your voice."

The call is cut off, and the silence is broken by the ironic voice of the telephone operator, who comments with the fanatic cruelty so unique to this moment in history, "You see, Citizen," invoking the insulting title given to those who, because they are not revolutionaries, do not deserve to be called 'Comrade.' "It's your friends over there, not us, who won't let you talk to your daughter. It's them! Not us!"

A month later, the mailman unhurriedly delivers a letter. It had been mailed from Colorado four weeks earlier, and is signed by a Franciscan nun. Isabel and her husband read it, searching for proof that Carmencita is alive. Each line is etched into their memories, like an epitaph chiseled on a shield.

Sacred Heart Home
2315 Sprague Avenue
Pueblo, Colorado

April 2, 1962

Mr. and Mrs. López
Dear Friends,
We are very happy to have your little girl with us. We are Franciscan sisters. Please do not worry about her, she is a good girl and once she is settled she will be much happier.

We have a very big, modern house. The Oratory is very pretty. The infirmaries are in the same building. We have a nurse, and when they need a doctor she calls him. Once a week the dentists visit. The school and everything is in the house, and the children don't have to leave for anything. The furnace is excellent.

We have had some snow and the Cuban children are delighted. Now we have 110 children: 43 are Cuban. I have 5th and 6th grades and have 11 Cubans. They are progressing well in their studies. Now they can write letters in English. The Cubans just arrived. They have a young teacher who just graduated from the University of Mexico.

We take them to the movie theater every two weeks. We also have a pool for them to swim in during the summer. The Rocky Mountains are nearby, and in the summer our bus takes the children there to have a day in the mountains.

I will write to you on occasion to give you news of your 'treasure.' Pray for us, that we may do the best for all of the CHILDREN. We are doing our best for you.

*Sincerely,
Sister M. Gloria O.S.F.*

P.S. María Carmen is a very pretty girl and she is not sad.

Joy and relief that came with this letter that Isabel read over and over in her anxious uncertainty. It didn't matter that accents were missing, as happens with American typewriters, or that whoever wrote it used some old-fashioned Spanish phrases.

After the first letter, another arrives written in a very careful hand. It is signed by a twelve-year-old girl they do not know, but who identifies herself as María Magda de Quesada. Her words reflect surprising maturity and responsibility. Some of the letter is written by her, and at times she guides Carmencita's hand, producing bigger print. From then on, María Magda's letters arrive every week, framing the passage of months and the first year with unshakeable hope. They carry news from Carmencita, who did not know how to read or write when she left Cuba because her mother was afraid to send her to school, worried they would indoctrinate her with communism. The letters hold trembling messages filled with a child's longing, like this one, which nurtures in Isabel's heart the comfort that she is remembered:

March 1, 1963

Dear Mami,
I hope you are fine when you receive this letter, and that you can come here soon so I can give you chocolate, butter cream and vanilla hugs and kisses like I used to in Cuba. Do you remember?
On Saturday we went to the theater and watched "King of Kings." It was the story of Jesus. I liked it a lot.
I'm sending this letter to wish you Happy Mother's Day. I am going to miss you a lot. This is the second year that we're not together, but I think next year we will be together, God willing.
I am behaving myself in school and am making good grades.
María Magda is still taking good care of me.
Sister Daniel is leaving the Sunday before Mother's Day. She is celebrating being a nun for 25 years, and she is going on a retreat, too.
It's been a long time since I've received a letter from you or Papi.
OK, now Professor Know-it-all" is going to write to you.

Dear Mami,
MAMI I LOVE YOU A LOT AND I'M SENDING YOU A CHOCOLATE KISS FOR MOTHER'S DAY. YOUR DAUGHTER MARIA DEL CARMEN.

Hugs and kisses from María Magda.

This is how Isabel and her husband, Rolando, survive: waiting for letters from their daughter and the little girl who takes care of her like a mother while in exile. They eek out a living secretly, risking years of imprisonment because anyone wanting to leave the country is fired from their job and subject to degrading humiliation. Rolando was fired from the electric company when the State took it over and severely reduced the salaries and benefits the workers enjoyed when it was run by a North American consortium. Isabel was fired from the post office. They manage to purchase their ration of food with the secret income Rolando earns fixing small appliances for his most trusted friends, the ones he is sure will not turn him in. He and Isabel survive by reselling chickens and eggs that they furtively buy from a farmer—even though these tiny resale operations constitute a crime in this rigid, socialist society. They help themselves further by selling shoes that Rolando makes behind closed doors out of discarded car tires. Little by little they sell off their belongings, hiding from the Defense of the Revolution Committee that watches them day and night. The pictures that used to adorn the walls of their home are also secretly sold and are replaced by landscapes taken from calendars. They sell their bedroom suits, knick-knacks, some of their best clothing. In this country, everything is scarce. It is against the law to sell any of one's possessions, which are now considered property of the State—a prohibition that weighs even more heavily on those who plan to leave the island. Between their fear of losing permission to leave, even after they obtain a visa, and the need to sell things in order to eat and pay their bills, poverty slowly overtakes them and to oppression is lent the added stigma of destitution.

    Later, at the beginning of 1968, will come a time when those who wish to leave the country will be sent to work the fields, sometimes for as long as three interminable years, submitted to the inhuman camps where they are underfed, forced to work long hours every day, and allowed to leave only one week-end per month. The despotic government fights to keep the people, now just slaves to the established State Capitalism, within its borders as a dehumanized work force. Meanwhile, Isabel sobs every hour of every day that she endures in abject sadness, missing Carmencita. And like her, thousands of mothers in the same situation cry in the silence of their homes, suffering hunger and the fear of never being able to leave Cuba to see their children because the country has been cut off from the Free World. There are but a few flights in and out of Mexico, Spain, and Jamaica, or sporadically from some other country. These mothers who have sent their children away to ensure their right to live, cannot communicate with each other because repression, distance and the hope of receiving word from their children prevent them from meeting one another. Meanwhile, the written press, the radio and the television, the required meetings and forced political study groups, and the enormous street propaganda echo relentlessly that Cuba, "the free land of the Americas," will never back down from the creation of socialism.

CHAPTER 22

Martín and Juan Ling arrive at their maternal grandmother's apartment in Tampa. She, too, is Chinese and has recently emigrated from Cuba. She has rented an apartment in one of the low-income buildings, known here as "projects." Their aunt has brought the boys from the camps run by Catholic Welfare where they were staying. Their grandmother, quiet and refined, hugs them, kisses them, and takes them by the hand to show them the two-room apartment where they will all live together. Their aunt lives there, too. She understands a little English and has found a job as a bookkeeper at a construction company. Another aunt's husband works at the same company as a bricklayer.

Their grandmother serves lunch in her unalterably serene manner, quietly at the edge of the family conversations. Signs of stress and worry, so apparent in the Western world, seem not to exist for her. She serves a delicious fried rice, assorted spring rolls baked in the oven, and a thick, Chinese soup. "How wonderful to have home cooking again!" thinks Juan, remembering the chicken, potatoes and salads so frequent at Father Walsh's camps. The aunt who does not work outside the home, the grandmother and the two boys sit down to lunch. Savoring the tender spring rolls, Martín announces his first decision made in exile, destined as he is to build the future of his well-lead family.

"I'm going out this afternoon. I want to find out where I can get newspapers to sell," his short, thick eyebrows arch over his almond-shaped eyes as he puts down his napkin to cross the thumb and first finger of his left hand.

His grandmother remains silent, saddened that she cannot provide the basic necessities for her family so that her grandchildren would be able to study without taking on jobs that delay their progress in school.

Martín leaves and returns a little while later. "Grandmother," he announces, sitting carefully in a chair that has a loose leg and crossing his right leg over his left. "I'm going to sell newspapers every day after school. I'm also going to sell subscriptions for the papers to people who want them delivered.

They didn't want to give me the forms in the office. They said I was too young to work." With the same determination he had at lunch, Martín turns to his aunt, "If I sell the subscriptions and write them on a plain piece of paper, will you sign them for me as if you sold them?

His aunt looks at him, admiring the boy's sense of responsibility that has been so carefully cultivated by his family's tradition.

"Yes, of course!" she responds. "Tell me where to go to ask for the forms."

Martín settles back a bit, hiding his eagerness to throw himself into the world of decision making and responsibility behind the disciplined self-control that has been taught to him for so long by his elders, and adds, "I asked around to see if there was some other odd jobs I could do, and I signed up to pick oranges on the week-end. I'm sure Uncle will want to go, too. If I can do all of this, by Sunday night I'll have earned seven whole dollars. That way, when Mamá and Papá can leave Cuba and join us, I'll be able to help them get started here." Martín drops the seriousness that marks his sense of responsibility, bites his lower lip as he so often does, and erupts in a smile so warm that it spreads to the others who have been listening to him with the tranquil composure of the East that seems to date back to the beginning of human history.

On this same cold, winter day offered up during the first months of 1963, Marta and Raquel de la Portilla, after a five-hour journey, arrive at the home of their elderly great-aunt Clarita in the beautiful city of Philadelphia. She is the only sister of the girls' maternal grandmother. The two had come, as girls themselves, to the United States during the first Cuban war of independence against the Spanish Crown from 1895 to 1898 in which the American armed forces were allies of the Cuban Liberation Army. They had lost their their parents in that war and were brought to the United States by Methodist missionaries who cared for and educated them. When peace was reestablished in Cuba, Clarita decided not to return to her beloved Caribbean island because she had accepted a marriage proposal from a Presbyterian minister from Pennsylvania. Her sister returned to their homeland alone, married, and began the family of which Marta and Raquel are granddaughters.

In Marta's and Raquel's eyes, filled with curiosity and emotion, and still misty with a deep longing for Cuba, the beautiful home of their nearly unknown Aunt Clarita seemed like any other typical American house. Perched on the white snow, with its lofty three stories defying a cold they had never before experienced, it reveals a pleasant interior enlivened by crackling flames in the fireplace, a soothing breath of heat, dark rugs stretched across the floor, high-backed, upholstered furniture, dim floor and table lamps instead of the ceiling lights common in houses on their island, high walls covered in wallpaper—something else not used in their country—and cold, glass doors that close off access to the outside world. All of this together presents a distinctly foreign heritage that worsens the sting of their homesickness. In every corner of the elegant living room they walk into, Marta and Raquel search for the familiar creaking of high-backed rocking chairs with cane seats where every Caribbean mother sings bedtime songs to her children. Accustomed to the casual cheerfulness of their childhood home, everything here seems silently frozen in rigid symmetry. The rugs, due to impeccable care, seem to have been put down precisely the day before, and they seem eager to gather up the shadows of family members, erasing their footsteps in the silent hallways that connect the rooms like the links of a chain, producing a tightly woven tapestry.

This distant aunt from Philadelphia, whom Raquel and Marta have never met, has rescued them from the foster home were they cried secretly in their bedroom each night. She has brought them to her home as the result of a desperate letter from the girls' father, whom the girls had called begging him to bring them back to Cuba. The girls study their austere aunt Clarita's features, recognizing a family resemblance in her round face and full cheeks as she comforts them, welcoming them into the inner circle of her world. Her simple attire reveals her dedication to keeping up her home, preparing delicious meals in her immaculately white kitchen and her unstopping religious devotion. She sews for the poor, visits and cares for the sick and immigrants in need, and hosts gatherings to raise money that the church uses to support the handicapped. Marta and Raquel take in everything around them, still discretely rubbing their ears, frozen from the cold. Both girls have lost the bubbly extroversion and light humor that once characterized them, as well as the optimistic playfulness of their newly begun adolescence, as if that fragile stage of their lives had been swallowed up by banishment and exile, keeping them from entering into its delights and enjoying it.

The first to approach and welcome them, is an old man with a venerable appearance who gets up from the piano where he was playing a prelude by Bach. The new arrivals believe he must be Aunt Clarita's husband. At his side is Louise, their daughter, who hugs the girls with a fondness that surprises them, making them realize that she intends to treat them as sisters. Speaking perfect English, slowly so they can understand her, she introduces a group of ladies from the Presbyterian Church they attend, who pause in their charitable sewing to welcome them warmly. After she kisses them, Aunt Clarita speaks to her grandnieces in Spanish, which is a bit rusty from lack of use. Her grammar is tangled and the prepositions are mixed up, like cable-car lines in a busy capital city. The sisters feel relief at being able to speak in their own language, after months of speaking it only between themselves. When she takes them to show them their bedroom, furnished with a huge bed skirted with pretty ruffles, their aunt hints at their new life, in which the girls discover a glimpse of hopefulness toward their uncertain future, and the piety that underlies the strictly maintained discipline and the quiet affection—unexpressed as it is so warmly by Latinos—that comes from constant religious observance.

"Marta and Raquel, you're going to see how beautiful Thanksgiving is. We didn't celebrate it Cuba, but I'll, *saben*, you know, *yo voy* a roast a turkey. In Cuba we called it *guanajo*, not a very pretty name. We'll have turkey at Christmas, too. Here, this is the door to your bathroom. There are new towels and washcloths so you can bathe before you go to bed. That's the best time to do it because of the cold. In the closet, there are boots and coats, and a new dress for each of you to wear to church on Sunday. You can go outside to make snowmen. Tomorrow you'll start school so you can learn English…you really must." Aunt Clarita turns up the heat and smoothes the impeccable bedspread.

"My husband, my daughter and I are very *alegría… alegres*? (I don't remember), very…*mucho*… pleased to have you here. You've seen how much they love you. Tonight my son is coming to meet you with his wife and my grandchildren. I know… *yo sé*… that you're good girls and you'll behave," adds the lady of the house, who has adopted an American restraint in her demeanor.

The sisters smile, reassured, and look at each other relieved at being accepted into the home of a family member. But suddenly, like a ringing bell waking a sleeping child, Aunt Clarita says something that leaves Marta and Raquel confused in a labyrinth of surprise.

"You won't attend the Catholic Church ever again here. You'll go with us to the Presbyterian Church where my husband is the Minister Emeritus. Our whole family goes to services on Sunday, in the morning and the afternoon, Wednesday and Friday afternoons, too." She stops to look at her nieces, "Please go get your mass-books and Catechisms out of your suitcases and give them to me. Give me your rosaries, too. No more praying to idols. We only pray to God. I've left a Bible on the night table. It's in English, and you can ask me the words you don't understand. You'll find the truth there."

Raquel and Marta look at one another, astounded by the thought of a world where they would have to live without them. Rebellion swells in Raquel, her face turning purple. "Here comes the 'red menace'," thinks Marta, seeing her sister's emotional reaction and remembering the nickname her family in Cuba used for her in similar situations. Meanwhile, she stands behind Aunt Clarita and opens her eyes wide at Raquel, warning her against an explosion that might cost them the warm welcome they have received in this new home. The girls' devout Catholicism is like the last ember of Cuba burning in them, the only thing exile has not taken away.

The prudence of the defenseless obliges Marta and Raquel to hold their tongues. "We have to go along with it. There's no other option. Papá doesn't want to come here and leave his elderly mother in Cuba," thinks Marta. "And grandmother doesn't want to leave her other children behind. This emigration is one big chain," thinks Raquel, never breaking her outward silence. The sisters turn over their missals and Catechisms, pull their rosaries from their suitcases and place them on the nightstand next to the black, delicately bound Bible. Aunt Clarita kisses their round cheeks, so similar to her own, and leaves the room with her bundle of rosaries, catechisms and mass-books.

When after having let them rest awhile the girls are called to dinner, Marta and Raquel are thrilled to see sumptuous dishes served, with delicious pies for dessert. When they sit down, they are surprised when their venerable uncle closes his eyes and invents a prayer. Louise and Aunt Clarita silently close their eyes, too.

Later, after exploring all three floors full of antique furniture and decorations, and spurred on by their curiosity about the residence, Marta and Raquel pretend they are going to wash their clothes in order to gain access to the basement, something they have never seen since homes in Cuba do not have them. Trembling and holding onto one another, they descend the wooden stairs, afraid that ghosts might appear since they have heard this beautiful mansion used to be a funeral home. Their youthful desire to explore wins over their fear and they go deeper. Looking around the immense basement, they find a printer with programs that will be distributed the next Sunday at the Presbyterian Church, stacked in perfect order. The vibration of washing machine renews their juvenile fear of ghosts, and Marta and Raquel clutch each other, bursting into tears.

"Oh, sister, sister!" they cry. "We're never going to learn English! Or be happy in this cold, with people who even pray differently than we do...!"

At this precise moment of realization, the experience of touching snow again in Buffalo and sinking into its softness on another long, winter day, finally brings a note of happiness to Ely and María del Carmen Vilano as they walk together to the church nearest the foster home where they are living during this first year of exile. The two timid, adolescent figures wobble in their slippery boots as their longing for Cuba swells amid the expanse of whiteness that seems to cover the city like a giant, frozen bedsheet.

Holding her little sister's hand, Ely walks and remembers the thick world history book she used to read in her big house in Guanabacoa. Increasingly able to trace her thoughts through the labyrinth of the English language, she thinks, "I am a citizen of the world," because at this precise moment she acquires a truly subtle understanding of the infinite magnitude of the world.

"In Cuba, I would never have seen snow," she whispers, enraptured by this still new experience that she dreamed of in her privileged childhood.

"Ely, where are we going to live now?" pants her little sister as she walks beside her. The question plunges Ely once again into the problem that governs the day: the Guatemalan foster-mother who took them in has decided to move to another state, and the priest is going to inquire at Mass if there is another generous family that will take them in.

"Don't worry. God will find us another home until our parents can get American visas and come here, or until Fidel falls and we can go back to Cuba." Ely has become increasingly accustomed to placing her faith in Divine Providence.

"And if God forgets about us or doesn't have time to worry about us today?"

"That's not going to happen. Have faith. God is merciful," affirms Ely, squeezing her little sister's arm and looking at her, trying to hide her fear that she will suffer an asthma attack brought on by the worry their foster mother's move to Boston has caused.

Slowed by the spectacle of the snow they had never seen in Cuba, the sisters arrive late to Mass, just as the priest is beginning his homily.

"Dear God, please find us a foster home with good foster-parents," implores María del Carmen in her silent prayers, vexed yet again by the specter of abandonment.

"Dear God, I know that You won't let my little sister and me end up in the street," prays Ely. "You know that Fidel won't let money or belongings or anything valuable out of Cuba, and our parents can't help us from there."

The priest finishes the homily and announces to his parishioners that two Cuban girls in their congregation need a new foster home. In the front row, a little girl with Italian parents whispers in her mother's ear, "Mommy, Mommy! Let's bring the two little girls from Cuba to live with us!"

CHAPTER 23

Rolando and Isabel re-read the letters that come from the orphanage where Carmencita lives, hoping that they will be able to obtain a visa from any country in the world so they can go and get her. But it almost always takes years for a visa to be approved, bogged down in endless bureaucracy. Sometimes, those in need do not have family members abroad to request the visas, and it is nearly impossible to get them from inside Cuba. Almost all of the Latin American countries have cut ties with this tragic island. They are afraid of being infiltrated by Castro's supporters, and since the Missile Crisis, there have been no flights in or out of the United States. Letters are the only consolation for desperate parents whose children went by themselves to Miami. Rolando and Isabel live in anticipation of these letters, accustomed now to their daughter being called by her first name.

Pueblo, April 30, 1963

Dear Mrs. López,

María treasures your letters and carries them with her until they are worn out and illegible. Sometimes I read them to her. She never forgets her mother, the precious jewel of her island. She also awaits anxiously the day you will be reunited. Please don't worry about María. We love her deeply and we care for her like a treasure. Rest assured that she remembers you and her devotion to you will continue to grow even stronger and more deeply in her here. We will make sure that it does. We pray that Our Lord Jesus and the Virgin Mother are with you in your suffering.

In the love of Christ and our Blessed Mother,

Father Jaime Friel, Chaplain

The post office delays these letters even more than usual. Some are never delivered. When they do arrive, hope returns and accompanies the parents who await in Cuba.

Pueblo, May 30, 1963

Dear Mrs. López,

María is a beautiful and intelligent girl who speaks perfect English.

When she came to us, she was so small and thin! Now she is 4 feet tall and weighs 48 pounds. She eats well, but remains quite slim. She drinks milk at every meal, and twice during recess, too. She hasn't been sick since she had the mumps. She plays well with the other children and is absolutely devoted to her studies. She is very smart and has a good memory. From the beginning, I have referred to her as 'my little doll.'

Our special petition on the day of her First Communion will be that you will soon hold your living doll in your long-suffering arms.

Father Jaime Friel
Chaplain

Rolando and Isabel are re-reading this letter when someone knocks at the door. Rolando opens it a crack, fearing that it will be some G-2 agent. Outside, he sees a tall, blond man with a thin mustache who is surprisingly well dressed considering the general poverty of the times.

"I am María Magda de Quesada's father," he whispers, reinforcing the mystery glimpsed on the other side of the door. Suddenly, the door opens and the man is welcomed like a king, although only a moment before he was a stranger. He admires the beautiful face of the lady of the house. "My, she's very pretty!" he thinks as he explains that he has come from the distant province of

Camagüey, where he lives. He has come to Havana with his wife to file yet another of the thousand requests he has already submitted, to obtain a foreign visa. María Magda sent him this address and asked him to visit her beloved "daughter's" parents. The new arrival introduces himself as Félix Roberto. He is one of the few men in the country who still owns his own business, a confectionary and café that have not been overtaken by the State. This rare situation is owing to a Communist from the party who blocked its confiscation, asserting that Félix Roberto had given a percentage of the earnings to each employee even before the Revolution came into power.

De Quesada invites his new friends to lunch with him and his wife, Curruca, at the *Capri* hotel where they are staying. The conversation between these two desperate couples turns on their daughters and their efforts to obtain visas in order to reunite with them. They all believe that their daughters have received scholarships to schools. Mercifully, no one has told them that they have been relocated to an orphanage. They discuss the well-intentioned lies they tell their girls about how well they are managing in Cuba.

The four suspect that their daughters also exaggerate regarding their emotional state. Curruca's health is precarious because of her aggressively advancing diabetes, which has nearly blinded her with retinopathy. But Curruca is lively and talkative, and has faith that they will be able to escape this country that has become a prison. She and her husband lament that María Magda barely writes. Isabel and Rolando sympathize with them for this silence they do not share.

May 10, 1963

Dear Mami,

Sunday morning I am going out with the couple from church that takes me places on Sundays. I love them a lot and they are very nice to me, but I love you more.

I got the letter with the medallion of the Virgin of Charity. Thank you for the medallion. I like it a lot.
When are you coming? I want you to come soon and I want to see you. I had the mumps last weekend and I spent a week or two in bed. María Magda didn't have them, but she came to see me every day in the infirmary and helped feed me sometimes.

The last few lines were written by Carmencita:

Dear mother How are you? I am fine and happy. I love you. How is my oncle [sic] Jesus?
Your loving child,
María del Carmen
and María Magda

The feeling that María Magda has apparently forgotten them compounds the Quesada's emotional suffering. In the street on their way back to the hotel, they feel the sadness of Havana, which has lost its charm, having become a bastion of Communist oppression. The unemployed women, who are active in the Defense of the Revolution Committees, watch every block, eagerly spying on people estranged from the Revolution whom they can denounce, and searching houses that might receive some unidentified package that could contain hidden arms or secret anti-government propaganda. Hunger assaults the city, evidenced by the long lines to buy a loaf of bread or a cup of coffee—black, because there is no milk—from the few establishments that have not been closed by the increasing nationalization of any commercial enterprise. Everyday stability, which until recently seemed immutable, has disappeared. A former beauty shop has been closed recently in the name of the Revolution and is now a military barracks. Where a store once was, there is now an office to regulate the rationing of food or clothing, or some other unimaginable regulation, proof of the bureaucracy and militarization that are destroying the essential flow of production in this tiny country. Flowerpots in a nearby park, their flowers wilted from lack of care, represent an arcane and superfluous gesture in the face of the basic necessities that this new existence regulates. In the distance, stanzas of "The International" waft from a rundown storefront where a group of poorly dressed people has just listened to a recording of one of Fidel's recent speeches on a loudspeaker.

> "Poor people of the world, rise up!
> Stand, slaves without bread...!"

The tragic hope to redeem the poor grows increasingly stentorian at the end of the beautiful hymn recently imported from the Soviet Union.

> "Let us join together
> in the final fight!"
> And let brave people rise up
> in support of the International!"

The increasingly scarce taxis and the already insufficient buses slowly meander down the streets, standing passengers holding onto their fenders and windows because there are no seats available inside. Fabric stores have almost completely disappeared, many of them converted into living space, which is severely limited. The businesses that remain open have very little stock, not even what is promised in the ration booklets. A military truck carrying soldiers to guard Western embassies and prevent political asylum brushes against the bus in which the Quesadas are traveling. On a corner, a group of revolutionaries has encircled a man and assault him with brutal insults before turning him over to a police patrol, accusing him of having complained while standing in one of the shortage lines that wrap around the country. In the streets of Miramar that before Fidel's dictatorship was the most aristocratic district of Havana, platoons of children on scholarship march in military order, scraping the pavement with their hard boots on the way from their barracks—houses once owned by emigrants—toward their classrooms, also in houses abandoned by the wealthy who now live penniless in exile. State scholarships keep these children far from their parents to indoctrinate them with the imperious ideologies of Marx and Lenin. On the next block, on a vacant lot, stand three hundred modern automobiles confiscated from families who have left Cuba. They will remain there forever, unused because there are no spare parts to repair them, proof of the economic disaster that has befallen this country. They are parked here, half-destroyed, just a few months after being converted into taxis to be driven by girls who used to work as maids. The people of Havana, once so happy and outgoing, walk in silence, afraid to invoke any commentary regarding the unbearable national situation. They are poorly dressed and suffocating in the implacable heat that bears down on the island this disastrous summer, unable to find a cool drink in the deserted cafes, They are oppressed by a sweeping vulgarity that has dethroned culture and courtesy, distained as the decadent values of those disaffected by the new order. Finally, a group of revolutionaries chant vile insults at the door of a church where a couple is being married. The students who pass by it stoop to pick up stones, which they throw inside while a car fitted with a loudspeaker stops to join them in their strident, revolutionary hymns.

"God knows that we're suffering because we're separated from our only daughter, María Magda," Curruca tells her husband. "But at least in Colorado she doesn't have to suffer this horrible existence."

From Camagüay, the De Quesadas correspond continuously with Isabel and Rolando until they are able to obtain their visas to Mexico, obtaining a third for one of their friends as well. In the Aztec capital, the three stay with on of Curruca's cousins who emigrated during the last Cuban war for independence in 1898. Isabel, who did not accompany them, remains in Havana. She is anxious for the long awaited visa, desperate to be reunited with her daughter and husband, even though it will bring with it the tragic consequence of abandoning forever the soil of her homeland.

CHAPTER 24

With the first check sent to support their American asylum, Martín and Juan Ling's parent buy their very first groceries at the nearest Winn Dixie. Counting and recounting the little bit that is left over, they buy four spoons and an equal number of knives and forks to eat with. Their mother, with steady hands, takes the ham from the table and places it in the oven to bake the way they like it. Juan, inspecting the ancient furnishings that populate the apartment, has already counted a staggering two hundred cockroaches in the corners and angles formed by the unpainted walls of the rat's nest lovingly shared by his harmonious Chinese-Cuban family

"So, when the ham runs out, what are we going to eat?" the boy asks in a worried voice, folding a letter from his grandmother who stayed with her daughters in Tampa.

"We'll work, and we'll buy more. Don't worry, son," answers his father, hiding his own anxiety.

"I've got an interview for a job this afternoon," says Martín seriously, uncrossing his leg from his right knee.

"Yes? Where?" asks his father.

"At a Chinese restaurant downtown."

"How are you going to get there?"

"I have to take two busses. I'll have to wait an hour for one, and a half hour for the other. Then I'll walk."

At the end of his long journey from the outskirts on the Northwest of the city where he lives with his family, Martín, who has just turned fifteen, walks quickly along the wide downtown sidewalks. He walks alone, guided by the street numbers and asking people he meets on the way. Finally, he reaches a corner where a young girl with Chinese features is waiting for him, leaning against a storefront window. As he is crossing the street, he nearly runs into a powerful, black horse ridden by an agile, blonde policeman.

The girl offers her cheek, which Martín kisses with tormented youthful desire. She is María, the girlfriend he left behind in Cuba, found by chance a few days ago in Miami. He gazes at her dark, almond-shaped eyes, gently caresses her cheek and takes her hand as they begin to walk together. After repeatedly swearing their love for one another, that no one will ever separate them again, and promising to get married when they are old enough, they tackle their day's work.

"I'm going to introduce you to the manager of the restaurant where my family works," she says, smiling at her boyfriend with a sensuality that dazzles him. "He told me that he'd give you the job."

"Afterwards, we'll go see a movie."

Martín kisses her cheek again, eager to begin life anew on this intensely cold afternoon when the downtown breeze smells of salt, just like it did in Cuba on afternoons spent in silent searching and anticipation of adolescent dates along Havana's boardwalk, the *Malecón*.

CHAPTER 25

"I'm going to see my Mamá! I'm going to see my Mamá! I'm going to see my Mamá!" The thought dances in Carmencita López's mind with the happy echo of castanets at a popular street party. Her straight, blonde hair, as fine as her delicate silhouette, bounces in rhythm with her enthusiasm. Her slight, little frame has stretched during her two long years of exile, like a bar of taffy in an indulgent grandmother's hands. Her eyes, accustomed to the melancholy of human longing, look out the frozen airplane window. Suddenly, she is dazzled by the whiteness of the sleeping snow that blankets the Providence Airport in Rhode Island's capital city. But her immeasurable joy is shattered as if by gunfire when she hears the stewardess's voice, suspended in the air like a soft carpet, announce that they cannot land on the runway.

The plane banks and climbs on its way to Boston, a city she has never been to, like so many other cities she has passed through. Carmencita remembers the difficulties she has been through since María Magda de Quesada left the orphanage in Pueblo, Colorado to join her parents in Denver. The measles, the pneumonia, the tonsillitis and a traumatic throat operation have discouraged her and increased her longing to kiss her mother again. But her gratitude to the nuns who cared for her with such loving attention grips her soul, so much so that it pained her to leave them behind when she said good-bye, a moment that continues to flood her memory.

In Boston, the stewardess takes Carmencita by the hand and accompanies her to Rhode Island on a train. They exit the train together at the station, submerged in the cascade of travelers. As they search for Isabel, they pass a woman who does not recognize them, but who quickly starts running after them.

"Carmencita! Carmencita!" shouts the woman until they turn around. In an unbridled outburst of emotion, she holds out her arms to the child, pulling her against her chest. "I'm her mother! I'm her mother! At last, I've found her!" the woman tells the stewardess. "Let's go home, Carmencita! My husband is waiting for us there!"

Carmencita looks at her, taken aback. The woman she sees has been stripped of every characteristic she remembers of her beloved mother in Cuba: the clothing, the beauty salon up-do so fashionable during the tumultuous sixties, the joyful smile, the youthful cheeks. This woman is short and chunky, shoddily dressed and without a warm coat, her face is withered, and beneath the girl's longingly expectant gaze, she seems ugly; and what is worse, unfamiliar.

"No! That's not my Mamá!" she shrieks, trembling. "My Mamá is tall and slim, and very pretty! I don't know this woman! I'm not going with her! I'm not going with her!"

The stewardess looks at them, not knowing who to believe in this unexpected confusion. The woman begins to cry, struggling to make them believe her.

"Carmencita! I'm your Mamá! I'm your Mamá!"

"No! No! My Mamá is beautiful! She's tall and slim! You're not her! You're trying to kidnap me! She's trying to kidnap me!"

A group of curious onlookers gathers around the two women and the girl. They are American and only half-understand the situation that is taking place. Carmencita and the stewardess are speaking in English and the unknown woman is speaking in Spanish.

"Let me see your documents," the stewardess manages in Spanish, her words squeezing out like the last drops of juice from an orange onto a parched throat.

The woman pulls out her passport, her work permit, an identification card from a factory, and another one issued to her husband who works on a road crew. The stewardess, suspicious at first, sees that the crying woman's information matches what she had been given about Carmencita's mother. But even more than the documents, she is convinced by the woman herself, in whom she senses profound sincerity and genuine suffering.

"But I don't want to go with her!" Carmencita whispers in her ear. "That woman isn't my Mamá! She isn't! She isn't!" she insists, clinging to the stewardess's dress and sure that this unknown woman is carrying out some dark plot to kidnap her.

The group of on-lookers parts for the woman taking Carmencita. They get into a taxi, the mother frightened and hurt by her incredible silence. At home, she shows her everything, taking her to her bedroom, overflowing with dolls and toys in spite of their extreme poverty—the hopeful poverty of immigrants. But Carmencita will not speak to her, or look at her, incapable of overcoming the suspicion and the alienation that two years apart has sown between them.

She does not recognize Rolando when he arrives, either. The only words Carmencita speaks are to excuse herself and go, alone, to her room where she longs to write to María Magda and the nuns at the orphanage. Isabel, in desperation, recounts memories of their life together. She sings her old songs. She shows her pictures of them together and dressed alike until Carmencita begins to open up to her, little by little. The girl understands at last that time and sorrow have erased her mother's beauty, and that she seemed taller when she was very young. Only after several days have passed, does Carmencita begin to believe that she is back with her mother. Just as—after many trials and much suffering as they advanced, fighting their way through Canaan—the fugitives from Egypt believed Josua when he told them they had finally reached the Promised Land.

A CUBAN GIRL IN AN AMERICAN HOME

I

Anita Rivero left the Florida City Camp in Miami, as per the relocation plan, and was on her way to a foster home in a tranquil Virginia town where an American family had offered to take her in. The young girl carried with her a fear of the unknown, of not being able to understand people speaking another language, of a country different from her island, of food she wasn't used to, and of living amid customs other than her own that were sure to cause difficulties.

Sweet, chubby Ana—timid, yet determined—sets forth to conquer with kindness and win over these strange Americans she will live with from here on out. First, she ventures a smile at the couple who will be her "parents" for who knows how long. Her real parents, unable to get a visa to anywhere, cannot get out of Cuba; and her father, having been an activist against Castro and is a political prisoner, shackled to the tragic Caribbean island unable to escape its bitter destiny.

—"Welcome to your new home!" announces the mother joyfully as she steps forward to take Anita's cold, sweaty hand and kiss the unruly dark curls that tremble on her forehead.

—"Thank you," replies the little girl. She had asked the social worker who brought her a handful of words in English in preparation for this moment. She whispered this first phrase so hurriedly that she forgot to extend her tongue in order to pronounce the "th."

—"May I give you a hug?" asks the charming woman. Anita doesn't understand her and looks toward the social worker, a question wavering in her dark eyes.

—"The lady is asking if she can hug you."

—"Yes. Yes," responds Anita hopefully. The "yeses" sound like roller skates gliding on the sidewalk in front of her house in Cuba. She balances on the tiptoes of her worn-out, patent leather shoes to give the lady an exuberant kiss on the cheek that pops like a tiny firecracker.

The social worker says good-bye, as Anita looks at her with the pleading eyes of a lamb led to slaughter. The American man, who is now for all intents and purposes her father, signals her to follow him through the house, showing it to her with the quiet kindness common to the region. She is surprised that he does not hold her hand, or pat her shoulder. Nor does he hug her very often, like her father in Cuba did. Following him through the house, she looks at him closely. He is very tall, with blond hair and clear blue eyes. The hair on his arms is blond, too; and he looks like the rowers who competed in the regattas during the blistering Cuban summers. She assumes, then, that he likes to row and that he will probably take her to the beach sometimes.

The house is not like the ones Ana knew in Cuba. She looks idly for quiet rocking chairs, surprised by stiff, high-back chairs and a reclining armchair that magically produces a little footstool as her new father demonstrates. As they pass the fireplace, she wonders if they will have a real fire in the winter like she has seen in the movies. But she is most amazed when she reaches the foot of the basement stairs. There is a family room with a television and cozy furniture; and even more incredible, in an adjoining room she finds a washer and dryer, luxuries available only to the wealthy in Cuba.

—"The house in Cuba, no *chimenea*, no *sótano*," she says, in her first attempt to communicate in English. She is relieved by their kindness; and her fear of this new house full of strangers begins to fade.

The American man recognizes that *chimenea* means fireplace, and he answers with words she does not understand. Ana's shiny black curls bounce as they head toward the kitchen. She sees that the woman, who has the reddest hair she has ever seen, has prepared a lunch of unusual foods served in such abundance that it makes her feel guilty, knowing that her family in Cuba has nothing. She asks herself "How am I going to eat those yellow potatoes, that huge salad and so much fruit? And am I going to have to drink one of those big cups of black coffee?" She sits down in front of a hamburger, the first American food she has begun to like. Instead of rice and beans, the centerpiece of every lunch she has ever known, she is faced with corn on the cob, something unheard of in Cuba, and some unexpectedly spicy beans. Her new parents speak to her in gentle, affectionate tones. She cannot understand them, but assumes they are asking if she would like something more to eat. She misses the croquettes and tamales from Cuba, but she still cannot understand her new parents when they ask her what foods she would like them to make for her. Seeing her so forlorn, her new mother offers her something to drink: a little bottle of Coca-Cola, just like the ones she used to drink in Cuba before Fidel Castro came to power and made them disappear like magicians' doves. As she takes a sip, she is overwhelmed by its sweetness, and with a sadness that washes over her with the suddenness of a summer downpour, she yearns for the magnificent slices of guayaba on her small, beloved island. Anita's new parents seem concerned that she does not want to eat, and her heart breaks like glass, feeling them so close to her, caring for her so lovingly while her real parents are in Cuba, having sent her here, surely to unburden themselves of her.

II

Just after three in the afternoon, the school bus stops in front of the house, dropping off a little boy; a bit taller than Ana, nine years old like her, and with the same red hair as his mother. He comes in, uncertain and circumspect, and looks over the new arrival warily. Ana guesses that her parents are introducing her to their son, whose name they spell out for her in English: B-R-Y-A-N. Anita nods her dark head and her unruly curls fall over her face as she tries to correlate this untranslatable name with something Spanish: Bryan. She tries to make associations with the word *vayan* or better yet, *brillan* so as not to forget it, since it sounds so odd to her. It is obvious that the boy is not thrilled with the presence of this strange girl in his house, thinking she has come to take his place. At snack-time, he gulps down his doughnut and glass of milk, staring at her coldly. She has chosen a popsicle, which to her surprise was homemade instead of coming from the ice cream truck like in Cuba—before Fidel confiscated them and they disappeared. When her new, red-headed mother speaks to

Bryan, he grudgingly goes in search of his toys and drops them in front of Anita. At night, as they watch television shows Anita does not understand, the little boy comes over to her, touches the black curls bobbing tremulously over her ears, and looks anxiously at his hands to see if they have been stained black.

III

At bedtime, Anita has a room to herself, a luxury few girls on her Caribbean island have. Suddenly, she is afraid of the glass windows that a robber could break with his fists, and she misses the heavy wooden shutters of her homeland. Wrapping herself in the bedspread against this too chilly summer, she looks at the cuckoo clock on the wall and feels a flood of emotion spill over the rims of her eyes, overtaken by the guilt of having left her friends behind at the camp in Florida City. But at the same time, she is comforted by the certainty of knowing she has been taken into a stable, loving home that shares so much with hers in Cuba: the Catholic faith and, by what she has seen today, the same provisions against sin. But here she misses the Cuban joy of living, their perpetual good humor and jokes. "My parents don't love me," she thinks again, crestfallen. "They sent me here alone and they stayed behind with my baby brother and little sister." The baby and a seven-year-old girl, thirty months younger than herself, rush to her memory as quickly as the nocturnal crabs who scuttle out of their caves on the sandy beaches. "They love them more. That's why they kept them there. Oh, God! Why did they do this to me?" And she begins to cry, alone in her bed, until slumber spreads over her like wine spilt on a beggar's table.

IV

When Sunday arrives, dancing against the glass windows, Anita anticipates a joyful celebration, like carnival one of Cuba's provinces. She is surprised by the reverence and quiet of the Americans' pass-times. First, they take her fishing on her parents' new boat, an extravagance reserved only for the rich in Cuba. In the afternoon, they visit their grandmother who lives very contentedly in a "home." Seeing her there, Anita questions the kindness of her new family, since to Latinos putting an old person in such a place would be an unthinkable cruelty. She is also able to pick a few words out of the conversation, words like "cancer," and realizes that they have told the grandmother that she has this disease; something else Latinos would never do. The next weekend, she is surprised to learn that one of her new uncles had his gall bladder removed, and no one went to stay overnight with him in the hospital.

V

The days pass quickly, and Bryan's jealousy fades. In a few months, he has become Anita's brother, a partner in mischief and someone to share childhood illnesses with.

Later, as autumn unleashes the fire that seems to be suspended in the trees, Anita crouches to gather the fallen leaves. Fascinated, she touches their reds, yellows and caramels; feeling during this season—so brief in Cuba—the same thrill she felt on the carousel across from her old house with its horses and benches that went round and round every evening. With the arrival of winter, a visitor never-before-seen by Ana, Bryan takes her to the patio to collect the firewood their father has cut and shows her how to build a fire in the fireplace. Then, up to their knees in the first snow, feeling like a finger poked in mashed potatoes, she listens as he explains how to make snowmen with this dazzling softness she has never known before.

Even now, there are things that surprise Anita about her new American home: the thermometer placed in her mouth instead of under her arm when she's sick; witches with broomsticks strolling the streets on a new holiday, Halloween; Thanksgiving, non-existent in her country; turkey instead of suckling pig on Christmas Eve and eating sugar cookies instead of imported Spanish turron; strange music by the Beatles that she is beginning to like and that is starting to take the place of the Cha-Cha's strident flutes and the soft, sweet dance music of her childhood memories.

Almost without realizing it, Anita is speaking—even thinking—in English. Although she is adapting to American life, the feelings of abandonment and the distance between herself and her parents are seared on her soul. They have become the core of her emotional life. Ever since that flight that cut across the sea toward the coast of Florida, Ana is afraid of airplanes and car seatbelts. She avoids tight spaces, honey-flavored candies, and plastic cups like the ones they used to serve Coca-Cola on the plane; and she does not like to get close to balconies or windows in tall buildings.

VI

The years glide past Anita like long-awaited rail passengers rolling through a country village. Adolescence smiles on her, and she is surprised when her parents allow her to go out with friends, unaccompanied by the customary Cuban chaperone.

One terribly frigid afternoon, the girl's Cuban parents appear, stiff with cold and poorly fed. Their arrival softens the rough edges of their absence, but not the trauma of abandonment. Seeing them in the doorway like a pair of wounded birds, she runs to embrace them amid a swirl of conflicting emotions: happy to see them again, unable to forgive them for sending her into exile alone, jealous of her brother and sister who have grown so much she hardly recognizes them, and pained by having to leave this American home and go back to a Latin lifestyle she is now unaccustomed to. She is overcome by a sense of yearning and withdrawal, faced with a return to Cuban customs and the Spanish language she has almost forgotten: endless discussions about politics and soccer, a constant preoccupation with what is going on in Cuba, and José Martí verses full of democratic ideals.

The Cuban family stays two months with Ana's foster parents in the best guestroom. Her "Yankee" father finds her Cuban father a job with a construction company, and her mother a job in a small cosmetics company. Anita's brother and sister begin to learn English and to listen to Beatle's music.

Living together day after day, Anita is bothered by the way her family talks so loudly, the greasy food they eat, that they play dominoes instead of tennis, and that their friends seem unable to pick up a phone and simply arrive unannounced. All of this makes the girl blush with shame in front of her American family. Finally, she is insulted when her father, much more authoritarian than her benevolent foster father, objects to her going out with her friends without an adult. On the other hand, and on a more positive note, she is comforted by their physical expressions of affection: hugs and kisses, sleeping in the same bed with her little sister, knowing that they would never leave her alone overnight if she fell and broke a bone or needed an operation.

When they all move to a little apartment, Anita takes to grumbling about their annoying habits. Very soon, the cold and snow push them to Miami, the epicenter of Cuban exile with its rallies and protests against Fidel Castro. The day that Anita hugs Bryan good-bye before returning to the Latin world, she drapes his neck with a garland of wonderful memories and he reciprocates with a chain of beautiful words. That is when Anita understands that as poor as she was when she arrived from Cuba, she gave her American parents something only love can give: the illusion of having a daughter. And to Bryan, who will spend the rest of his adolescence alone, the joy of sharing his life with a sister.

RENÉ, THE BOY WITH TWO MOTHERS

I

Margot López takes René's hand at the Miami airport and guides him to her car, bought second-hand since she is just beginning her exile. René's hand is still cold from the snow that surrounded his orphanage in Montana, where he had been sent. "It's so cold here. I miss Mamá and Papá so much! I want to jump out of a window," had been Rene's plea in a letter to Margo, one of his mother's best friends who had taken him out on Sundays when he was at the Florida City camp near Miami. "God didn't bless me with children, but now I have two," thinks this energetic woman enthusiastically as she arranges her blond hair in her old car's rearview mirror and settles René in next to her with a mother's tender care. Her deep compassion grows, feeling that this nine year old boy, whom she watched growing up in Havana, needs her now that homesickness has siezed him. When they get out of the car in front of Margot's apartment near downtown, the neighbors gawk, surprised that this blonde woman with delicate features and milky-white skin, so perfectly coiffed and elegant, is walking hand-in-hand with a black boy. Their disbelief swells to overflowing when she introduces him as her son.

In the apartment, everything is perfectly clean and tidy. Margot is still holding René's hand, cold from Montana's arduous climate, as she leads him to a pretty bedroom with two beds, many toys and a television in front of which sits a white boy, engrossed in a cowboy movie.

"This is Luis. He was at the Florida City camp. I brought him here to live with my husband and me, and now he's your brother.

Margo opens the boys' closet and shows them the clothing she has bought for them: McGregor shirts, winter sweaters, suits, vests, jeans, dress shoes and tennis shoes.

"You're brothers now," she tells them. "So you need to get along, love each other and look out for each other." In her decidedly irrepressible way, Margo walks from one spot to another, fixing random details and straightening their stack of illustrated, storybooks on the desk. "And always remember that I love you both equally!" Margot stops to look at René, seeing something princely in him, like a stamp of spiritual aristocracy. This boy's natural elegance, his kindness, his manners, all reveal a solid upbringing and intensify the tenderness he inspires.

At this moment, there is a loud knock at the apartment door. Opening it, Margot sees the building manager. She has a hunch she knows why she has come.

"Ma'am," the newcomer says as she crosses the threshold, "there's a problem."

"What?" asks Margot, her voice taking on a battle-hardened tone as she pretends not to know what this is about.

"When I rented you this apartment, you didn't say anything about bringing a black boy to live here. The neighbors have complained..." The ugly racism of the sixties erupts between the two women. Margot stiffens, and her posture shows that she will not back down from her intentions.

"Listen to me, lady," she responds in a voice that confirms her irrevocable decision. "This black boy is my son!"

"He can't be! You're white and blonde!"

"I am his legal guardian. I had his mother request the document verifying it in Cuba. She worked very hard to get it for me because there they don't respect the right of emigrants to get official documents. Even less so if they're black. Fidel Castro thinks that black people are sure to follow him because he says he's given them rights they've never had before.

"You'll have to move, Ma'am."

"I'm not moving! I have a lease signed for one year and I'm staying here!" Let me know if you'd like me to call a lawyer!" Margot's indignation at something she considers cruel and unjust rises in defense of René, her son now that his parents are in Cuba and he desperately needs her.

II

The second Monday that he is at school, a phone call stops Margot López just as she arrives home from her exhausting work at a hat factory.

"Ma'am, this is the principal at René's school. I have been trying to contact you all day.

"Yes, Sir," her voice hardens in defense of her black son.

"René is a good boy, well-behaved, very intelligent, but…there's a problem."

"A problem?" Margo feigns surprise. "No one has ever complained to me about my son!"

"It's… it's his race, Ma'am. The other mothers have complained… When you came to register him, you didn't bring him with you. We thought he was like you.

"So?" Margot's tense voice hardens further, backed by her impassioned nature.

"Your other son, Luis, can stay with us. But you'll have to enroll René in a school for black children."

Margot spends the hard-earned money from her exhausting work at the factory on her two sons' wellbeing. She does not have money to pay a lawyer, so she resorts to a lie.

"I've already consulted my lawyer! He told me that you have no legal right to discriminate against blacks! My son will continue to study at your school! And make sure, Mr. Principal, that the children don't discriminate against him, because if they do I'll raise holy hell in court!" Margot hangs up, more decided than ever to continue her personal campaign against any situation that arises. Such was her irrevocable decision to provide her black son an equal place in white society, making those who would impose their backward prejudice back down. Margot, this fiery Cuban woman from Havana, has in her defense only frankness and a fearlessness stronger even that the norms of the society she has entered or the one she belonged to. She, who never considered herself a social activist, now waves the flag of human rights in support of one individual. That individual is a child: her spiritual son.

III

Four years later, René's parents arrive from Cuba: María Josefa and her husband René Pinillos. Now Margot's battle is to find a place in one of the white neighborhoods of Miami that will rent them an apartment. She spends three days criss-crossing the city, but wherever there was an apartment available, when they see María Josefa, they tell her that it has already been rented. Sitting in her car, next to her white friend, María Josefa remembers the comments made by Cubans who watched her say good-bye to her son in the Havana airport when she sent him to Miami four desperate years ago.

"Look at that little black boy. He looks like a prince," said one woman sarcastically, "all dressed up in a suit and tie, and expensive shoes. Wait 'til he gets to Miami. They'll sick the dogs on him."

"Yeah," replied another woman, with equal sarcasm. "They'll make that little black boy sell suckers and newspapers over there."

"Those 'worms' that are leaving are so lucky. Their plane is taking off before the one taking our children to Bulgaria."

"Hopefully that plane to Miami will crash," was the final comment, as cruel as an unjust verdict.

"My God! Ignorance is such a curse!" María Josefa thought, struggling to shake off the anger that she never allows to enter her feelings, and remaining silent so that her son would not lose his way out of Cuba. "My people think Fidel is going to give them all their rights, but they don't understand that he's manipulating them just to stay in power. Dear God! There's nothing worse than ignorance!"

"Look, María Josefa!" exclaims Margot victoriously as she stops her car at a quiet Miami corner. "The singer, Orlando Vallejo and his wife are the managers of this building. We're going to talk to them.

The problem is resolved and María Josefa can finally count on an apartment. Margot laughs happily with all her natural enthusiasm. She laughs, talks, walks, comes and goes between one spot to another. She sets out to decorate the apartment with used furniture she has gotten for them.

"You are my white sister," María Josefa tells her, giving her a big hug. The black woman's serenity is unshaken, as are her dignity and her elegant manners. Her dark eyes shine with gratitude behind her spotless glasses.

"And you are my black sister," Margot tells her in a rush of emotion. "We've been sisters since we were neighbors in Havana. Prejudice will never separate us. Never! Never! Never!"

René walks by them, holding the handlebars of the bicycle his white mother has given him.

"René! Help me take out the trash!" calls his black mother.

René smiles in his princely way and says, surprised. "I'll do it, Mamá. But I want you to know that Margot never made me take out the trash!"

CHAPTER 26

Mr. Wifredo Chirino arrives in Miami suffering from an illness that has recently become serious. He brings with him the shared heritage of every exile: the inability to speak English. This brings with it the impossibility of continuing his career as an attorney in this country whose laws are different from those he spent so long studying in his own country. His advancing age is third on the list of reasons pushing him to abandon the brilliant professional life he led in Cuba. There, before *Fidelismo* cut short his advancement, his excellent work singled him out and Wifredo Chirino was set to be promoted to the post of Public Prosecutor in the Criminal Court in Havana, an extremely important position in the nation's judicial system. Giving up his work as a prosecutor causes him the same personal frustration that is collectively felt by his people, oppressed by Communist tyranny.

Mr. Chirino's wife, Josefina Rodríguez was a beauty queen in Pinar del Río, the western-most city on the island, when she was eighteen years old. She looks wistfully at the Miami pharmacies, missing the one she managed in Cuba. Helpless to resume her career for the same reasons that hold back her husband, she soon finds employment here and there in the drugstores that specialize in shipping medicines to Cuba. Wifredo and Josefina bring their youngest daughters with them: Fefita, who demonstrates an intense religious and humanitarian calling and who is four years younger than Wifredito; and Ana Lourdes, who is twelve years younger than her brother. Marilé, four years older than Wifredito, beautiful and extraordinarily loving, cares for her first-born son proudly demonstrating her deep devotion.

Wifredito is almost fifteen, and without his family asking him, takes on the responsibility of helping them. He still has warm memories of every morning giving back the change from the taxi that would take him to the LaSalle School in Pinar del Río, the capital city of Cuba's western province, some twenty minutes from Consolación del Sur where the Chirino family lived.

Wifredito's heart burns with the wavering question of Teresita's well being. He writes his young sweetheart nearly every day, still lamenting that he was unable to dance with her at his cousin's fifteenth birthday party and carrying with him the burden of losing his first love. He continues living in *Casa Carrión,* under the generous care of Father Walsh, for the five months it takes for his family to rent an apartment and get settled.

Wifredito's transformation, from a rebellious and mischievous boy into a serene, optimistic and tremendously responsible young man has been surprising and complete. The good example set by his stable family and their high moral standards has matured within him. The trauma of exile and his open and friendly exchanges with Father Walsh, with whom he has lived for several months, have built on this foundation. Therefore, Wifredito considers his family responsibility an obligation that he must accept as the only son, surrounded by three sisters. To these qualities that define him, are added his joyfulness, his religious conviction, his optimism and his absolute determination to establish himself as a musician even though he cannot pay to study formally.

During the first days that he is reunited with his family, Wifredito decides to sell newspapers while his sister, Fefita, sells doughnuts. They leave the family's apartment on the corner of Seventy-Fifth Avenue and Flagler to begin selling their products door-to-door, struggling to adapt to this new existence, so different from their protected and comfortable life they led on their island.

Wifredito knows, feels, is certain that life is a path he is going to follow with commitment and love. He relies on the self-assurance possessed by men driven by burning creativity, and that is how he prepares himself to become a triumphant musician.

To achieve this, the first thing he does is make arrangements to study at the LaSalle School, now that his parents' arrival on American soil excludes him from the scholarship program run by Father Walsh. At LaSalle, he agrees to wash dishes in the kitchen every day in exchange for his studies. There, too, he decides to form a band with aspiring musicians to play for the student body on special occasions. Although he is not old enough to hold a job, he arranges to play drums at a disco on the weekends. Later, he takes on jobs that keep him busy from nine-thirty at night until three-thirty in the morning. Never complaining, he splits his sleep between then and seven in the morning, and in the afternoon between five and seven-thirty. Sometimes he falls asleep at his desk in school, his eyes red from lack of sleep. Oftentimes, his mother, still beautiful in spite of the burdens of exile—among which is seeing her husband without work—and her younger sister, Esther, who is also Willy's godmother, advise the youth with the concern typical of the Cuban middle class for their children whose parents were overprotective and kept them at home, close to them, until adulthood came to take them away.

"Be careful, Sweetheart. You know that world of musicians is a dangerous one," says Josefina.

"My Dear, we love you so much! Keep an eye on your friends and watch out for the temptations of that world where we can't protect you," adds his godmother, kissing him.

But music continues taking shape in Wifredito's mind, resulting in compositions that begin to characterize his style while he plays in bands that accompany international stars like Olga Guillot, Celia Cruz, and Lucho Gatica. He brings home his pay every day and places it, in full, on his mother's dresser. He earns twelve dollars and eighty cents a night, from which he never withholds even so much as to give himself the pleasure of having an ice cream.

Any obstacles to his destiny are powerful levers that Wifredito applies to his art; and the trials he faces on the way, he transforms into songs.

From the classrooms of his high school, Wifredito heads to college. Time consumes his increasingly intense and fervent activities until he is able to finish his Associate's degree at the Miami Dade Community College North Campus. When he graduates, the young musician decides to leave for New York to seek his fortune like so many artists who thought they would find gold lining its streets, as abundant as the cars, people and noise.

So, Wifredito arrives in New York, hired by the Julio Gutiérrez Orchestra. With his dazzling, youthful enthusiasm, he sits at the drum to extract is best tones. One day, Gutiérrez decides to record an album for an important company. The owner, a famous Cuban, who through hard work has built an important business in exile, arrives unexpectedly at the studio where the musicians are playing a song that he stops to listen to carefully. Suddenly, he asks Julio Gutiérrez,

"Who's that tall, skinny guy back there?" he asks, referring to Wifredito.

"Wifredito Chirino," responds Julio, trying to protect Willy. "He's eighteen and really talented."

"Get rid of him. I don't like him."

"You don't know what you're doing! He's incredibly talented!"

"I'm telling you that I don't like him! Get rid of him!"

When Wifredito hears that he has been let go from the orchestra, he departs with a prediction that reveals the confidence with which he has determined his destiny.

"I'm going back to Miami because there's no work here. But remember what I'm telling you today, Julio: One day this famous businessman is going to beg me to record an album for his company!" and Wifredito leaves the studio with a youthful bounce in his step.

CHAPTER 27

In the Guanajay prison at the western-most point of Cuba, Sara del Toro swears to her companions that she has heard a voice telling her that they are going to be moved from there. As morning stretches into day then lulls into afternoon, the "girls" assure her that she is mistaken. Barely a moment later, a guard's voice orders, "Gather your things! You're being relocated!"

"I told you! I wasn't wrong!" confirms Sarah

In their sad, yellow prisoners' uniforms, several "girls" are lined up and loaded into a bus that leaves on an unknown course. But Sara recognizes the countryside of the Havana province, and when they cross into the *El Chico* region, just before reaching the Capital, Sara tells her companions, "They're taking us to *América Libre*! It used to be my home!" Sara was aware that Castro had established a women's prison at her beautiful country estate.

"How do you know we're going there?" her friends ask her sadly.

"Because I recognize this countryside, these palms that filled my life."

In fact, the bus pulls into the palm-lined drive and stops in front of the old bowling alley where Sara used to spend most of the day, knitting and caring for her children. They come out of the bus surrounded by machine gun carrying rebels, and the shocking contrast between her former life and what is happening now is so intense that the air rushes from her lungs and she must lean against the bus to avoid fainting. From among the rebels who guard the prison, emerges a black man who runs to Sara to embrace her. It is Pepito, one of her old servants, who is soundly rebuffed by the jailers for having greeted an enemy of the Revolution.

"She bought shoes and gifts for my children at Christmas time," Pepito explains uselessly, as they will not overlook his public outburst of affection.

Sara's face contorts and the other prisoners, who see her gasping for breath, shout to the guards to help her.

"Communists! Hurry! Quickly! Sara del Toro is dying!"

With the nonchalance of the powerful, the guards escort her to the doctor for the forced labor camp, who is not far away. Dr. Carlos Rubí Malaver, a patriot, a gentleman and a political prisoner himself, attends to her. He listens to her with his characteristically gentile kindness, and he talks with her, trying to lessen the weight of her pain, as rigid as a block of ice. Later, they install Sara in the old bowling alley of *Hurra!*, stripped of the alleyways and converted into a large cell that houses a hundred women. Opposite it is the balcony of the bedroom she used to share with her husband. She sees a hole in roof where Amador had placed tiles over the family silver and crystal, hiding them and hoping to recover them after the fall of *Fidelismo*. They tell her that at some point a guard broke the flat roof with a basketball and the silverware and crystal rained down on him. Sara looks at the palms, the trees she planted with Amador, the terrace where she used to knit. The barbeque and the swimming pool are still intact, used now by the rebels. Across the way, the pigsty where the pigs she visited every day used to live, is inhabited by a group of prisoners. Walking toward the dining room, Sara spots a toy tractor, left behind a tree. "That was Freddy's," she thinks. "I wonder if his hair has grown back or if he was just telling me that in his letters? And Javier, is he still suffering from insomnia and having nightmares? I'm sure Silvia is still suffering for her father and me. She's so sensitive!" Then, she remembers the day when Marianne, her youngest, jumped into the pool by herself; and Rufino, the waiter, jumped in to save her. "The other servants told me later that it was Rufino who turned us in," remembers Sara, disturbed by her memories. "This is my sixth year in prison," she thinks, and suddenly she realizes that she has grown accustomed to her profound homesickness. With the helplessness of someone watching their daughter being raped, she sees the trees and benches in the distance to which she is denied access. She notes that the guards have stripped away the lights and music that surrounded them, but they have left the bar, the pool and the clubhouse intact for themselves. The two-story house, with its arches and terraces, now contains an office, a radio station and a meeting place for the militant *Macarenas*, female rebels currently guarding the political prisoners. The breeze brushes gently against her cheek, just as it did on the night when she hosted the fabulous engagement party for Fidel Castro's sister. "My children must have grown so much! If only I could see them! If only Amador could see them! And my grandchildren, they must be so big! Are César and Sarita really doing well? I'm sure Sarita has kept studying, she's so driven to learn and understand the world. I wonder if Any Laury still collects nativity scenes, and if she's still so motherly and generous in spite of this ordeal? Mary Loly wrote to me saying that after Amador and I were arrested, six months went by before they heard any news of us. They didn't tell them where we were; not even if Amador had been sent to the firing squad. Dear God, have mercy on my children, the poor things! Have mercy on Amador, who is still a prisoner, there in the *La Cabaña* fortress. He's old, and his health is failing."

Albertina O'Farril walks past Sara.

"What's wrong with Albertina?" asks Sara, seeing her pained expression.

"Since this morning she's had a feeling that her mother is going to die, and they won't let her out of her to go see her," explains one of the "girls."

Pepito approaches Sara as the line of prisoners walks toward the dining room. Passing by, in his militia uniform, he whispers, "I've hidden two avocados behind that bush. Pick them up when you have a chance."

"God bless you!" she manages to whisper back emotionally. She dreams of satisfying the constant hunger she endures as a prisoner, sharing the two avocados with the "girls." Suddenly, an announcement over the loudspeaker pulls her from her trance.

"Citizen Amador Odio, a land-owner who exploited the people of this region has just entered *América Libre*. We have invited him to come admire the transformations made by the Revolution of his former estate by dedicating it to the service of the people.

"Amador!" shrieks Sara, seeing him appear next to the pool. He is handcuffed and escorted by two soldiers carrying machine guns. He hears her and searches for her. She struggles to reach him, until the guards restrain her.

"Amador! Amador! I'm here!" The "girls" cheer him, momentarily joyous at the thought of this unexpected meeting.

"Long live Amador! Long live Amador Odio! Amador, we love you!"

Sara is escorted to the pool, and they remove Amador's handcuffs. They allow them to sit, holding one another as they cry. He, accustomed to giving her strength, tries to give her solace. But, overcome by grief, he only manages to share her tears. They talk about their children, still sobbing, and exchange what news they have heard from them. They discuss the prisons where they have been kept and the lack of news from the outside world during the nearly six years they have been apart, during which they are not allowed to read newspapers, watch television or listen to the radio.

"Did you hear that César brought a boat to pick us up at Camarioca when Fidel authorized people to leave Cuba freely from that port? Did you hear about that? Poor thing, he fought and fought for them to let us leave the country with him, but they wouldn't allow it. He also asked to take a friend of mine, and I saw when they released him. He took him with him."

"I heard," Sara confirms. "This morning I heard a voice telling me that César was in Cuba. The "girls" didn't believe me until some guards took me to the prison office and asked if I was willing to be rehabilitated, even for just a week, in order to leave with César. I told them never. I'll never give up. So they didn't let me go. Amador, César is such a wonderful son! He can't rest so long as you and I are prisoners. He's suffered so much!"

A rebel brings Amador a coffee, which he and Sara share like they used to when they were free and happy.

"What do you think of what we've done with your estate?" a rebel asks Odio, his voice vibrant with revolutionary enthusiasm. "*Hurra!* used to belong only to you but now it belongs to the people."

"Well, I always thought that my estate truly served the people. We hoped to see a school or a hospital here for the farmers—not a women's prison."

Two guards handcuff Amador again and take him away. From a distance, he reminds Sara to take care of her health and keep her spirits up. "Poor Amador!" she thinks, her heart breaking with sadness. "He's always protecting me and the children! Oh, God! Have mercy on Cuba! Enough already!"

When she is escorted back to the bowling alley, she sees Albertina O'Farril, still beautiful, even shrouded in her political prisoner's uniform. She is surprised not to find her in her usual good humor. Albertina has a feisty and energetic personality: happy, dynamic and frank. She is one of those people who tell the truth point-blank with a grace that forestalls any bitterness from those who hear it. Sara tries to comfort her, but the heartache that has weighed on Albertina all day, erupts as evening falls.

"I've got a bad feeling about my mother," she tells Sara, her anxiety building. "I know that she's going to die tonight and I can't be with her." Albertina rushes to the warden, pushed by her characteristic fervor and asks to be taken to Havana to see her mother before she dies. The warden does not want to listen to her, but Albertina insists, tormented by the fear that her mother will die without her there. Thus begins a long bureaucratic process of the guards contacting one superior after another who can authorize the prisoner's travel to nearby Havana. Albertina stops in front of the guard station, and a rebel takes out her gun as she approaches. She continues toward the wire fence, electrified with a current that could knock her down. In her desperate anxiety, she wants to chase away the night as she watches the guard patrol the grounds that surround her abandonment. The guards stall the process, and Albertina begs again and again for them to take her to see her dying mother. In support of her petition, the other prisoners crowd around her, hemmed in by the fences that encircle them.

"If you don't take her, we'll strike!" The ever-increasing group becomes unanimous when all of the "girls," as the prisoners refer to each other, demand to see the warden so that Albertina will be taken to say good-bye to her dying mother. Outside the warden's door, the air is electric with the treat of a rebellion. The guards fear prisoner rebellions. Sara remembers the last one that occurred here, brought under control by club-wielding guards. Night falls, like a shovelful of dirt thrown atop a coffin; and a little while later, rebels come for Albertina to put her into one of the closed cargo trucks known as "cages" in Cuba. She is dressed in her worn, blue prisoner's uniform, and the truck takes off, the road disappearing under its wheels like a snake cut down by a sharpened machete. The December cold grips her chest and shoulders, making her feel even more abandoned. Albertina cries silently, without even a word of solace as she approaches this moment of supreme loss. Three armed rebels guard her: a man with a machine gun, and two women. Along the way, she swallows her emotions, which crash against each other as if in a whirlpool, robbing her of any objectivity while facing the echo of her own drama. "It's my fault," she tells herself. "I knew that Mamá was sick when I got involved in the conspiracy. I don't regret it; I had to do it and I'd do it again and again. But I'm sorry for Mamá's sacrifice. I knew she'd end up alone if they caught me. And now she's dying all alone in an asylum." She breathes heavily because the oxygen is running out in the sealed compartment of the truck. The silhouettes of her three children emerge from the night and appear at her side, in the truck. Each one looks at her with reproach. "I sent them to Miami all by themselves to save them from the reprisals that they would suffer if I got caught. But who knows how many times they've needed me there!" Finally, a conclusion draws over her feelings like a blanket over a corpse, "It was what I was facing, and I had to act: I sacrificed my family for Cuba! And I'll say it again, I don't regret it! But I'm sorry that my loved ones have suffered!"

  The lights of Havana twinkle beyond the cane fields that line the road, giving Albertina hope that she might find her mother still alive. Albertina feels the lights, although she cannot see them through the truck's metal panels that shut out the countryside like a rampart. "Mamá is going to die tonight, and I need to see her," she tells herself over and over, her soul in agony. "Dear God, see my desperation! Let me get there in time!" she pleads again and again. The truck brakes violently and stops abruptly. Albertina is thrust into the open night out between the two female guards. The darkness envelops her and slows her down, but she pushes through the shadows until she finds herself at the gate that blocks the main entrance of the Paula Asylum where her mother is. The cruel night has vowed once again to betray her. Albertina, standing between the guards, pounds desperately at the gate begging to be heard.

Her fists hit the hard wood again and again, like the bell strikes of a tower clock echoing away. No one hears her, no one opens the door, no one comes to aid her in her haste. Finally, the door opens to her cries, and Albertina runs through the dark, empty hallways. As if guided by a thread of love to where her mother is, she finds her on her deathbed. When the nun caring for the elderly woman sees Albertina appear, she exclaims, "It's a miracle! It's a miracle! We have prayed to God that you would come!"

The man with the machine gun and one of the female guards remain at the door of the ward lined with the beds of the sick. The third guard passes her weapon to her colleagues and follows Albertina, who his sobbing at her mother's side. Her honey-colored eyes do not open to greet her, and Albertina realizes that her elderly mother is already unconscious, exhausted by waiting for her. Crushed by the knowledge that her mother cannot see her now, she talks to her, she kisses her, and sits with her. Albertina tells her good-bye, gently kissing the weakened, old woman's hand like a dove taking in a drop of water. Albertina says good-bye, doubting that she has been recognized. And when the old woman passes away, Albertina holds her still warm, flexible body in her arms, enduring the most tragic moment of her life.

Later, they bring her back to the prison for a few hours before taking her to the funeral home for a while. They take her out again before the burial because they are afraid of the amassed prisoners who could riot in protest. And when the wire fence that surrounds *América Libre* welcomes her home, her fellow prisoners draw near to embrace her.

Albertina's pain is interrupted by a visit from the Minister of the Interior, Ramiro Valdés. He is preceded by an enormous group of armed rebels. His tall, slim silhouette stands in front of a microphone, preparing to deliver a speech. "He never looks you in the face," thinks Sara, unimpressed by this sinister man whose pointy beard makes him look like pictures of the devil that children used to pass around. Later, the devil was forbidden, too; because his existence, by opposition, would suggest the existence of God—fervently rejected by Marxism.

"This estate demonstrates how the landowners who lived here exploited the people," affirms Minister Ramiro Valdés, looking contemptuously at Sara.

A small group of rebellious prisoners pick up stones, ready to throw them at him, but Sara quickly stops them.

"Don't go looking for trouble," she tells them. "His words don't offend me. I don't care about his insults. It's as if I hadn't even heard him."

The year of imprisonment at *América Libre* ends on October 27, 1967. A group of rebels calls Sara into the office—her former home—, and one of them steps up to speak to her. Staring at her, he asks, "You don't remember me?"

"No, I'm sorry," responds Sara.

"I'm Juan Torres. My father, who had the same name, used to work on this estate when it was *Hurra!* and belonged to you and your husband. I've never forgotten something bad that I did to you at Christmas time one year."

"To me?" asks Sara, confused.

"Yes. You told all of the workers' children to write a letter to the Wise Men, asking them for the toys we would like to receive, and to give the letters to you. I asked for a bicycle, thinking that it would cause you trouble because it was an expensive toy."

"What happened?" asked Sara, not remembering the event.

"It turned out that you gave me a bicycle. I never forgot that," the rebel's tone softens. "And since you will complete your six year sentence tomorrow, I am going to arrange your passport so you can leave Cuba soon and be reunited with your children, like you want.

"Oh, God! You are glorious!" thinks Sara. "Thank you for this! Thank you for helping me survive! Give Amador strength so we can be reunited in Miami when his sentence ends in six more years!" Sara keeps this plea in her prayers, like a precious, crystal vessel, molded in the shape of hope, as delicate and weightless as the fragrant smoke of incense.

CHAPTER 28

Ely and Mary Vilano are very happy in the home of the Italian family that has welcomed them as daughters. The other two Cuban girls that came with them from the Florida City camp were lovingly taken in by another Catholic foster home also in Buffalo.

In the house were Ely and Mary now live, two of the couple's three daughters are sharing a room so their young guests can have some privacy in their own room. For their part, the two new arrivals happily join in the household routine, learning to make spaghetti and pizza with their new Italian parents. The happiness that fills the weekdays grows on the weekends when the whole family goes to their country house outside of Buffalo, naturally including their two newest members. Other times, in the winter, they go to the mountains.

When she finishes high school, Ely receives the fabulous news that she has been awarded a scholarship to study Child Psychology at a college in Buffalo. This is a step toward fulfilling a long-held dream: to set up a charitable home for orphaned children, which ideally would follow the example of her generous great-aunt, Sister María del Carmen, dedicated to caring for children in Granada. She is so inclined to charitable work that the nuns at the college she attends invite her to visit their convent as a possible future path. But the young woman decides against religious life, in spite of her ardent Christian faith, because she also hopes to fall in love and create a home that would allow the magic of having her own children. Perhaps Ely has a feeling that her childhood dream will deliver to her, like some precious jewel, one of the hundreds of young men who fill the cheerful classrooms at the college. Wondering who among them might be that special person, Ely goes to a college dance one splendid Saturday night, carrying with her the ardent fantasy shared by every girl hoping to fall in love. Camilo Cienfuegos is now just a distant, although unforgettable shadow at the threshold of her adolescence, extending his hand to help her mount a golden horse at the festival in her hometown of Guanabacoa near Havana. Thinking of his hand and his smile as she stands at the door, Ely sees a very

Nordic-looking young man appear as if from nowhere. He is tall, athletically built, and very blonde. His extraordinarily blue eyes flash with an inextinguishable spark of hearty and infectious enthusiasm. He has a hawkish nose and thin lips. He is happy and outgoing. His attitude reveals a decisive, perhaps even daring, spirit. Everyone greets him affectionately, and he reciprocates wholeheartedly, obviously a very popular individual. Ely is pleasantly surprised to see him walk toward her smiling and ask her to dance to "Moonlight Serenade" the famous Glenn Miller song as smooth as velvet that she heard so many times in Cuba and imagined dancing to with Commander Camilo Cienfuegos. Ely follows the handsome American and allows herself be carried away by the mood of the dance, caught up in the cadence of a cosmic breath perfectly in rhythm with her own.

"I heard that you're Cuban," he tells her in Spanish, the light, English 'r' slipping between the correctly pronounced syllables.

"Yes, I'm Cuban," she responds, captivated and smiling slightly as he, too, is taken in by her charming sweetness. "Where did you learn Spanish? It couldn't have been here!"

"In Colombia." The two look at one another carefully, each seeing the other's beauty and grace. He is taken with Ely's dark, curly hair and her eyes alight with tenderness. He flashes her an easy, brilliant smile. She is a singular beauty; the delicate features of her slightly olive-toned face, her fashionably thin, arched eyebrows, the graceful, flowing dress that accentuates her femininity all add to her allure. Fantasy swirls around them like a whirlpool.

"Are you Irish?" Ely asks, already smitten and trying valiantly to hide the flurry of emotions that assault her like sudden gunfire in the woods.

"My family is. They came from Ireland."

Their conversation continues in a blend of Spanish and English, this language that Ely now speaks, and even thinks in, so easily. The most insignificant words become transcendent to them, like a bridge they are crossing together, leaving the mundane world of everyday life and entering a world of possibilities where everything is carried to extremes. They tell each other their names:

Tom and Ely, and share their best memories as he adapts his athletic body to the rhythm of a Cuban rumba. As quickly as a dream can be imagined, they imagine theirs: the marvelous dream of being in love.

Love is born of friendship and kindness that deepen between those who are most alike, or between couples in which each partner makes up for the deficiencies, big or small, of the other. That love, born of a need to understand one another, to be together, to communicate with one another, touches Ely and Tom at the most beautiful moment of their youth. Love is also born of need and the joy of hopefulness. The sum of these human forces can lead to ecstasy or, sooner or later, be torn apart in failure. This night, they come together in the best possible way for Ely and Tom, the recently exiled Cuban and the son of Irish immigrants. This gift, as fragile as a crystal goblet and as powerful as a general, is shared a few days later when they first kiss after Tom finishes a tennis match, and is exchanged repeatedly between basketball games in which Tom also plays. With each new week, their kisses multiply, interspersed with the jokes Tom frequently tells or the many times he uses the word "fantastic," evidence of his inexhaustible zest for life. Finally, their youthful relationship is sealed with the university emblem, which she doesn't understand when he gives it to her a month later, when the cherished love they share has matured beyond their initial friendship.

"Ely got pinned! Ely's got a boyfriend! Ely's Tom's girlfriend!" Her friends' reactions surprise her when they see Tom's pin on her jacket, and they explain to her excitedly that giving her his pin is a preliminary step to giving her an engagement ring. It is a symbol of the love Tom has begun to feel for her.

A little while later, Tom takes Ely to visit his family and introduces her to his father, a district attorney, and his mother, who is half Irish and half German. A friendship blossoms between them as quickly as orchids growing on the branches of a tree. Their romance fills Tom and Ely's hearts. During the first weeks that they are together, she uses the savings from her job as a receptionist at the college where she is completing her first semester and sends a money order to her parents in Havana to purchase the plane tickets that will take them to Spain. They will have to do it that way because there are no flights between Cuba and the United States since the terrifying days of the October Crisis. Visas to pass through the Peninsula have been arranged by the aunt who is a nun in Granada.

Tom has been at Ely's side throughout every step of the long process as he begins his training as a pilot in the United States Air Force. Together, they set up a tiny apartment for her parents, bringing in furniture donated by the Salvation Army. Happiness reigns over their everyday activities as they prepare, and one pleasant Saturday afternoon, Ely and Tom set out from the university to visit the foster home where María del Carmen remained as part of the happy Italian family when her older sister moved into the bustling, college dormitory. Following the introductions, conversation begins in English, which the lovely Cuban girl finds increasingly easy to speak and understand, and which is increasingly becoming her dominant language. Looking around, she asks about her sister, whom she has not seen the past few days.

"Mother, where is Mary?"

"Mary's in her room, but…," the woman hesitates before she says something she knows will be difficult, like a pill too big for a child to swallow, "she doesn't want to see you." The last words batter Ely's feelings like hail on a fragile, glass roof.

"Doesn't want to see me?" asks the girl, her arched eyebrows knit together in surprise.

"No. She wants to be adopted by an American family."

Her world collapses around her when Ely hears this abrupt and cutting statement. To hide her tears, she excuses herself quickly and walks out to the street where loneliness quickly overcomes her in the silent, snowy landscape of this generous and welcoming country that has nonetheless suddenly raised up to unexpectedly slap her.

"Tom, I don't have anyone left!" Ely sobs, sucked in by a growing depression. "My parents are left without a daughter, and me without a sister!"

Tom consoles her with the calm warmth that he is able to provide when faced with others' misfortune, and in so doing to share it.

"Let's go see Mr. Cipriani, the social worker. He's surely had cases like this before with other Cuban children."

When they meet with Mr. Cipriani, the new social worker in charge of the Cuban children and teenagers who have immigrated to Buffalo, Ely interrogates him with the worry of a traveler who has lost their way on the route to their promised land.

"Mr. Cipriani, why doesn't my sister want to see me, or my parents, or be Cuban?" The open, gentle man seated across from her, lights his pipe and smiles at her, demonstrating his understanding of this problem he has seen before.

"It's just a phase, Ely. It's been three and a half years since Mary has seen your parents. Between twelve years old and fifteen and a half, Mary has become a teenager. The change was more dramatic for her than for you. Don't worry. Look, to make your parents' arrival easier, I'm going to find them a hotel room. That way it will seem less strange to your parents when they don't see her right away. Tell them she has the flu." His understanding renews the girl's hope that they might find a solution.

A few days later, Ely, Tom and the social worker are waiting at the airport when they see her parents emerge. Shocked, Ely watches them approach, barely recognizing them: they are old and sad, shabbily dressed and unprepared to face this cold that is worse than anything they could have imagined. They are wandering aimlessly through this crossroad of life. The Revolution has confiscated their furniture, their jewelry, their car and all of the money they worked so long to save. Upon leaving Cuba, their house was taken away, the last vestige of their years of constant labor where one old hunting dog remained, dragging his long ears down the hall. Now they are victims of banishment, like a bird in the jaws of a beast. Realizing that they have aged so much in this long absence that has spanned just under four years, Ely's sadness, caused by her sister's absolute refusal to meet them, grows.

The group melts into a tearful embrace, and Tom, who is so able to understand, say and do what is needed most, speaks to the new arrivals in Spanish to soften the pain of their despair. Among the many surprises of this encounter, is the forgotten island accent Ely notes in her mother's speech. Each one's gestures, habits, and personal style are rediscovered by the others, who now fear not being able to accept them.

"Where is María del Carmen?" their parents ask impatiently.

"She has the flu. No, it's nothing serious," Ely hurries to assure her concerned parents as she stalls for time, trying to explain this unexpected situation. "You'll see her tomorrow."

"Is she sick and you just don't want to tell us?" they ask, worriedly. "Is she… is she dead?"

Ely assures them that she is not, and they say good-bye to the social worker to go together to the hotel as the evening falls like an untrustworthy, scurrilous friend ready to divulge secrets. There, in the hotel room decorated in a style very different from that of Cuban homes, Tom turns up the heat so they don't catch a cold and says good-bye with the warmth of an old member of the family, winking at his girlfriend in a hopeful gesture. It is then that Ely and her parents begin to rediscover each other, in the difficult process of reunion that so often turns out to be disappointing.

"Ely, where is María del Carmen?" her mother asks again, spurred on by her growing concern.

"She has an awful cold, Mamá. That's why she couldn't come. But you'll see her tomorrow," Ely resorts to a white lie to avoid telling them that her little sister does not want to see them. She knows that her mother does not believe her and is painfully trying to come up with the truth.

"In your letters, you told us that everything was fine here," her father's voice trembles. He is torn by the need to know what really happened to his daughters while they were in exile as the distance, time and isolation that Fidel Castro imposed on Cuba held him on the other side of a wall where he could not run to protect and guide them. "So tell me, Ely. I need to know if everything you told us was true, or if you only said those things so we wouldn't worry."

"Yes, Papá. I wanted to help you get through the separation. You couldn't leave Cuba because no matter how hard I tried from here, I couldn't get you a visa to any other country. Almost every country has quit issuing visas to Cubans, afraid of being infiltrated by Fidel's followers who organize militias everywhere. Besides that, they can't keep up with the requests for visas for Cubans; there are millions. But the truth is that what happened to Mary and me was very different from what I told you. I was very sick with Measles and double pneumonia. We were terrified during the Missile Crisis because we thought you were going to disappear from the face of the earth along with Cuba. We were homesick, afraid, unsure of what was going to happen, and had problems in our first foster home. What can I tell you, Papá? We've been through a lot!"

"We have, too," her mother says with a seemingly incurable sadness. "We were hungry because there's not enough of anything in Cuba. We were persecuted. We worried about your cousin, who is very sick and still in prison. We were terrified that we wouldn't get a visa to anywhere in order to reach you here and see you both again. At night, we couldn't sleep, afraid that you weren't well cared for, that someone would take advantage of you, that there would be a war in Cuba and we would die, leaving you alone. But, do you know what dirty trick your father pulled on them in the end?"

"I shot a turkey vulture," her father says, "I plucked it so you couldn't tell what it was, and I put it in the freezer so the women on the Defense of the Revolution Committee would eat it after we left."

"Oh, Papá! The things you come up with!" laughs Ely.

"Your father cried every time he hear Debyssy's *Claire de lune* and every time he walked by your piano and saw the keys closed," her mother continues.

"Now, we're old and we have nothing. We can't speak English. We can't start a business here because we don't have the resources. We're exhausted and all we have is you, Mary and Tom. And we can tell, although it hurts too much to say, that Mary has forgotten us and didn't want to come meet us," her father's voice is silenced by a sob.

"The three sink into the darkness of exile weighed down by the sadness of the past and the helplessness of an uncertain future.

CHAPTER 29

"This is the coldest winter of my life," murmurs Martín Ling, looking at the thermometer hanging at the front of his grandmother's house in Tampa. Martín goes into the cold house that has no central heating and decides not to take off the sweater he is wearing since it seems even colder indoors than outside. As he enters his parents' bedroom, he finds his mother in bed, covered with a heavy bedspread.

"It's been three days since I've left this room!" she exclaims. "This cold is killing me!" Martín steps closer to rub his hands over the pot of boiling water that provides some heat to the room.

"I've got good news," his mother's voice emerges from under the old, worn out bedspread.

"What?"

"We're going to rent an 'efficiency.' It's just across the street."

"One of those 'efficiencies' that people call shotgun houses?"

"Yes, "Filomena's 'shotgun'," named for the old Greek woman who owns it."

"Can we afford it?"

"Yes, We've saved three hundred dollars."

"Poor Papá!" thinks Martín. "He's had to pick tomatoes, cut sugarcane and wash dishes in Miami just to rent a shotgun house."

Martín crosses the street in his typical, rapid gate and looks at 'Filomena's shotgun.' "It's just a one-bedroom," he thinks to himself, hearing a ruckus that grates at his Eastern sensibilities. In the 'shotgun' next door to where his family will live, Filomena and a boy who seems to be her son, are shouting and arguing in a mix of Greek and English that Martín cannot understand. Suddenly, he feels a comforting presence close to him. He turns around and sees his father waiting.

"Let's walk a little," he offers, and they set out together. "What do you think of 'Filomena's shotgun'?"

"It's good, Papá. This way we won't have to feel bad for Grandmother. I'm going to get a job, too. But I want my brother to go to school."

"And what sort of work do you propose we do?"

"We can sell eggs, Papá. I've done it before. I know a place where they sell them cheap. We can buy them and resell them."

"Good idea. Show me the place."

They walk with the stride of immigrants looking to make a new life for themselves, buoyed by unbridled hope. They are still walking when they come across a man washing an ancient stationwagon. The Chinese-Cubans ask if he will rent it, but he says no.

"It doesn't matter, Papá," Martín decides. "We'll sell the eggs on foot."

The two of them launch their egg business together. They start, in fact, walking door to door offering eggs to strangers. Little by little, they begin to build a clientele and learn more and more about their little business. They can buy different classes of eggs: A or B, sometimes even C. They look to see if the yolk is whole to tell them apart. They also inspect the thickness of the shell and notice that sometimes the chickens strain to lay the eggs and leave them stained with blood or feces. There are machines that wash them during the 'candling' process, but the Lings do not have one of those. They buy the stained eggs at a discount and scrub them perfectly clean with a brush and fine sandpaper. Then, they sell them to their clients, who soon are so numerous that they can barely keep up on foot. As well as the egg classifications, they learn about marketing and how best to sell them.

"See, these eggs are really big, but they have a thin shell, so we don't recommend that you boil them."

Sometimes their fragile inventory breaks if they brush too hard. Once they have moved into 'Filomena's shotgun,' the neighbors see them through the curtainless windows in the evenings. They work with the eggs so much that a rumor starts that they are raising chickens in their house.

One day, Martín's father rents a stationwagon for thirty-five dollars a month, and drives it home, although he has never driven before. He does not have his driver's license and almost runs over a little black boy who runs to take escape to the sidewalk on the opposite side of the street.

After that, the Lings build their fledgling business by selling cookies and Cuban coffee. Once they have saved a bit of money, Martín decides to go back to school. He keeps working part-time with his father. Short, chubby and reserved, he never admits to his new school friends that he sells eggs, hoping to avoid being teased and called 'egg-boy' by his classmates.

This same frigid winter, the citizens of Buffalo welcome the Vilanos with compassion, friendly understanding and marked generosity. But this family's reunion holds unexpected surprises as well, like María del Carmen's refusal to speak Spanish in the home where the four of them are finally together after being separated by the absurd social and political program engendered in Cuba by Fidel Castro.

"It's her way of telling us that we betrayed you two by sending you into exile alone. She can't understand that we were trying to save you from the horrible war we expected in Cuba. If he lost, Fidel had sworn he would blow up the whole country before surrendering," says their mother, overwhelmed, as she continues sewing in their tiny apartment filled with used furniture.

"She'll get over it, Mamá. Don't give up. You'll see. She'll come around," Ely fusses over her, draping a heavier sweater over her shoulders to lessen the impact of the brutal cold that the recent arrivals are unaccustomed to.

"How am I going to make it to work tonight?" thinks her father, looking through the window at the snow that is sticking to the street, the sidewalk and the roofs. "I have to go. If I don't, how are we going to pay the heating bill? We can't go without that." Undeterred, he picks up the shovel that Tom has thoughtfully brought, wraps the scarf that Ely gave him around his neck, and goes outside to clear the snow that is blocking the door so he can get to his shift pricing stock from seven in the evening until three in the morning. He is not embittered by having lost the fruit of so many years of labor in Cuba, or that he is no longer being the owner of his own business and must do manual labor for hourly pay. His inability to speak English bars him from any other work; and his age and complete lack of resources stops him from any other more profitable work.

"Mamá, the people here have been so good to you, to Mary, to me," says Ely. "They're the children of European immigrants and they've taught me the strength of this country. It's made up of people who love freedom."

"Yes, Dear. We're very grateful to this country that gives us freedom and hope when we were slaves in our own country."

But finally, Buffalo's unending cold eats away at the Vilano's hope of being able to stay in this welcoming city. When the school year ends and Ely finishes her freshman year in college, her exhausted and aged parents have reached the decision to settle in Miami. Ely decides to follow them, to help them get started.

CHAPTER 30

Ely finds a job at an upscale department store in Miami where the older saleswomen try to block her advancement, either because they are jealous of her youth or for fear that she could be promoted to positions beyond their reach. But the demanding lessons of exile have taught Ely something: she is a citizen of the world, and there are no obstacles that can stand in her way. She makes a quick decision and moves to Chicago to train as an airline stewardess. She completes the course at the top of her class and is immediately sent to New York where she begins her travels across America and Europe. Her life is a flurry for this one brief year until her boyfriend Tom, with whom she is more in love every day, finishes his pilot's training and begins serving in the United States Air Force.

Then there is the bliss of their wedding, complete with his uniformed comrades' sabers forming an arch over the aisle, as romantic as any girl's childhood fantasy. The honeymoon is a dream-come-true. In Tom's car, they travel through California, Oregon, Tacoma and Washington, surrounded by scenery so beautiful that it takes their breath away. Tom's happiness, his enthusiasm and love for life is expressed in a word that is like a leitmotiv of his vocabulary: "Fantastic." The honeymoon is "fantastic," as are the sights and their plans for the future, and his promise to Ely of a beautiful life together. His affection for her and the world around them—far from diminishing in the bustle of everyday life as so often happens, revealing an unexpected personality change in one spouse or the other—is one of the links that joins Tom to those around him, making their home an oasis of happiness. They set up their apartment in Alabama, where between kisses Tom teaches Ely to cook "fantastic" dishes, in a seemingly endless honeymoon that is no less "fantastic."

As their happiness grows, Ely is gripped by a tragic premonition. "I have to give Tom a daughter right away. He's going to die. I want some part of him here on earth after his death." Frightened, she pushes the dark thought aside, like a child trying to fend off a ghost. But like a dagger thrust into their perfect happiness, Ely continues to feel this foreboding that she dares not share with her husband. When they are together, she surrenders herself to him, obsessed with giving him a daughter, while at the same time she struggles to quiet the irrational fears that assault her.

One day, as she is roasting a duck in the "fantastic" way Tom has taught her, she opens the oven door to check on it and is assaulted by a wave of nausea. She steadies herself against the table, trying to overcome the dizziness that threatens to overwhelm her. Tom, seeing her like this, comes to her side. He holds her and kisses her, and the two smile happily at this new certainty.

"Tom, I want it to be a girl. And I want to name her Bridget."

"Why Bridget, my love?

"Because when I was a stewardess, I visited Saint Patrick's Cathedral. I felt that someone was watching me. When I turned around, I saw a statue of Saint Bridget. Let me name her Bridget, Tom."

"Of course! I love it. Didn't you know that Bridget is a traditional Irish name?"

On the night Ely delivers, Tom is at her side every moment, helping her through her labor.

"What a mess I've gotten you into, Sweetheart!" he exclaims, surprised by the magnitude of sacrifice implicit to giving birth, something few men fully comprehend—sometimes suppressing their own responsibility in this necessary, yet happy, trauma; and other times anesthetized to a pain they are relieved not to have to experience.

The birth goes smoothly and when it is over, Tom takes Bridget from the nurse's arms, wraps her in an operating room blanket and carries her to a window to see her tiny face more clearly. In this climactic moment, there is no trace of worry or dark intuition like that suffered by Ely before conceiving the child. Or perhaps the same unwelcome premonition touches him, but he says nothing to avoid hurting his wife. On her part, Ely insistently forces back the dark shadows that hound her like a bad omen. She prays to God with her unflagging devotion, "Please, God. I've finally built my life in this generous country. I've found the ideal man. Lift this dark weight from me. Let it just be some irrational fear."

But the unchanging days draw on, bringing their grave intentions. When Bridget is five months old, Tom is called to serve on the front in Vietnam as a captain in his country's Air Force.

CHAPTER 31

Tom accepts his deployment to the war in Vietnam, happy to serve his country and knowing it is a battleground between the free world and dark forces that are spreading across the planet, taking it prisoner. Before he leaves, youthful and smiling, his pure heart impervious to bitterness, Tom decides to take a road trip across the United States. He takes Ely and their beloved daughter with him. The plan is to visit his extended family and introduce Bridget to them. He also wants to say good-bye because whether or not he will return from this mission looms over him like a dark uncertainty. Together, they visit Tom's parents, his Irish grandparents, his aunts and uncles, cousins and friends. Their trip ends in Miami at Ely's parents' house. She goes with her husband to the airport, an unanticipated colophon to their perfect bliss. They tell each other good-bye, smiling and exchanging assurances that they will be reunited. Neither one of them reveal any sense of foreboding. When his Captain's braids, khaki hat and loving wave disappear at the top of the boarding ramp, Ely fears for Tom as she would for a deer crossing a hunter's line of fire.

Ely is back in Alabama with their daughter when Tom's first letter arrives, written from the frontlines of the war. Amid the numerous assurances of love and loyalty extolled in his letters, Ely reads her husband's perspective on his presence in Vietnam: "It's one of life's great ironies!" he writes. "I'm over here risking my life for my country when I could be risking it in Cuba to win back your homeland!" He goes on to tell her about his days, flying reconnaissance missions for bombing squadrons, or engaging in dogfights. The young pilot relates that his missions are carried out at such low altitude that he almost clips the treetops.

Faced with the inescapable uncertainty of knowing at exactly what moment Tom's life is at risk, Ely dedicates herself to mentally protecting her husband and helping him survive the dangers as she cares for their daughter. Every morning, she prepares a little package to send him: Cuban-style green plantain chips that he's grown to like, gloves to protect his hands from the cold, a handkerchief embroidered with his initials interlaced with her own, a picture of Bridget…She offers this proof of her love up to the heavens, like the verses written by José Martí, remembered throughout her snowy exile:

> "I have seen the wounded eagle
> soar to the bluest air
> and watched the poisonous viper
> die in the depths of his lair."

Death! Again the threat of death because of that horrible Communism! Camilo Cienfuegos disappeared on some plane because of Fidel Castro's jealousy. She remembers another of Martí's poems that echoed through the infancy of her generation:

> "Buried in my brave heart
> a pain secret from all eyes,
> Son of a country in shackles
> who lives for it, is silenced and dies."

The loneliness of snow-covered Alabama pushes Ely back to Miami where she is comforted by the tropical breeze. There, not far from her family, she rents a one-bedroom apartment in Coral Gables, visiting her family and her sister often as she waits the life or death result of her husband's fate.

In Tom's letters, his pen continually returns to the leitmotiv in which his emotional life is rooted—his wife; and in the logic and absurdity of the international situation that seems evident to him: "Ely, why couldn't they have sent me to Cuba to fight Communism there? I'd be ninety miles from my own country, instead of here, so far away that my countrymen don't care if the people are Communist or not." Very soon, he sees the war for what it is: "This is a dead-end, but it's my duty and I'm not backing down."

Every day Ely receives Tom's letters and cassette recordings from the front, where the world fights for freedom. The television inundates viewers with news. Horrified, they watch images of flag-draped coffins and military funerals. Overwhelmed, Ely remembers a statement Tom made when they visited Washington before he left: "My love, if anything happens to me, I want to be buried at Arlington." Ely turns on the television and sees a dramatic scene play out on the screen: a car crashing into a barrier on a bridge, breaking through it and plummeting into the abyss. A moment before the accident, the driver had been looking at his watch—nine o'clock at night. Unnerved by the scene, she turns off the television and looks at her watch. It is exactly nine o'clock in the evening. "What a coincidence," she thinks. Then, she begins to re-read the letter she received from Tom that same morning. It contains a poem in which he assures her that he will be thinking of her every night at exactly nine o'clock. Images of Tom pass again through Ely's memory: Tom, singing in the university and Air Force choirs; Tom, singing as he slaps his thighs and chest to the beat of the song; Tom, humming wordless melodies. Their little girl is asleep in the bedroom. "He's thinking of me right now. Tom, I love you." Suddenly, the telephone rings, startling her. She answers and hears her mother's voice.

"Ely, an American officer is at my house. He's trying to verify your address. He had the one in Alabama. He wants to see you."

She waits anxiously, her frenzied worry intensifying. The baby wakes up crying, and Ely tries to help her back to sleep, patting her back. Finally, there is a knock at the door. Ely opens it and ushers in an officer in full uniform. His presence looms, like that of a giant's shadow, outside a child's bedroom window.

"Why are you here?" she asks him in English, feeling her knees buckle as her fear mounts. The officer responds, looking at her with the impeccable detachment of one who must fulfill his duty devoid of emotion.

"I am here to inform you that your husband has died."

"You're wrong!" exclaims Ely, her normally quiet voice rising. "You're lying! They didn't kill my husband! It's a mistake!" she says between sobs she cannot contain. She picks up a vase from the coffee table and hurls it at the wall, not noticing the shattered pieces of glass that ricochet back at her. Then, she looks the officer in the eyes and demands: "How did he die?" She repeats the question over and over, meeting the stoic gaze of her unflinching visitor through her desperate tears.

"In combat," he replies simply.

At that moment, Ely's parents arrive.

"It's a lie! It's a mistake! I want to see it in writing!" the young woman cries over and over, feeling the officer hold her tightly by the shoulders, trying to reestablish her self-control. Then, she watches him extract a document from his briefcase and hand it to her. Ely reads it, crushing it in her hand as she runs to get her daughter.

"How could this happen to me?" she whispers, still unable to believe it. "How could this happen to this little American girl?" she asks as she takes the child from her crib, holding her tightly and sobbing. "Once more Communism has destroyed my life! That damned Communism, again!"

CHAPTER 32

At her Miami apartment Ely Vilano waits with her parents for the return of Tom's body. She watches through the window as the mailman passes by, like a puppet moving across a stage. A moment later, he knocks at the door and delivers a letter from Tom that Ely opens, trembling. The others are surprised to see her jump up with unexpected cheer.

"Oh, it wasn't true, my God! It was a mistake! Tom's alive!" and soaring with enthusiasm, Ely shows them her husband's letter, dated September 16, even though the death certificate showed that he had died on the fifteenth.

"Look! Tom's alive! He's not dead! He's not dead!" and she shows the cherished letter to her family. Hope springs up in every one of them, and like Ely they are elated. Ely runs through the hallways of her building, letter in hand, knocking on her neighbors' doors. When they answer, they hug her and congratulate her on this fabulous news that has saved her from facing early widowhood. Once her happiness has inundated her building, Ely takes to the street and runs several blocks to the house of an old friend, to show her the letter. She arrives, happy and out of breath, like someone who has just escaped hell and happily returned to life.

Once more at home, surrounded by faces beaming with joy, Tom's father tells her by telephone that he has requested information about his son's case from the American State Department. Their hope for verification starts out optimistically, but as the hours pass, their worry returns. Finally, a day after receiving the letter, the devastating official response arrives, like a train barreling down on a child with his foot caught in the tracks.

"There was some confusion because of the time change. As I understand it, there are fourteen hours difference between the United States and Vietnam…so the sixteenth here was the fifteenth there."

Later, Ely asks a friend who is a Captain like Tom to tell her what really happened when her husband died. The friend visited the place where Tom perished. "It was a terrible accident," he says. "He was taking off for his reconnaissance mission, and an allied pilot from South Vietnam took off before receiving the order. He hit the tail of Tom's plane, knocking it off and causing it to crash."

Tom's body arrives in Buffalo in a sealed coffin. Not being able to see his face is a terrible, emotional burden for Ely and his family. His coffin is draped with the U.S. flag for a funeral that lasts two days. Finally, the funeral ceremonies proceed: the squadron of airplanes that fly over the cemetery, three volleys fired in the distance, the officer who presents Ely with the flag that covered Tom's coffin, the twenty-one gun salute, the wail of Taps which is the saddest melody she has heard or will ever hear again.

After the funeral, all of Tom's family gathers, demonstrating the typical Irish serenity with which they face death, feeling that it is simply a continuation of life.

But Ely is not comforted by this idea. "This is the saddest thing that has ever happened to me. The saddest thing that ever will happen," she thinks, hugging their tiny daughter. She turns to Sister Silvia, who was her favorite teacher in Buffalo, and asks her, overcome by her tremendous loss: "Why did God do this to me, Sister Silvia?"

"Don't lose faith, Ely," responds the nun, trying to bolster her convictions. "Tom, at his young age, accomplished everything anyone can: he loved and was loved, he married in the Christian Church, he had a daughter, he served his country, he found his professional vocation. His death isn't in vain, dear Ely, because he died for freedom in this world. One day, when that freedom shines for your daughter, she will be proud that her father gave his life so that humanity could be better, and happier."

But Ely sobs, clutching her daughter. In her quivering memory, she sees Tom at the top of the airplane's boarding ramp the day he left for the war. His death seems like the greatest injustice of her life. She knows that Communist imperialism and its furor to take over the world caused it. But she believes that "the United States government also is responsible for it, that they should have freed Cuba, just ninety miles from their own shores instead of declaring war in Vietnam, riddled with countless tactical failures."

"I've always suffered because of history's mistakes," she whispers. "Communism in Cuba is one of history's mistakes. Because of it, I had to abandon my homeland and witness the disappearance of Camilo Cienfuegos. How sad to see the people you love die because of history's mistakes, because of absurdities, because of the whims of leaders and others! How terrible! My God! How many stupid things are we destined to suffer for?"

PRELUDE TO A PEDRO PAN PRIEST

I

As a boy cavorting in the streets of his beloved hometown of Jovellanos, Cuba, Felipe Estévez never felt the call of a religious vocation, and no one could have predicted then that one day, given his unbounded love of life which he saw as a wondrous expression of his God, he would be ordained as a priest.

He did not feel called when they declared communism in his country, either. Nor when he served as a quiet, chubby alterboy at mass, foregoing the traditional chasuble because of the poverty that had descended on the Catholic Church under Castroism. Felipe still was not thinking of becoming a priest when Fidel's agents detained him for several hours when they saw him visit the parish priest in San Miguel de los Baños. It happened during the time when southern Cuba had been invaded by a small army of ex-patriots clinging to the dream of liberating their homeland. Felipe was only thirteen-years-old; his arrest, his nonchalance in the face of danger, and his participation in various social protest activities worried his parents, who decided to send him to Miami to avoid having him thrown into prison.

He arrived in Florida at the age of fourteen, embarking on the journey filled with fantastic adolescent dreams that were certainly evidence of his invincible faith in the joy of human existence.

That morning in 1961, Felipe trusted in God that someone would appear at the airport to take him where he needed to go. Soon, a priest came and took him to one of the camps established by Father Walsh's untiring efforts.

There, faced with hopeful expectations of unknown adventure, Felipe immersed himself in the delights of exploration and adolescent mischief, like one striking out on an heroic quest. His adventures included learning English, a walk through a snowy landscape, and relocation with twenty-four other boys who had emigrated from Cuba, to Fort Wayne, a city situated in the north of the friendly state of Indiana. In Fort Wayne, the twenty-five

Cuban boys were assigned to a wing of a Catholic orphanage where they slept in three perfect rows of beds squeezed into a single bedroom. The orphanage consisted of eight old, two-story buildings housing themselves and three-hundred American orphans, all minors, black and white alike, who attended grade-school there while the newly arrived Cuban boys sat at their desks at Central Catholic High School.

Inside those high walls, a backdrop to the solid discipline maintained by a group of strict nuns of German ancestry and persuasion, Felipe witnessed the adolescent fury of his twenty-four companions erupt and intensify, like the winds of a hurricane in a forest. They were boys, stifled by the strictness of the orphanage, and tormented by homesickness for their families and the desperate uncertainty of the future. Their close quarters resulted in violent behavior toward one another, and their conflicts multiplied, like the dangerous tentacles of an octopus. But Felipe, ever optimistic, was not drawn into these problems. His spirit was comforted by the daily mass; and he enjoyed each newly found region of the country where he launched his youth, every moment that he looked out the windows to admire the city streets, every outing in which members of the Catholic church took him for Sunday walks, every new encounter with another of God's creations. During the course of his forays into the boundless corners of the world, Felipe saw serenity in the face of death at the funeral of an old English immigrant and compared it to the passionate cries that resonated through mortuaries in Cuba. He fixed that day, alight with new understanding, to the walls of his memory as a testament to strength in the face of hardship.

While still in high school, Felipe began washing windows with the hope of scraping together the twenty-six dollars needed to pay his brother's passage from Cuba on the crowded route to freedom. His brother, five years older than Felipe, arrived in the United States and found a job in a hospital to finance his medical studies, which he happily would finish soon thereafter. After a year on his own, Felipe's parents and his nine-year-old sister arrived from the Island that they continued to yearn for. The family's reunion was filled with warmth and happiness, free of complications or traumas born of the long-held grievances of many children who felt abandoned by their parents when they were sent alone to Miami. Then, in Fort Wayne—under the same wide sky that hung over the sober orphanage Felipe had recently abandoned—was ignited the wonder of his youth, filled with first dates, American girlfriends and dances, all the rites of passage in the social life of American youth in the sixties. Friendly and outgoing, Felipe was accepted as a welcome companion by Americans and Cubans alike.

II

Later, during his whirlwind college days, Felipe came face to face with the question of his future vocation. It was then that he realized he wanted to become a priest to serve the vast diversity of people who had awakened such deep love in him. His father and brother opposed his desire to take vows, afraid of losing him just when the family needed him the most. Watching him say goodbye and leave them was almost like watching him die, and they did not want to relinquish the joyful comfort of his presence that permeated their home to drift away like a wayward kite entangled in the odd events of daily life.

But again, Felipe approached this step, in keeping with his inherent optimism, as a colossal adventure. With that attitude, he cheerfully said good-bye to his family and set out for a seminary in Montreal where his perspectives broadened and his humanity soared. The sixties carried with them an ideological identity crisis that forced a complete rethinking of what its proponents considered progress. The Quiet Revolution flew in the face of the Church and society, sweeping like a storm across the previously tranquil borders of Quebec. The nuanced shades of deep-seated reforms colored the classrooms of the seminary, preceded by a radical questioning of traditional Catholicism and social customs. It was tragic, seeing beliefs held for centuries fall from their altars and watching the very foundations of the Church attacked from within its lofty towers by the same men who had vowed to God to uphold it. This spirit of denunciation devoured any affirmative impulse, and amid daily desertions, Felipe observed the successive questioning of everything, including the celibacy of the priesthood. But the young seminarian sustained his faith throughout the storm, like a pilgrim protecting his sandals during his long religious sojourn.

As he witnessed these difficult events, Felipe confronted cultural paradoxes, and meditating on them again and again, arrived at some certainties. Having learned to understand philosophy from a broad Christian perspective framed by love towards one's neighbor, he was drawn to the emotion expressed in literature and embarked on the study of psychology as a means of serving his fellow man. Ultimately, he studied the writings of Carl Rogers and incorporated the open psychology of Transcendence, believing that it was more important to support existential solutions than to run the risk of directing them. Such was the democratic inclination with which he approached his consecration as a priest.

III

Following his ordination on May 30, 1970, Father Estévez tried to return to his homeland, to serve God where misery and horror enveloped the people like some tragic, inescapable bioplasm. But the massive restrictions imposed by Castroism denied him entry into his own country. Temporarily postponing his return to the beloved soil of his roots, he looked to serve as a spiritual guide to other peoples oppressed by poverty and was sent to Honduras in Central America where he practiced his ministry with heartfelt joy.

When he was sent back to the United States, this passionate priest was appointed to a professorship in the Bilingual Seminary of Saint Vincent de Paul in Boynton Beach, Florida. From there he was sent to Rome, where he received his Doctor of Theology, writing on a topic rooted in Cuba: "The Spirituality of Father Félix Varela." Upon his return, he became Rector of the Seminary, the first Cuban ever to receive this distinction in the United States. Later, he brought the comfort and aid of his religious faith to hundreds of Hispanic-American immigrants in Saint Agatha Parish in Miami, and was chosen to serve as Student Chaplain at the

International University of Florida. He worked with tireless enthusiasm, disregarding his sometimes-frail health, and always accompanied by great joy, his most steadfast spiritual mantle. His humility and intense service, as well as the long list of his innumerable activities, keep his ministry forever young, given the amenity and sincerity of his feeling. The benevolence of this charismatic priest reveals that he has achieved the full measure of his humanity, a trait characteristic of a great majority of Pedro Pan children. It is fed by his never-failing love of life that is inseparable from his love of God, because he knows that God is eternal life.

CHAPTER 33

Wifredo Chirino, motivated by his deep desire to start a family, (one of his most deeply felt inclinations) marries Olga María Rodríguez, a serious and responsible young woman he met at a mixer held by "Cherished Cuba," an organization of young Cuban exiles organized by Father Chabebe, an enthusiastic and patriotic priest dedicated to ensuring that this generation of young people from his island do not lose their attachment to their homeland. Olga María continues working for "Cherished Cuba" during the day while Chirino works in discos and hotels at night, playing the music that has not yet brought him fame. The young couple is happy together and they have three daughters whom they name Anjeanette, Olguy Mary, and Jessica. Soon, as a concession to the language of the country he is intent on conquering, Wifredo changes his name to Willy.

On one of those days that is so typical that no one would suspect that anything out of the ordinary could happen, Willy steps out of their home in Hialeah, gets into his car and takes Fourth Avenue West, which runs parallel to a canal swollen with dark rainwater. The car in front of him accelerates through the drizzle. The pavement becomes as slippery as a griddle covered in melted butter. Inspiration is dancing in Willy's head, like it so often does when he drives, and a song begins to take shape, crafted by intuition and emotion.

If anyone were to analyze Willy, it would not be difficult to identify the core elements of his personality. He is a steady, self-assured man who knows what he wants and will fight to achieve it. He is wholesome and decent, dedicated to home and family. He is happy and trusting, a good-natured prankster and joker. He demands a great deal of himself, a trait that will be put to the test a few seconds later when suddenly the car in front of him skids into the canal and sinks. Willy does not hesitate for a moment; he stops his car and jumps into the canal, intent on saving the lives of those in danger. In the water, like a doll floating in a basin, Willy swims to the submerged car and within seconds begins a series of life-saving maneuvers. He opens his eyes and sees that the car's windows are rolled up. He beats at them futilely with his fists; and drawing on the last breath of air in his singer's lungs, he finds a rock on the canal bottom and uses it to break the windows. Water floods into the car and Willy helps the two men trapped inside escape. Then he pushes them toward the surface. When he sees them emerge from the water, amazed by this unexpected miracle, he helps them to the shore. When the two men Willy saved—still in shock from the ordeal—manage to voice their thanks, the singer realizes that he is still holding the rock from the canal in his right hand. Soaked and happy, Chirino returns to his car where the euphoria of having cheated death and saved two lives inspires the end of the song he had begun to compose.

A few days later, the two men Willy saved present him with a trophy they have had made for him which incorporates the rock the singer used to break the windows of their submerged car. As they say good-bye, they ask him to keep it so he will never forget his courageous act of human kindness.

At one point in this intense period, Willy begins recording his first record, titled *One Man Alone*. Not having found a producer, he records it on his own—playing all of the instruments in the ensemble himself after long hours of practice at home to keep down the cost of studio-time. Willy sings his own songs, filled with a passion born of sacrifice for his art. The demo tape is steeped in the singer's joyous emotion, his love for life, and the well-deserved rewards of honest, hard work.

The famous record company owner who had fired Chirino in New York when he was playing in the Julio Gutiérrez Orchestra arrives as Willy is leaving the studio, the echoes of his own songs woven into his mind like a crystal braid. Any recollection of the Cuban, or Willy's boyhood face, had been erased from the rich businessman's memory. The freewheeling playboy jokes with the sound technician as they greet each other.

"Come here. I'm going to play something for you. You're going to like it," the technician tells the famous music producer as he cues up the newly recorded tape. Willy's voice spills from the speakers, singing his original compositions.

"Damn!" exclaims the newly arrived producer, surprised by Willy's harmonies. "Who is this? And what band is it?"

"You're not listening to a band," replies the sound tech, "It's just one man. That's why he's going to title his album *One Man Alone*."

"Who is he? Where can I see him?"

"He's playing at the *Sonesta* hotel in Key Biscayne."

That night, the renowned producer appears at the hotel in Key Biscayne and approaches Willy, who is playing his own songs.

"Hey, buddy, I wanted to talk with you a sec'," he addresses him casually using popular slang. "I heard the tape you made today and I've gotta tell you, your music sounded great—and playing all the instruments yourself. I'd like to produce the record."

Willy looks at him and responds calmly and politely, with a sense of satisfaction at having been recognized for his music by this famous producer who had rejected him years ago.

"Do you remember a skinny kid you fired once in New York?"

"Sure, buddy."

"Well, I'm that skinny kid."

Just as Willy had hoped, the producer begs him to sign with him.

A fantastic period of fame and fortune ensues. Willy establishes and directs his own orchestra. They perform in huge venues. There are ovations, tours, and media attention, a show in Curacao filling a 15,000-seat stadium. His fans sing the songs through which he defines himself as he frolics amid the notes of the staff.

But life's great paradox again imposes pain on this joyous period. One day during this happy time, Josefina, Willy's mother, begins to lose her memory and coordination. She forgets where she has left things with increasing frequency. In the ensuing months and years, events, ideas, people and names are rapidly and irreversibly swept from her memory, as if by a windshield wiper whisking away raindrops and leaving dry glass behind. Her vocabulary, once brilliant and expansive, filled with the concepts of a doctoral degree, shrinks in on itself like a glove devoured in flames. As the days rush by, her primary physician seals the verdict on her aged silhouette: Alzheimer's disease. Dr. Chirino tells his children that how he has an infant at home, his wife.

The tragedy of this family's sadness is faced with religious faith, as are the days that bring Dr. Wifredo Chirino's suffering from chronic Chrohn's disease, and his death in 1980. In his last days, he is comforted by his children in a Miami hospital following a surgery that left him in tremendous pain. In 1983, as Ana Lourdes marries and Fefita is establishing herself professionally, there is another painful event. Esther Asunción, Josefina's younger sister, called *Madrina* by her nieces and nephews because she was Willy's godmother, undergoes an operation for cancer. She fights her illness, unwilling to admit that she might not be able to continue caring for her older sister, whom she has loved more dearly than anyone since their mother died when Josefina was only nine years old and Esther only five months. Josefina, when she married Dr. Chirino, decided to continue living in the family home in order to care for her seven younger siblings. That is why Esther maintains that she cannot succumb to the cancer because Josefina needs her. She undergoes chemotherapy, determined to defeat her illness out of love for her sister. Esther had always lived with the Chirinos, as happens in so many families of Hispanic ancestry, where aunts help raise their nieces and nephews as if they were their own children.

The tight-knit family endures this difficult time, drawing together even more to protect their weakened members. That is why Marilé, always so kind and nurturing, brings her mother and her sick aunt to live with her. Willy, Fefita and Lourdes help their older sister, hiring a woman to come and care for Josefina and Esther, who thankfully recuperates from her operation with no recurrence of the removed cancer.

Such was the last chapter in the life of Josefina Rodríguez, Willy's mother—a woman who was crowned a provincial beauty queen, earned a doctoral degree when only a handful of women dared to undertake graduate studies, and who brightened her son's songs with her flowers and her smile.

JESÚS, THE RENEGADE

I

When he arrived at the Miami airport, he felt even more sharply the discrimination that had segregated him in Cuba, and he could feel it tearing at his silky, cinnamon-colored skin like scornful daggers. In Father Walsh's camps he was comforted by the commitment to racial justice held by the teachers and staff, although not always by his white peers who cruelly referred to him as *Zebra*, or by the girls who refused to dance with him at parties in spite of his dashing good looks.

It was this racial oppression that made Jesús García begin questioning democracy. It pained him to see, again and again, how the Americans looked down on him on the busses—and the humiliation of being forced to the seats in the back. Or being turned away at the movie theaters when he went with a group of white teens from the camp, who also had to miss the movie because of the standards of equality set by their instructors.

Jesús never had a foster home in the United States; and he knew that it was because of his race. It weighed on him, multiplying his homesickness for Cuba and his family, whom he had left in that little, wooden house, perched on a corner at the outskirts of Havana.

Later, the snow-covered landscape of Pennsylvania depressed him, and his spirit faded to gray as he looked out the orphanage windows at the American children who discriminated against him again and again. There, a nun forced him to change his name, because Jesús, a common name in Cuba, was sacred and reserved exclusively for the Son of God. No human being should sully it, carrying it with them through the sordid streets of the world.

II

As time went on and he set out on his own, he went by Joseph instead of Jesús. He still spoke English with an accent since he had arrived in the United States at the age of seventeen. The white consulate workers who processed his requests refused him a visa for his parents or his siblings in Cuba. He listened to the thundering tirades about Castroism on Miami's Cuban radio and television stations and began to believe that they were exaggerating the problems in his country because he could not imagine that daily life had changed so much on his island.

Joseph-Jesús was not the studious type, so he decided to make his millions working and saving so he could invest in business opportunities later. He went to Miami, looking for a climate that would not force him to shovel snow or put chains and snow tires on his car just to get to work.

In the Cuban neighborhoods of Miami, Jesús worked day and night in garages, restaurants, in plumbing and road construction. He saved every penny, even skimping on necessities in order to save for the future. In the little restaurant where he worked nights flipping burgers, Jesús-Joseph met Jennifer, a blonde, white, American girl who responded sweetly to his flirtation and compliments, words floating between them like dreamy snowflakes outside a window or hovering miraculously like a full moon over the desert.

For months, they spent passionate nights in Jesús's little room, which he decorated each time with the fantasy that his love inspired. In those days, his doleful racial complexes receded and a tiny flicker of hope grew in him.

III

Maybe he was just not destined to be happy. Life seemed to have one unhappy surprise after another in store for him. Unhappiness first siezed Jesús the afternoon that his American girlfriend's father discovered that his daughter was in a relationship with the bi-racial youth. The man's reaction was brutal. His threats rained down on the young Cuban, and the daughter was shut away and punished with unprecedented severity. Jesús, disregarding the threats, fought to see Jennifer. To rescue her from the misery of her punishment, he sent her clandestine messages telling her that he would marry her and use all of his savings to take her far, far away, where she would be safe. But Jennifer did not respond to his messages, or show up for meetings he proposed, or break her curfew to see him. Her silence crushed him, until he heard through the grapevine that Jennifer had been sent to some unidentified city so far away that she would never be able to see him again.

Jesús waited and waited, hoping she would get word to him of her whereabouts so he could go to her, free her, and take her away with him. He suffered the uncertainty of her absence for days, months, a year. Finally, it struck him that Jennifer had accepted her family's decision to send her away. The sorrow Jesús felt when he came to this realization would never completely fade away.

During this painful time, his determination to become rich consumed him. Jesús redoubled his efforts at work and began to investigate which businesses he might invest his savings in. At last, he decided to open a nursing home for the elderly. He took out a mortgage on a house, hired three shifts of nurses, a cook and a janitor. But no old, rich, white people came to live in this supposed paradise of senility. For his part, Jesús was not a good manager and began to encounter problems he did not know how to solve. If an employee did not show up, he did not know how to replace them. And when the cook missed a day, chaos rained over the home, sparking complaints from everyone: the elderly residents, their families, even the other employees. In the end, Jesús's lack of organization drove his business into bankruptcy.

This exile's hope ran out when, after extraordinary efforts, he obtained visas for his parents but found they could not join him because Fidel Castro had decreed a prohibition against leaving Cuba.

IV

In spite of this new circumstance, Communist propaganda caught up to him in the wake of his failed foray into capitalism and took him as its quivering prisoner. He believed the perfectly crafted messages about hospitals built for the people, scholarships for poor children, medicine taken out into the countryside. He began to believe that capitalism was an inhuman system that devoured a person's mental and physical energy. He lost faith that progress, social integration, new laws supporting black people and time would one day ease the racial discrimination in the United States. His yearning for Cuba and for his parents further aggravated his inability to adapt to life in American cities.

One day, a letter arrived with news that his mother was seriously ill. The distance and silence that separated them was too much for Jesús. Telephone calls to Cuba were forbidden in those days, and there were no boats or airplanes traveling between the two countries either. Letters took months to get from one country to the other. His failures and his disillusionment steered Jesús toward return. So one day when the growing disappointments of capitalism threatened to suffocate his spirit, Jesús took his gun and bought a ticket on a flight from Miami to Mexico. When the plane flew over Cuba, he burst into the cockpit, held the gun to the pilot's temple and demanded that he land the plane on the island.

V

His actions were hailed by the only two newspapers in Cuba as acts of heroism and patriotism. The news was covered on television, and journalists published interviews with him relating his story. The regime capitalized on the news that a bi-racial Cuban, disillusioned by discrimination and beaten down by the evils of capitalism had return to his homeland enlightened by hope for the future. But he was watched carefully after his arrival in the country for fear that he might be an infiltrator from the ever-feared

Central Intelligence Agency—always on the lookout for ways to get into Cuba.

During his absence, Jesús's family had witnessed the marriage of his siblings and the birth of grandchildren. When he returned, this broken man realized that he would have to reestablish a place for himself in the family. His mother, having recovered in the hospital, came home and worried about how to make up a little bed for him in the living room, since the bedrooms were very small for such a large family and there was no hope of getting a bigger house at the overcrowded Office of Urban Reform.

Jesús's friends who welcomed him back after his strenuous journey home—proud that their respective Committees for the Defense of the Revolution saw them rubbing elbows with someone who had rejected capitalism—fearfully began to avoid him when they heard his first criticisms of the "Socialist" system in place in their country.

When the clothes and shoes that Jesús brought with him from the United States wore out, he found himself reduced to standing in lines on the sidewalk for days to collect the miserable annual quota permitted by his provisions book. He found out that his situation at work would be affected if he went to church. He had no say in choosing a doctor, and if he needed medicines, they were very difficult to find. If he wanted to go out, there was no available transportation, or hotels, or tourist attractions because everything was now in the hands of foreigners and the country's political elite.

VI

One day, at an assessment and self-assessment meeting, Jesús, who felt himself watched constantly because of the suspicious life he had lived for so many years in the Capitalist world, struck up a friendly conversation with a white girl whose straight, blonde hair and blue eyes reminded him of Jennifer. Hope, as lost as a soldier in battle, returned to comfort him. The girl's father was a political leader whom Jesús expected to be free of racial prejudices since he was a militant member of the

Communist Party. But in this area of his life, he was once again surprised by the unexpected: neither the girl nor her father would accept a bi-racial suitor.

More quickly than he could have imagined, Jesús was disillusioned by Cuba's Communist experiment and wanted to make his way in some unknown country. But emigration from the Island was forbidden; and the mere desire or discussion of the desire to do so was a serious political crime. Because of his desperate desertion of the Free World, Jesús was a man caught between the world's two political systems. Finally, frozen by the inertia of his country that blocked his every initiative; frustrated by the official lie of having eradicated racism within its national borders, and by the impossibility of finding freedom someplace else in the world, Jesús resigned himself to living as a spiritual cripple. "I don't belong to this system or the other," he thought. "They both destroy a man. It's the same with race. I'm not black and I'm not white. I don't know who my people are. I'm alone."

And hearing his own complaints, bitterness set upon his emotions like a hook snaring a fish in the vast immensity of the ocean.

CHAPTER 34

Miami was readying itself to celebrate Halloween, and life's paradox surprised Willy Chirino again, bringing his mother's last days. As he kisses her thinning hair, Willy hears his sisters comment that of Josfina Rodríguez's children, he looks the most like her.

"He has *Mima*'s face, but he's quick-witted like *Pipo*," says Marilé, the oldest sister whose piano their father would never let Willy get near when he was a boy, trying to avoid distractions along the future that had been planned for him: to become a doctor or a lawyer like so many men in his family. His second sister, Fefita, the Theology professor at Belén College, takes her Bible and reads aloud the Twenty-third Psalm: "The Lord is my Shepherd, I shall not want... Yea though I walk through the valley of the shadow of death, I will fear no evil..." The youngest of the family, Ana Lourdes, leans against her husband for support at this difficult moment. He is Cuban, of German descent and is a successful businessman.

Willy kisses his mother's hair again and remembers her walking along the violet-filled patio, telling him not to ride his pony bareback. He remembers her running to pick him up when the pony bucked him off and he broke his arm. His mother's shrunken body had reliquished her mental abilities long ago, and with them were gone the memories of happy family events she could no longer share with her loved ones. Her vocabulary was reduced to the name of her oldest daughter. So when someone, trying to gauge the extent of her memory loss, asked her a question such as "How old are you?" she would respond with three heartfelt syllables, "Marilé." "How many children do you have?" they would ask, and she would again respond, "Marilé." "What is your son's name? The musician?" And still she would answer, "Marilé." Nevertheless, the exquisiteness that had carried Josefina to a young beauty queen's throne had not fled her face, shining mirror in a frame of worn wood.

Willy thinks back to his father's death seven years ago. He envisions him, withered after twenty-nine days in a hospital bed after he suffered a heart attack during the last operation to treat his longstanding intestinal condition.

"Look, *Pipo*, you have to rest now. We can accept it now," Willy remembers telling his father in Kendall Regional Hospital. He repeated this loving logic for an hour as the clock approached six o'clock in the evening. His father died at six o'clock in the morning the next day. "That was my oldest daughter's birthday, and Lisette gave birth to our first daughter," Willy alludes to his second marriage to singer Lisette Alvarez Chorens, the daughter of the famous Cuban singers, Olga and Tony. As a show of support for Willy, a club in Panama closed that night and hung a sign on the door that said, "Closed due to the death of Willy Chirino's father."

It is five o'clock when Willy decides to leave.

"Marilé, I have to play with the band at nine o'clock tonight. I can't break my contract. If Mamá dies, don't tell me."

And they did not tell him. In fact, he was performing on stage when Doña Josefina passed away. But his fame betrayed him, and the painful news reached him because the anchorman, Guillermo Benítez announced it on television. In one of those moments in which performers approach heroism, answering their vocation and their artistry, Chirino continued playing until the clock struck two in the morning. Then, he hurried to Marilé's house to grieve with his family.

Chapter 35

The enormous cafeteria of Lasalle High School in Miami is open for a performance by Willy Chirino, one of its former students who has returned amid cheers to sing a benefit for *Love in Action*, a non-profit organization dedicated to helping poor children. One of Willy's two younger sisters, Fefita, endowed with a deep religious vocation to serve humanity, is a tireless member of the group and has just finished her Master's Degree in Theology. When he arrives on the platform, with his typical dynamic energy, Willy addresses the audience, flashing his lively, joyful smile, shining with sincere happiness.

"Gentlemen, what a difference!" he exclaims in his unmistakable Cuban accent. "When I was coming in, I almost turned to the left to go to the kitchen—I used to wash dishes there every day when I was a student here—But I caught myself and turned right instead...and here I am on stage."

Willy earns the applause of the crowd that loves him. From the stage, he sees Lissette, his second wife, the woman who shares his love of music, of playing dominoes until the wee hours of the morning, the memory of crossing the Straits of Florida alone, without their parents. Willy constantly admires in Lissette, among many other traits, the ability to select songs when she performs. Before he met her, he had heard her on Cuban radio singing a trio with her famous parents, Olga and Tony. In those days, Willy imagined her standing on tiptoe in front of the microphone singing "The Mickey Mouse Song" which she made famous in his country. At the same time, Lissette recalls the first of Willy's songs she recorded and how many times he called her when she was on tour in Puerto Rico.

Looking at the standing crowd in a break between songs, Willy reflects, "The journey is more important than the destination. More than getting there, I like to think I'm on my way, walking just for the sake of walking." Again, his sincere joy and his talent spark applause as the first cords of Chirino's best song ring out. His exile's voice retraces the path from tyranny to freedom, undertaken nearly thirty years ago when his father sent him into exile to save him from the hammer and sickle, and the oppressive color of olive green.

"If only *Mima* could see this!" thinks Marilé as she applauds Willy. "If only poor *Pipo* could see it!"

"Fefita, overcome by filial emotion whispers in her older sister's ear, "One day they'll see it in Cuba! When we're free, they'll see it!"

CHAPTER 36

Willy Chirino is standing in the middle of a large group that is applauding him. Today, a handful of his compatriots is honoring him by dedicating a star in his name on Eighth Street, the most Cuban of Miami's thoroughfares. It is a traditional honor given to outstanding Cuban exiles.

More emotional than his family has ever seen him, Willy dedicates the star to a tall, robust priest wearing a dark jacket and pants, a crucifix resting on his black shirt. This priest standing next to Willy is Father Walsh, who watched over him like a father at *Casa Carrión* in Brickell when he first arrived in Miami as an exile. Father Walsh, because of his immense charity efforts has been honored with the title of Monsignor. His words trembling with emotion, Willy, who has his father's presence and his mother's dark eyes, speaks in abrupt syllables that sound like sobs. "I want to tell all of you that this priest's conviction moves me. Coming from a rich family in his home country of Ireland, with every privilege a person could have, he decided to live with true Christian humility." Willy holds the microphone close to his perfectly trimmed beard as the famous singer, Olga Guillot, smiles at his side. "I want every Cuban to know of this priest's work. It's because of his tireless efforts that many children who arrived alone from our country have become good people. I was one of those children, and I'm here to tell you that Monsignor Walsh's work was incredible," continues Willy, hiding his emotion behind round, dark glasses. "We were separated from our parents who had stayed in Cuba and could not get to the Free World; Monsignor Walsh was our father and was a magnificent role model for us to follow. He raised us well. He played with us like a friend. Our concerns were his concerns. He supplied our material and spiritual needs in every way. The part of my youth that I spent living with Monsignor Walsh was very important to me, and to everyone else in my situation. He helped us all grow up and he taught us that things weren't easy. So, since you have all so graciously offered me this star on Eighth Street, I dedicate it to him and say, 'Thank you, Monsignor, for helping thousands of destitute Cuban children become upstanding citizens. Your work, Monsignor, is a labor of love. It is the work of God, Our Lord, a blessed project that you started and carried out as a hero of our exile.

THE FERNÁNDEZ SISTERS, GEORGINA AND MARISELA VERENA

I

They crossed the streets of Pinar del Río amid trucks full of bare-chested men calling for all enemies of Fidel Castro to be lead to the firing squads. And together, they were sickened by the revolutionary hymns that poured from crackling loudspeakers. More than once, they heard in the early morning silence through the doorways stripped of their gates by the new social order, the heads of men shot by the Communists thud against the pavement and their bodies dragged from the nearby military barracks to be buried before their families could claim them. At school, if they went into the bathroom, they were followed and watched very carefully, by those who feared they might hide a pipe-bomb or scrawl some anti-Communist graffiti, although neither girl would have ever considered such things.

Georgina, the older of the two, was not allowed to enroll in her last year of school where she had been studying to become a teacher because they knew she was not a supporter of Castroism, nor would she wear the militia uniform or go to cut sugarcane on Sunday public work projects. Before the Bay of Pigs invasion, the two sisters prayed together that the invaders would be successful. They were seized by the same frightening feeling of claustrophobia when Fidel defeated the brigade, which he disparaged as "mercenaries," and then cut off all contact between the Island and the rest of the world, burying signs of progress with the epitaph of the Revolution.

One morning, the Fernández family awoke to the rumor that secret Visa Waivers were being sent from the United States to allow children passage out of Cuba. Georgina—at fourteen years old and acting against the wishes of her father who tried to convince her to remain in the country for the short time that Castro's government would last—decided to request one of the Visa Waivers along with friends and anti-Communist family members so she could immigrate to the democratic country.

Without knowing who had initiated the project, or who was sending the visas from Miami, Georgina managed to get one, and waited three agonizing months for the telegram sent by Fidel's secret service that would allow her to leave Cuba.

In the "fishbowl" at the Havana airport, she faced the menacing interrogation by the rebel with the evil scar on his temple all alone, as well as the search of her three changes of clothing that spilled the discretely packed feminine products out of her "worm."

From inside the airplane that carried her away, she saw her country like this:

> They sealed the door, I felt an emptiness...
> My Island remained behind.
> I "discover" it from the air
> more beautiful than before,
> its infinite sea linked to the sky even bluer,
> the foamy arm of its coast even whiter...
>
> My Island remained behind, defeated,
> but part of me stayed on my Island;
> and within that part of me
> that fled from there,
> in that part, there still lives,
> my Island.

II

After Georgina left, her twelve-year-old brother, Carlos said good-bye, as did Marisela Verena a few months later, her ten-year-old sister who hoped to join Georgina in one of the girls' camps in Miami.

In the memories of the three siblings, Cuba's coastline slept like a precious grain of sand that solidified in the distance, under the suffocating breath of the sun. George, who seemed friendly, optimistic and hurried when they met, picked them up one by one at the Miami airport. When Marisela arrived, she did not know that Georgina had already been relocated to another part of that vast, country in the North. Shivering because of the required vaccine she received at one of Father Walsh's camps, Marisela was completely overcome by a sadness much greater than her ten years. She asked for her sister Georgina as she looked around, feeling for the first time the smallness of Cuba as compared to a world that a seemed as amazing to her as it was foreign. One by one, she counted down her cruel days of longing, telling herself, "Today makes sixty days of being homesick, sixty days of sweat and exile. Today makes three hundred days of being homesick..." She felt these words swirl throughout the sad melody that drummed dramatically in her head, an unnamed tenet of the dynamic nature that guided her through life.

At the time, Georgina was enrolled in a school in Iowa, surrounded by a cold, snow-covered landscape that was as strange to her as the sounds of the English language and the loneliness that followed her through the long hallways. A generous scholarship from Catholic Charities supported her studies. Amid the flood of children who were arriving alone to the northern country, like a spray of human buckshot shot out of the asphyxiating barrel of Castroism, Georgina did not know where Marisela Verena had been sent, although she knew from a letter sent by her parents that she had left Cuba. At night, both sisters fell asleep wondering how they would find each other.

One day, the school principal sent for Georgina and asked her a surprising question:

"Do you know where your sister is?

"No, Sister," answered the devastated girl.

"She's at an orphanage in another city in this same state. Would you like her to be sent here to be with you?"

Georgina begged her to reunite them, and very soon Marisela arrived. She was frail and had matured during under the deluge of separations she had endured. She had grown up and was so serious that she had almost lost her smile in her snowy surroundings. Georgina could just make out a hint of her first song, trembling in her soul: "We struck out for hundreds of miles, stripped bare..." This verse grew every night in her thoughts, like a bell sounding the alarm. She would finish it many years later in a pale corner of her exile:

> We struck out for hundreds of miles, stripped bare.
> Stripped of justice and liberty.
> We were looking for refuge
> asking only for the luxury
> of earning a living with dignity.

The loving sister that she was, Georgina took Marisela and introduced her to the younger girls in another wing of her school. But the boon of having her close by could not quell the feeling of desolation that surrounded her. In fact, Georgina was certain that Marisela had changed from when they lived surrounded by the peace of their home. Separation from their family had changed her. She had abruptly left her childhood behind, faced with being responsible for herself. Watching her again and again, Georgina realized that she had suffered greatly. In letters to her family in Cuba, she barely mentioned the issue, resorting to the cheery tone taken up by most of Father Walsh's children, always hoping to spare their families additional worry. As they struggled to regain some level of stability, Georgina wrote the following verses about exile, perhaps for Marisela:

> you,
> like me, suffer for our homeland.
>
> (your childhood cut short
> between two worlds)
>
> and perhaps, like me,
> you yearn to go back
> to what you remember
> Cuba to be.

At the time, Marisela obsessively pieced together her feelings in a rhythmic melody, like repeating links of a chain that struck her like an arrow piercing a waiting target, recalling the days leading up to her exile. This melody stayed with her always, and she continued adding to it layers of insomnia and months of searching that buried her and her people under a mountain of monstrous emotion. Years later, it would take shape in poetry and music:

> Three hundred sixty months
> spent walking.
> Three decades of work and perseverance.
> Thirty years of discrimination,
> even though we belonged.
> How sad the song
> sung by my wandering generation!

Later, Georgina dedicated herself to getting her brother Carlos, who was in the Matecumbe camp in Florida, transferred to Iowa as well. The boy had felt out of his element from the first day he arrived at the camp in Florida. He had come across a snake he thought might be poisonous since he had never seen one like it before in Cuba, and he had felt a watchful panther's breath at his back. Finally, aided by Father Walsh's desire that all of the siblings in his camps be kept together, Georgina was able to find him a foster family with eight children near her school in Iowa. As the months passed, that cherished light of Marisela's joy returned bit by bit.

It was during that time when history was marred by the assassination of President Kennedy, unleashing the fury of opinions throughout the world. The pain that his death caused the Irish nuns who cared for Georgina surrounded her. The girl watched them cry for the dead president, of Irish descent like themselves, with the same feeling of loss as if they had lost one of their own. Seated in the school auditorium with the other students who watched the somber burial procession on television, Georgina, although not unmoved by the sorrow expressed by the nuns, thought of those who died at the Bay of Pigs having embarked on a mission that turned tragic because of this president's cowardice. Perhaps Georgina was mourning her own circumstances so deeply that she could not add the weight of this death to her burden. Additionally, the girl was facing a new moral dilemma and thought of her parents, subject to imprisonment because they did not support Fidel Castro, and now even more at risk of not being able to leave Cuba because since the October Crisis all flights between the Island and the United States had been suspended. Georgina took up a pen to write to her parents, searching for Marisela's head among the lines of the younger girls. "We're not getting any news from Cuba," she thought. "We don't get any newspapers that cover what's going on there." And forgetting about the Kennedy funeral, she focused on a fervent prayer: "Dear God, bring my parents from Cuba soon!" Meanwhile, Marisela, seated in the same auditorium, mentally knit together a response to the others' sobbing because of Kennedy's death. She could not forget that he had been the architect behind the armed invasion at the Bay of Pigs, or that in a supreme act of cowardice he betrayed them when faced with threats of Soviet imperialism, the defender of Castro's regime as the operation began.

> Armed with hope instead of machine guns
> there in Girón,
> confident in the promise made by the Power
> that armed and dispatched them
> but once deployed they found themselves...

Years later, when life had taught her the meaning of the verb "to corner," she finished the verse:

> they found themselves cornered by impotence.

III

Finally, two years after arriving in the U.S.A., Georgina received the news that her parents had arrived in Miami, and at last she and her two siblings would be able to join them and rekindle the warm family unit. They embraced when they saw one another, happy to celebrate the feat of arriving in the Free World, even as they shared the fear—rampant within the isolated island of

Cuba—that communism was on its way to becoming the sole master of every continent.

The Fernández also took in two cousins exiled from Castroism, who brought the total number of people living in their small apartment to seven. Georgina, who had finished high school, decided to join her parents, performing exhausting work in the tomato fields that surrounded Miami. At their side, worked Cuban doctors and lawyers, former ministers of the Batista government, and even millionaires who had been ruined by Fidel Castro's nationalization plan.

IV

It was then that Marisela's artistic talent became evident. In Cuba, she had studied piano, an instrument that did not inspire her; but in Miami she learned to play the guitar by ear. She was playing and singing when she began working with a woman who hosted children's parties. The exile that pained her impassioned soul turned upside-down in her music. So she presented herself in this way to her increasing fans:

> I come from a country blessed
> with nature as its ally,
> a monopoly of sunshine,
> Spanish ancestry
> and people whose blood is sweetened with sugar.

Whenever Georgina saw Marisela dressed as a clown—her tiny face hidden by make-up, and ready to go perform at a party—she felt a mix of joy and pain. She was overwhelmed by this emotional paradox until one day she heard Marisela say how much she loved the interaction with people. That was when Georgina knew that her little sister's artistic vocation was real. Another time, she watched her pick up her guitar and move to Puerto Rico, where she took her middle name—Verena— as her stage name. The young artist broke onto the scene playing in piano bars, small venues and hotels that catered to Hispanic tourists. The heat of Cuba smoldered in her music, defending her own human identity.

> I belong to a people with an easy smile
> who could always laugh at any mistake.
> The curtain raised and fell,
> interchangeable governments
> playing he who laughs last laughs the loudest.

Later, her career carried her to Spain, where she played for five or six years and where the record company, CBS, signed her to record her songs. There, her desire for Cuba's liberation flowed through her verses.

> My country is a sparrow cage,
> but you can't lock up a sparrow.
> If he's kept captive
> there's no alternative
> but to escape the cage and fly away.

When Marisela returned to Puerto Rico, she joined an international song festival in which she represented Spain. She won the top prize, placing first out of twenty countries. Her lyrical sermon on Cuba continued, her immigrant's heart spreading across the whole world:

> Three hundred-sixty months of humiliation.
> Three decades of censorship and repression.
> Thirty years of dictatorship,
> of prisons, of bitterness.
> What a sad song
> my generation must sing!

And her pain grew, accentuating her recollection of the past. Her pity for her sold-out country linked with her pride in the triumphant attitude of Cuban exiles:

> Thirty years since a cornered tyrant
> sold my sun to a land of shadows.
> My people boldly
> lift their heads
> where ever the snail settles.

Every word of her greatest patriotic song resonates with the alienation of exile:

> Three hundred-sixty months of speaking a foreign tongue.
> Thirty years of not seeing the sun that witnessed my birth.
> My generation clings
> to a root with no soil.
> What a long song
> my wounded generation sings.

V

Today, Marisela still expresses her yearning for Cuba in the songs she writes and performs. Georgina, who became a journalist, expresses herself in powerful, tender words that join together in article after article, testimony after testimony of children who came alone from Cuba and became successful men and women. She expresses it as well in the poetry published in her book *Claroscuro*:

> My Island was happy.
> Its bosom flourished with valleys of fresh fruit,
> and emerald suns on mischievous streams
> that splash into rivers.

> My Island was happy.
> Sugary sand sweetening its seas
> and people of different colors holding hands
> as the sound murmured through the streets.

> And so, caught unaware,
> how happy was my Island
> and how tragic her luck!
> Unexpectedly, with a hearty laugh,
> Death sprang upon her…

Georgina is moved as she listens to Marisela relate the exile of the Pedro Pan children in words that seem more like lyrical prose than a song. She expresses them in her warm, clear voice so as to reaffirm her message of hard-won victory, "Faced with the impossibility of changing the fate that befell us, we were dealt the challenge of enduring a difficult time, and therefore, of growing up and maturing before our time. Destiny offered us a choice between dissolving in a foreign sea or reaffirming our origins, assimilating into ourselves everything possible that the strangers had shown us. We have learned to dress in the appropriate costume for every occasion. Instead of drifting away, we came together. Instead of watering down our identity, we unified our origins. Instead of cursing, we blessed. But we are in transition, and that's precisely why we are experts of survival, why we overcame every misfortune that befell us in our youth. That is why we defeated the negative forces of the political and social history that tried to break us."

CHAPTER 37

A fine rain falls on the boulevards as Paris joyfully turns on her lights, culminating with the corners of Montmartre, where artists spend each day painting portraits of tourist until they say good-night.

Ely Vilano Chovel enters the living room that belongs to her daughter from her second marriage. She has come from Belgium for a very special occasion; her daughter is going to be a high fashion runway model in one of the highlight shows of fashion week.

Maternal pride washes over Ely as she sees her daughter realize her goal. Seated in the gallery of the main runway, awaiting the spectacle that they have come to see, she envisions two silhouettes that shaped her youth passing over the luxuriously carpeted runway: the faces of Commander Camilo Cienfuegos and Tom—communism's human victims catch her eye first. Then, the verandah of her home in Cuba, filled with birds. Her second marriage to a European nobleman, from whom she separated when their youngest child turned three. The sun in the Canary Islands, where she lived during the happy years of that marriage, grazes her memory. "The coincidences that have ruled my life," reflects Ely. "I love the ballet and my oldest daughter is a ballerina. My mother was born in the Canary Islands, and I lived there for several years. Camilo and Tom, both killed for opposing communism. I was a child who emigrated alone, and now I'm involved in the construction of "Catholic Children's Village" with Monsignor Walsh, to take care of other children in need. Freedom made it possible for me to realize my destiny."

Ely's second daughter, Bronwyn, emerges from the curtains that open to make way for the models. She is modeling an elegant white suit. She enters to a Cuban song performed by Celia Cruz, whose strong voice sings about the brilliant dancer, Isadora Duncan. Ely sees her daughter go by and smiles, "Another coincidence," she thinks. "Coincidences have a meaning. This one today corroborates what I felt as a child when I finished reading that book of world history: 'I am a citizen of the world,' like Confucius said." Her inner world spreads out into the universe, a common occurrence among the men and women who as children emigrated alone from Cuba. "That has been my life," Ely concludes softly. "A road to oneness," she affirms with the passion of her memory, and she smiles again at her daughter.

CHAPTER 38

The festive *Cuban Café*, situated in Plumtree Center, Boca Raton, Florida is decorated for a reception honoring men and women who came alone to Miami as children between 1960 and 1962. They came from Cuba, and now, more than thirty years later, they know what was unknown to them then; that the massive exodus from their Island was called *Operation Pedro Pan* and that a priest named Father Walsh, who now bears the title Monsignor, sent their Visa Waivers to Cuba, authorized by the American government. They also know now that people like Penny Powers, a British woman who still lives in Cuba and who was integral to the plan, knit together a secret distribution ring for those visas. All of these men and women are now aware of the role Mongo and Polita Grau, now exiled in Miami, played in getting them the visas; and that it was the Florida press that dubbed the activity *Operation Pedro Pan*. There are many other things that they now know about that time: that the Dade County Department of Welfare provided buildings in southeastern Miami for the Cuban children's housing which had previously been used to house indigent children and juvenile offenders; and the diocese donated 150 acres of land for a camp twenty miles south of Miami. Father Walsh rented several apartment buildings in Florida City and had them fenced in for the children's safety. The United States government assigned them retired military barracks from World War II in northeastern Miami. And some three hundred people helped Father Walsh in his efforts, including hundreds of state and federal organizations, as well as the directors of Catholic Charity organizations who took responsibility for many children.

Ely Vilano Chovel crosses Boca Raton Boulevard and enters the *Cuban Café*. Smiling, she pauses to take in the warm and welcoming atmosphere of her homeland. Ely runs *Operación Pedro Pan Group, Inc.*, an organization she founded in Miami to connect those who came alone as children from their Island oppressed by Castroism. The woman who thirty years ago had asked the priest to give her the last rites and begged not to be buried in the snow, and who thought she had found the ideal husband when she fell in love with Tom, is still characterized by her slender gracefulness, youthful bob, finely arched eyebrows, and easy smile.

Ely eyes the humorous mural painted by the famous Scull sisters that decorates the restaurant, adding the ambiance of a traditional Havana street. She touches the gates that harken back to the colonial period of her Island. She admires the paintings of palm-lined landscapes and tobacco fields, the postage stamps and coins that crossed the ocean to arrive in Florida—as lost as the Pedro Pan children—immigrants themselves in search of sacred freedom.

"Hey, my friend!" Come and have a cup of roadside coffee with me!" laughs Carlos Rico, the cheerful owner of *Cuban Café* and himself a Pedro Pan child. Seeing Ely come in, he takes her by the arm and escorts her to a table to sit down.

"I just heard that your first grandchild was born in Brussels, Ely. Congratulations! Although no one would believe you're a grandmother, as young as you are.

"I just got back from Brussels. My daughter from my second marriage had a baby. I left Cristián here with my oldest daughter, who I had with Tom."

"Where did they send you, my sister, when you left the Florida City camp?" asks Carlos Rico, a tall, well-built and lively man, filled with unflappable optimism and the self-assurance of a winner.

"They sent me to a foster home in Buffalo. Before I got there, I thought it was going to be a prairie full of buffalos."

They laugh at the memory.

"When I left Father Walsh's camp, they sent me to Albuquerque, New Mexico," explains Carlos. "It wasn't a good experience. I spent four years there with two other Pedro Pan girls. They didn't treat us well there; but here I am, and I see the girls all the time. I love them like sisters."

Looking around, Ely Vilano Chovel realizes that Carlos Rico has tried to recapture the homeland he lost as a child, recreating a sense of Cuba in his restaurant. She also intuits that by treating everyone with such kindness, he is compensating for the emotional indifference that surrounded him in Albuquerque.

The door opens and in come the De la Portilla sisters: Marta and Raquel. They are still as lively, outgoing and cheerful as when they were girls, glowing with warmth and sincerity. One of Raquel's daughters is with them, a tall, slender girl as blonde and friendly as her mother. Obviously, as an American she wants to learn about Cuba. She is an architecture student and is supporting Mrs. Gloria Nodarse, one of the Florida City camp housemothers, by the arm. The four of them stop to read a poem about the "Parisian Gentleman," that crazy, romantic beggar who ruled the streets of Havana, wearing his black rags and his world emperor's cloak.

"Josefina Leyva gave me that poem for my café," says Carlos Rico, coming over to greet the women as Raquel blushes from the emotion of being surrounded by "Pedro Pans."

"Well, the 'red menace' is here," laughs her sister Marta, like she did when they lived with their Aunt Clarita in Philadelphia, and she watched her turn crimson at the thought of changing religions and adapting to new customs.

"In the end, we realized that the Presbyterian Church was good, too," says Marta longingly. "Poor Aunt Clarita. She was so good to us, but she's passed away now. They recognized her husband, whom we called 'Dad,' at a ceremony at the church when he turned one hundred years old. Raquel and I attended. It was so lovely! He was a wonderful man, so caring and giving. Aunt Clarita and their children were so kind to us!"

"But at first, we rebelled when Aunt Clarita told us were could only go to the Presbyterian Church. And now we go to both," explained Raquel.

"A few years later, our parents came with our brothers and sisters. We went to live with them in a big house in Philadelphia," remembers Marta, who has suddenly become melancholy, as so often happens when "Pedro Pans" talk about their past.

"Marta and I married Americans, and our children barely speak Spanish," continues Raquel.

"I got divorced and live in Miami with Bryan, my only child and my best friend," adds Marta as Carlos Rico formulates a question and extends a warm hand to her.

"What did you take away from the trauma of coming alone from Cuba?"

"The optimism to survive," responds Marta de la Portilla, smiling. "I look at the positive side of everything. Even if I'm in a traffic jam, I just tell myself 'Oh, great! I can rest a little bit!' and I turn on the radio and listen to music."

Mrs. Gloria Nodarse remembers her days as housemother at the Florida City camp.

"I had the youngest girls. I loved them so much. God didn't bless me with children, but my husband and I loved all of the girls like they were our own daughters when we were house parents. I wanted to adopt one of them, but we couldn't afford it."

"Not one 'Pedro Pan' was ever adopted," remembers Marta de la Portilla. "The ones who were never reunited with family, because their parents couldn't come from Cuba, stayed in Father Walsh's camps until they were grown up."

"That was the case for us," says Gerardo Simms, who had arrived unnoticed. Simms is a slender, elegant man whose handsome, ebony face has the air of an intellectual. Today, he is a district attorney in Miami. He was this group's first president. At his side, is Juan Couriel, who led the nighttime adventure at Sears while Father Walsh searched the city for him. Juan is tall, strong and dashing, with the attitude and grace of a gentleman. He graduated from the University of Miami with a degree in Political Science, and runs a ceramics business.

"Oh, that night at Sears!" remembers Juan, laughing. "I made so many shots that night that for a few hours I believed that pool table was mine!"

"Juan was the ring leader among us," says Gerardo Simms. "One time he swam in the fountain at the house in San Rafael where we were living with Father Walsh, after we moved out of *Casa Carrrión*! And Monsignor swatted him with the leather paddle.

"And when my older brother, who's as adventurous as I am, got a job behind Father Walsh's back. Father Walsh found out he'd bought a car…"

"We weren't allowed to work," explains Gerardo. "We were in high school at the time, and at the camp in Opa-Locka where we lived, they provided everything for us."

"Well, Father Walsh called my brother. They talked about it, and he let him keep the car and the job since he understood his point of view," said Couriel. "My sister, Silvia, is different. She's not as adventurous as we are. I love her like a mother—although Mamá finally left Cuba and came to live with us. And Papá isn't a prisoner any more."

Other men and women from the 'Pedro Pan Group' arrive at the luncheon organized by Ely Vilano Chovel. They include Teresita Ayo, with her two young daughters who are used to hearing her stories about the New Bedford orphanage where a boy slapped a nun. Georgina Fernández also arrives, with her tiny journalist's tape recorder and her camera. After her, Sara Yaballi, one of the nurses at the Matecumbe camp arrives.

"Oh, those chicken pox outbreaks during the heat of a Miami summer!" recalls the nurse, sitting down. "Seventy children sick all at once!"

"And the sores from the mosquito bites, and the pinkeye," laughs a priest recently ordained in Venezuela. His name is Pablicito and he is a good friend of Willy Chirino going back to the happy days of their childhood in Cuba. Father Pablicito has been invited to the luncheon since he is visiting in Miami. He is one of the twenty-seven "Pedro Pans" who have joined the priesthood.

"We're Cubans and we love both cultures: American and Cuban," says Georgina Fernández. "Sometimes we speak English, sometimes Spanish. We want Cuba to be free, because the suffering there pains us. Many of us will go back, to help rebuild it when it's free. We don't want anything, just to help."

Two "Pedro Pans" step into the *Cuban Café*, first José Frank Aspillaga and then Martín Ling.

"Buddy, I think I know you," says Martín, the Chinese boy who sold eggs in Tampa and lived in Filomena the Greek's shotgun.

"I remember you," Frank responds, calling on his prodigious memory. "I met you when we were hiding in the brush at Matecumbe, trying to escape the initiation they had in store for us."

"Yeah, man, of course! Now I remember!" says Martín, shaking his hand. The two men are similar in appearance; neither one is tall, or thin. They both seem very observant; and as they talk, they discover that they both served in the U. S. military.

"I was a cook. I learned how to make some delicious dishes there!" explains Martín, stroking his perfectly trimmed beard that is starting to turn gray and which accentuates his almond shaped eyes and impassive, Eastern serenity.

"Come over here...didn't you have a brother?" Aspillaga asks him, his expressive eyes widening behind his glasses.

"Yes, my brother Juan. He's a doctor and doing very well."

"And what do you do, Ling?"

"I have my own accounting firm in Miami. I started it when I graduated from the university. I'm married and have kids."

Carlos Rico interrupts the joking and laughter to announce that lunch is ready.

"No, wait! Monsignor Walsh isn't here yet," says Ely from the sidelines of the group where she is taking care of some hosting details. "Something must have happened to him."

"I'm convinced that since none of the thousands of children that passed through our camps died or was injured, it was because Divine Providence heard our prayers and protected us. Your generation was well brought up in good homes. We never had any assaults or anything like that. You all had solid morals!" Sergio García Miro's voice catches the attention of Ling and de Aspillaga, who turn to listen to him. They look at him curiously until they recognize him, as slim and loving as before.

"Man, you were a teacher at the Matecumbe camp," says Martín.

"You had been a medical student in Cuba and you saved us from the initiations," Frank pats him affectionately on the back. "I see you're a priest now. So you didn't finish medical school?"

"I did. I finished and specialized in psychology," Father Sergio responds humbly. "I work at Catholic Charities in Miami."

Father Walsh arrives, hurriedly. His car had broken down, causing him to be late. He is wearing his customary, black suit, and has his hands in his pockets. His boys gather around him; and always ready with a joke, he takes Juan Couriel and Gerardo Simms by the scruff of the neck, like when they played at the camps. Time has faded the blonde hair of this Irishman who gave so much to the Cuban children in exile. But there is no questioning his vitality or his desire to continue working for others. Marta de la Portilla comes to greet him just as Ely Vilano Chovel approaches them.

"I don't know if you two knew each other in the camps," the Monsignor tells the two women as he introduces them.

"It can't be!" they exclaim and embrace each other, overjoyed by their reunion.

"You're Ely!"

"You're Marta!"

"Hurry, Raquel! Look, it's Ely!"

They cry happy tears as they remember bits of their Florida City friendship and the letter that Marta wrote to Ely's mother encouraging her to find her parents in Cuba.

"The things that happened to these children!" smiles Monsignor Walsh, filled with emotion.

"That's nothing!" comments Teresita Ayo softly, giving each of her daughters a candy. "I found out that María Magda de Quesada and Carmencita López, who were like mother and daughter in that Colorado orphanage, bumped into each other in Miami." And as if summoned by her words, Carmencita appears among the "Pedro Pans," exhibiting the same lively sensitivity. Her straight hair is a bit darker and her features remain sharp, although she is no longer so thin.

"I brought the doll they let me bring with me from Cuba," she says. "The wind blew her hat off between flights and María Magda searched between the planes until she found it for me. I love María Magda like a second mother."

"Let us see her, Carmencita!" say the others as they gather around, touching the Shirley Temple doll's face and her time-faded sun hat.

Isabel, her mother, is with her and is still as beautiful as María Magda de Quesada's father had noted that day he knocked on her door in Cuba.

"María Magda's mother died in Denver. The poor thing, she was such a wonderful lady! I have a bad heart and Carmencita tries to keep me from becoming too emotional. But even if it pains me, I want to say that if I had to send my six-year-old little girl alone to Miami again to save her from communism in Cuba, I would do it. I want all of you to hear me. I would do it! I would do it!"

The exquisitely Cuban luncheon starts with roast pig, rice and beans, yucca root with garlic sauce and twice-fried plantains. Carlos Rico is moving from table to table, waiting on the group's members, when he sees two women approach Monsignor Walsh. One of them is black and hugs the priest as he stands to greet her warmly.

"How is René, María Josefa?" he asks.

"Fine, Monsignor. He sends you a hug."

"Is he still working at the bank?"

"Yes, Monsignor. And you should see how my granddaughter has grown!"

"How wonderful!"

The two new arrivals sit with Georgina Fernández and tell her René's story and how he grew up with both of them as mothers.

"René's wife died giving birth, poor thing!" remarks the black woman delicately, exhibiting the dignity that characterizes her every word and gesture. "I'm raising his daughter, who's already in high school. Monsignor is our spiritual father. He's been with us every step of the way; he was with us when she died; he baptized my granddaughter..." and she turns toward Margot López to introduce herself.

The group continues sharing memories of the traumas caused by their abrupt departure from Cuba and their adaptation to the United States. Anita Rivero, who lived in a typical, American foster home, has become a psychologist and practices in Miami. She is the one who begins recounting their difficulties.

"In Cuba, we bore the brunt of our parents' fears that the government would take away their parental rights and send us all to the Soviet Union. It was painful for us to see them take over our schools and kick out the nuns who used to teach us in the parochial schools. After that, our parents were terrified to send us to the schools that Fidel controlled because they were afraid they would brainwash us and turn us into communists."

"I remember the firing squads, too. I could hear them from my house at night," affirms the journalist, Georgina Fernández, emotion evident in her mild, soft-spoken manner. "We lived with them following us around at school to make sure we didn't try to sabotage anything or pin up any anti-Castro posters. Finally, many of us weren't allowed to continue studying and were kicked out of the high schools and normal schools where they prepared teachers, because we weren't communists. Being separated from our parents and sent into exile alone at the age of five, or fourteen, was the greatest trauma of our lives; and it affects all of our emotions. We tend to be very emotional when we have to say good-bye, and we're the only ones who really understand what we've been through. That's why we get together regularly to talk about those experiences, as if we were brothers and sisters, or as my sister Marisela says, 'travel partners.'" The elegant journalist adjusts the scarf at her neck, ready to listen to others' stories.

"I never could understand why my parents sent me into exile alone when I was only five-years-old," says a slim, rather young 'Pedro Pan' woman. "I've often wondered if it wouldn't have been better if they had kept me in Cuba. But an uncle of mine who left not long ago told me about the agricultural work camps and the factories where the students had to go every year so they wouldn't be expelled from their schools and universities; about the privileges granted to the Communist Youth in order to get into universities or how they spied on their peers, about the required military service and military training and having to pass a political test to gain admission. If someone says they believe in God, they're not let in. And I'm appalled by the 'permanent record'."

"What's the 'permanent record'?" the others ask her.

"They start it when the children are in pre-school and continue throughout grade-school and high school. Their entrance into the university depends on it; and it's secret. It's considered counter-revolutionary if the parents ask to see it. They won't show it to them. It includes the parents' political views, which are investigated at their work and by the Defense of the Revolution Committee on their block. If they don't pass, or they're religious, the student can't enroll in the university. We escaped those horrors, and having to go to Angola to teach for two years during the height of their civil war, like thousands of students from the Pedagogical Institute. And we escaped the mandatory military service that has sent so many young Cubans to die in wars in Ethiopia, Angola and other countries. That has been one of Castro's greatest crimes."

The "Pedro Pans" reflect on this silently until Anita Rivero mentions the emotional problems they've suffered.

"Divorce is common among us." Everyone looks at Dr. Rivero, who is no longer plump and whose dark bob is traced with gray. "Some 'Pedro Pans' have divorced two or three times," she states. "We seem to unconsciously repeat the act of leaving our parents by breaking up with our spouses. That separation trauma made marriage difficult for us," she declares.

"We had a role-reversal," says Teresita Ayo, holding her youngest daughter on her lap. "We parented our parents. First, when they were in Cuba, we told them that everything here was good and that we were fine. When we were reunited, we taught them English, found them jobs, arranged apartments for them and worked to help them..."

"When we left our parents, we felt like we grew up overnight," says Georgina Fernández. "We became adults without ever being children."

"Some of us were away from our families for more than seven years," notes Anita Rivero, "and in my case, like so many others, the reunion was very difficult. We couldn't forgive them for sending us away. Because we believed that they had abandoned us! We didn't understand the scope of was going on in Cuba. I went through a huge rebellion against my parents, and truth be told, we can't live together, although I visit them very often and I've overcome my anger toward them. There's no doubt that the trauma of being separated from our parents left its mark. In my case, it became the center of my emotional life. Among other things, good-byes are very hard for me, and they upset me more than they should."

"Another 'Pedro Pan' like us once said 'I boarded a plane a child, and got off an adult'," continues Georgina Fernández.

"But we learned to make decisions and to fend for ourselves early on," adds Juan Couriel. "There's my sister Silvia, who at twelve years old made the decision for us to leave the house where we were staying and go to the camps, even though we didn't know anything about them. Look how fast she grew up! I admire her and respect her so much!"

"Our psychological development skipped some stages," Teresita Ayo interjects again. "But we got used to taking on responsibility at an early age. That was good."

"And we're all alike in that we want to give our children everything so they never feel like their parents aren't there for them, like we felt. On the other hand, we also want them to appreciate the value of things," says Carlos Rico, asking his waiters to serve coffee and a dessert of guava shells with cream cheese.

"My sister Marisela says we became experts at survival," interjects Georgina. "We flourish wherever we end up. Who's ever seen a 'Pedro Pan' who wasn't a fighter? We're doctors, lawyers, business people, university professors, musicians, and composers... Successful, productive members of society for the most part."

"We learned to become citizens of the world," concludes Ely. "Although we know, and feel, that our roots are in Cuba."

The gathered "Pedro Pans" sing one of Marisela Verena's songs, as Monsignor Walsh listens to them smiling, like when they had impromtu parties at the camps.

> And so I inherited the mistakes
> and then I had to leave my country...
> ...Three hundred sixty months of yearning
> are three decades of exile and sweat.

Thirty years of cruel banishment
of living somewhere strange.
What a sad song
my wandering generation sings.

The "Pedro Pans" continue remembering and sharing.

"What ever happened to that little girl who came on Ely's flight? Her name was Sol de la Luz? Do you remember, Raquel?" Marta de la Portilla asks her sister.

"I don't know. I never heard from her again. I remember she used to look at herself in the mirror a lot and smile.

"Who knows where she ended up! And thousands of other 'Pedro Pans.' Who knows where they've settled, what they studied, what they're doing...!"

After dessert, Ely Vilano Chovel stands to introduce two elderly women to the group, both heroines in Castro's prisons. One is Albertina O'Farril, the woman whose intuition moved her one cold night to travel from the "Free America" prison to Havana to say good-bye to her mother who was dying in a nursing home. She is escorted by her husband, Samuel Teúrbe Tolón, a kind and well-mannered engineer who has doted on her throughout every day of their exile, trying to make up for those tragic years she spent in prison. Albertina, still as beautiful and passionate as in those years when she fought and was imprisoned, is presented with an award honoring her patriotic activities. She shares an emotional explanation for her secret, anti-Castro activities, "...the Revolution nationalized the sugar cane plantations that were the base of our economy. Land, industry, businesses, apartment buildings newspapers, radio, television, universities and schools—all of it was run by the State and there was just one leader, Fidel. The whole country became a dark cave where we struggled to shine a light... In that tragic decade of the sixties, the forces of darkness and repression had taken over half of the world, and in Cuba they crushed our sacrifice and determination. Today, history has restored the balance; and Cuba is among the last remnants of international communism. While we await the day of our liberation, I am happy to see that the children who left our country thirty years ago have become successful men and women because they were able to live in freedom."

"Those gathered applaud Albertina. Then Ely introduces a woman who is surprised when her name is mentioned and she is asked to speak, since Ely had kept it a secret.

"Sara del Toro de Odio is with us today, the first Cuban whom Monsignor Walsh entrusted with Visa Waivers to be secretly distributed in Cuba. She is the mother of five 'Pedro Pans.' She spent six years in prison because of her anti-Castro activities, and her husband served twelve years of hard labor. They called for the death penalty for him. Sara spent her last year at their former estate, which had been turned into a prison. She was reunited with her husband there. He passed away two years ago."

Sara stands, as open and energetic as ever. She is as elegant as before, and smiles with a vitality that the prisons were unable to extinguish. Calling on her characteristic humor, she says, "The first thing I want to tell you is that when I was distributing the Visa Waivers I received from Monsignor Walsh in Cuba, I didn't know that I was involved in an operation called 'Pedro Pan'. I wasn't planning to speak today but Monsignor Walsh wouldn't let me out of it, so here I am; I did it for Cuba and not for me." Her youthful good nature and her fantastic energy remain intact. She has never succumbed to bitterness or resentment.

The group laughs as they listen to her. She laughs, too, before continuing.

"I'm happy, because I have ten fabulous children. And I thank God that I was reunited again with Amador. The last thing I want to tell you is that I keep fighting for Cuba. And I'll always keep fighting."

Those in attendance applaud Sara del Toro again as she receives a certificate of appreciation from the group. Returning to her seat, Sara thinks of her husband, Amador. Her vivid memory recalls his vibrant silhouette as he sat beside her in their home. The memory is of a Miami evening two years ago. They were in their small living room talking, having been reunited after the completion of their six- and twelve-year prison sentences. It was dusk and Amador had just spoken on the phone to their daughter, Silvia, the poet. Suddenly, he turned to Sara and said:

"Don't keep driving the van."

"But so many women here earn their living driving children. I like taking them to school and back," she replies.

"Don't drive any more." And as he said it, his head dropped forward. When she reached his side to help him, she realized that he had unexpectedly passed away.

"Death came so quickly that afternoon!" thinks Sara, rapidly gaining control over her longing for him with her characteristic strength. "Amador, my dear husband. And I never drove again. Never. Maybe he had some premonition concerning me before he died."

They ask Monsignor Bryan Walsh to close the meeting. He stands, surrounded by his former children; and smiling, puts his hands in the pockets of his dark suit, as is his custom. He bows his head humbly as they applaud, and still smiling at the children of the Cuban exodus, urges them to continue working for others.

"My dear children, I feel that my work with you is not over—I still baptize your children, or officiate at your weddings or listen when one of you comes to me with a problem. But given that you're all well established, I want to encourage you now, to begin working together to build the Catholic Children's Village. In it, we will house hundreds of children from many countries and of every race, to help them become successful adults. To undertake this project, we're calling on people of good will who want to help us to come together. This is our work for humanity."

"Let's build the Catholic Children's Village! That way, when we return to a free Cuba, we will leave behind something for other children who are alone in the world like we used to be," exhorts Ely Vilano

"To the Catholic Children's Village! For Father Walsh!" cheers the group.

And Monsignor Walsh smiles again, because men like him do not rest on their laurels. They are always looking toward the future, eager to keep working.